KEDLESTON ROAD

Japan and the Pacific Free Trade Area

As the end of the century approaches, the Asian-Pacific region is becoming the most important economic area in the world. Since 1965, when the idea of a Pacific Free Trade Area (PAFTA) was proposed by Kojima Kiyoshi, there have been rising levels of integration and co-operation between the Asian-Pacific countries.

Pekka Korhonen examines the nature of Japan's economic rise since the Second World War and its economic and political relations with other nations in the Pacific area as a result of its new-found economic strength. The study explains Japan's and the region's rapid economic development as having followed the pattern of Akamatsu Kaname's flying geese theory. This in turn led to an optimistic world outlook for Japan in terms of its prosperity and security. Political and military tensions could be wiped away as a result of sustained regional economic growth and the formation of an interdependent structure for Asian-Pacific countries.

With the so-called Pacific century nearly upon us, this highly original work will be of great interest to all those engaged in the study of Pacific economic growth and integration.

Pekka Korhonen is a Junior Research Fellow of the Finnish Academy and is currently based at the University of Jyväskylä, Finland.

Sheffield Centre for Japanese Studies/Routledge Series

Series editor: Glenn D. Hook, Professor of Japanese Studies, University of Sheffield

This new series, published by Routledge in association with the Centre for Japanese Studies at the University of Sheffield, will make available both original research on a wide range of subjects dealing with Japan and will provide introductory overviews of key topics in Japanese studies.

Other titles in the series:

The Internationalization of Japan
Edited by Glenn D. Hook and Michael Weiner

Race and Migration in Imperial Japan
Michael Weiner

Japan and the Pacific Free Trade Area

Pekka Korhonen

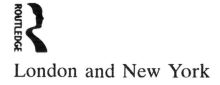

London and New York

First published 1994
by Routledge
11 New Fetter Lane, London EC4P 4EE

Simultaneously published in the USA and Canada
by Routledge
29 West 35th Street, New York, NY 10001

Reprinted 1996

© 1994 Pekka Korhonen

Phototypeset in Times by Intype, London

Printed and bound in Great Britain by
Antony Rowe Ltd, Chippenham, Wiltshire

British Library Cataloguing in Publication Data
A catalogue record for this book is available from the British Library

Library of Congress Cataloguing in Publication Data
A catalogue record for this book is available from the Library of Congress

ISBN 0–415–10828–4

Contents

List of tables	vi
Acknowledgements	vii
List of acronyms	ix
1 **Introduction**	1
2 **Themes**	13
A small country	16
Economism	28
Growth	38
Development	49
Asia	63
3 **Integration**	72
Re-entering the world	74
Regional co-operation in Asia	87
Kojima's concept of integration	94
An Asian vs. a Pacific orientation	113
Asian dynamism	128
The PAFTA proposal	133
Japan, the bridge	145
Exposure to international discussion	153
4 **Conclusion**	167
Bibliography	182
Index	197

Tables

2.1 Years when pre-war (1934–6) levels of economic activity
were attained and doubled   39
2.2 Per capita gross domestic product by major regions   40
2.3 Gross domestic product by major regions   42
2.4 Average annual compound rate of growth of gross
domestic product by major regions   43
2.5 Growth and structure of gross national product in
Japan between 1955 and 1969   46
2.6 Geographical distribution of Japan's trade; percentage
shares in total Japanese exports and imports   70
3.1 Statistical characteristics of the Pacific Free Trade Area,
1963   137

Acknowledgements

This study has been a long process, and many individuals and institutions have helped along the way. The beginning of the study was made possible by a two-year grant by Japan's Ministry of Education for 1986–8. The time was spent in the Faculty of Law at the University of Tokyo under the guidance of Professor Sakamoto Yoshikazu. Teachers at the University of Tokyo's Center for International Education, especially Kusaba Yutaka and, later, Mrs Sakamoto Kikuko provided for inspiring and demanding Japanese language education. The library staff of the Faculty of Law and the Japanese Economic Research Center co-operated splendidly. Students of the highly unofficial Transnational Network provided for an intellectual community, and particularly fruitful were discussions with Endo Seiji.

In Finland, the Department of Political Science at the University of Jyväskylä provided the intellectual and institutional setting for the work, whether I was employed there or not. I would especially like to thank Professor Kari Palonen for general encouragement, and Jouko Salonen for discussions on methodology. The Department of Political Science, the University of Jyväskylä, the Emil Aaltonen Foundation, the Ellen and Artturi Nyyssönen Foundation, the Finnish Cultural Foundation, the Finnish Academy, and the Japan Society for the Promotion of Science provided financial backing on different occasions. The staff of the University library were always helpful and co-operative.

This book is based on a dissertation published by the University of Jyväskylä in 1992. I have since rewritten and updated the manuscript for Routledge. Most of Chapter 2, pages 49–63, will also appear in the *Journal of Peace Research* in 1994 prior to the publication of this book. I am obliged to the editor for permission to use the material here.

Kari Palonen, Kojima Kiyoshi, Raimo Väyrynen, Olavi K. Fält,

Ilmari Susiluoto and Glenn D. Hook have read different versions of the manuscript, and their comments have been very helpful. Alice Moore has checked my English. My final thanks go to my wife, Mutsuko Korhonen, for help with the Japanese language and support throughout the writing process.

Jyväskylä, Midsummer 1993
Pekka Korhonen

List of acronyms

ALA	Asia and Latin America
APEC	Asia–Pacific Economic Co-operation
ASA	Association of Southeast Asia
ASEAN	Association of Southeast Asian Nations
ASPAC	Asian and Pacific Council
CACM	Central American Common Market
COMECON	Council for Mutual Economic Assistance
EAEC	East Asia Economic Caucus (formerly EAEG)
EAEG	East Asia Economic Group
EC	European Community
ECAFE	Economic Commission for Asia and the Far East
EEC	European Economic Community
EFTA	European Free Trade Association
EPU	European Payments Union
ESCAP	Economic and Social Commission for Asia and the Pacific (formerly ECAFE)
FAO	Food and Agriculture Organization
GATT	General Agreement on Tariffs and Trade
GDP	Gross Domestic Product
GNP	Gross National Product
IBRO	International Bank for Reconstruction and Development (World Bank)
IMF	International Monetary Fund
JANFTA	Japanese–Australian–New Zealand Free Trade Area
JERC	Japan Economic Research Centre
JICA	Japan International Co-operation Agency
LAFTA	Latin American Free Trade Area
MITI	Ministry of International Trade and Industry

NAFTA	New Zealand–Australian Free Trade Area
	North American Free Trade Agreement
	North Atlantic Free Trade Area
NATO	North Atlantic Treaty Organization
NIEs	Newly Industrialized Economies
NPR	National Police Reserve
OAEC	Organization for Asian Economic Co-operation
OEEC	Organization for European Economic Co-operation
OECD	Organization for Economic Co-operation and Development
OPEC	Organization for Pacific Economic Co-operation
OPTAD	Organization for Pacific Trade and Development
PAFTA	Pacific Free Trade Area
PAFTAD	Pacific Free Trade and Development
PBEC	Pacific Basin Economic Council
PECC	Pacific Economic Co-operation Conference (since 1992 Pacific Economic Co-operation Council)
SCAP	Supreme Commander for the Allied Powers
SEATO	Southeast Asia Treaty Organization
UNCTAD	United Nations Conference on Trade and Development
UNESCO	United Nations Educational, Scientific and Cultural Organization
USSR	Union of Soviet Socialist Republics
WHO	World Health Organization

1 Introduction

I was fascinated at first sight by the strange beauty of the idea of the Pacific Free Trade Area (PAFTA). The idea was originally proposed in 1965 by Kojima Kiyoshi, a professor of economics at Hitotsubashi University, and meant creating a free trade area among the United States, Canada, Japan, Australia and New Zealand. The PAFTA proposal became the foundation on which was built a huge body of literature and political activity during the 1970s and 1980s relating to various forms of co-operation and community-building over the Pacific Ocean. That activity was accompanied by various slogans such as 'Pacific Age', 'Twenty-first Century', and 'Pacific Century', which depicted a transference of the economic and political centre from the Atlantic to the Pacific area.

My fascination with the original proposal arose from the combined rationality and strangeness of the idea. It was rational because it followed logically from the economic situation in the Pacific area during the 1960s as seen from Japan. The countries mentioned were at the time the only industrially advanced countries in the region, and were already engaged in mutually complementary trade. It was strange because in its bold economism it seemed to transgress all other conditions I had learned to associate with regional integration, whether referring to the European Community (EC), European Free Trade Association (EFTA), the Council for Mutual Economic Assistance (COMECON), or the failed Nordic Economic Co-operation (NORDEK) of the North European countries (see Turner and Nordquist 1982). Not being an expert on the theory of integration, I had in my mind such simple and concrete prerequisites of regional integration as physical proximity, as well as a measure of political, cultural and linguistic similarity between the participants. Such non-economic factors were not totally lacking in the case of PAFTA; at least politically the countries belonged to the same grouping of capitalist countries in the Pacific area, linked through political co-operation with the United States – a factor not given much explicit consideration by Kojima. It was his concentration on purely economic argument that aroused my curiosity.

However, this study is not only about Professor Kojima Kiyoshi and the original PAFTA proposal. The original interest grew into a larger project on the history of Japanese discourse on regional integration. The present study analyses the post-war period from 1945 to 1968. Kojima Kiyoshi, the most important intellectual studied, did not work in a vacuum, but was part of a larger community of economists discussing the problems of Japan's international economic relations. Another economist, Okita Saburo, and a politician, Miki Takeo, are especially important to the development of the idea of the Pacific Free Trade Area. Thus, this study covers the first phase of the discussion relating to Pacific economic co-operation.

The situation of international integration in the Asian Pacific area has been very different from the situation prevalent in Europe, and very few major decisions have ever been made. European integration has proceeded as *institutional* integration, and its history can be written as a process of distinct decisions and agreements leading to various institutional structures. The integration process taking place in the Asian Pacific area, on the other hand, has been mainly *functional*, characterized by slowly deepening co-operation between economies – rather than states – in various fields, accompanied by a continuous process of discussion among various professionals, which has only occasionally come into the spotlight at the state level. Even nowadays, in place of institutional structures capable of making decisions, in the Asian–Pacific area there are only various discussion clubs, and a general process of dialogue that produces ideas and images; ways of mentally constructing the world within various useful categories.

Two different concepts of politics will be used in this study. They can be called a sectoral way of understanding politics, and politics as action. Politics understood as a sector refers to the ordinary manner of dividing national activity into various sectors, such as the political, economic, military, or cultural sectors. Academic disciplines usually follow similar divisions. Although some overlapping occurs, they are often treated separately, each of them the domain of appropriate professionals.

Sectoral imperialism is usually at play in this situation. For instance, political scientists expound the autonomy of politics, evaluating – not always unpejoratively – the domain of other sectors from the point of view of political science. Similarly, Japanese economists tried to maintain the autonomy of economics, emphasizing that they were interested only in the economic aspect of different situations, and considering economics to be the discipline that most accurately organizes the relevant aspects of reality. They tended to regard other sectors pejoratively, especially the political and military ones, as dealing too often with irrelevant matters, or as being outright dangerous.

Since this is a study in political science, another concept of politics will be used, too: namely Kari Palonen's 'Politics as a dramatic action situation' (1983). Politics as action refers to using one's own power in the context of the powers of others as a way of pushing through one's will in social situations. These situations are not necessarily the dramatic ones of conflicting passions crashing against each other, one of them emerging victorious, the others lying defeated among the ruins of the emotional battlefield. Politics as action is understood here as the-not-so dramatic situation of social discussion, where various arguments are proposed for others to accept or refute. The various disciplines do not appear here as sectors, but as overlapping layers, where none is more important than the other. There are periods when certain matters become more political, acquiring a political coloration, while at other times the same matters may be coloured more by economics, or by cultural or military aspects (comp. Morgenthau 1929: 67).

For instance, when someone who happens to be a Japanese economist publishes a treatise on abstract economic theory, he may be engaging in politics among his fellow scientists, trying to make them see abstract economic matters as he does, but the political coloration of this situation is not necessarily intense; with respect to national politics there may hardly be any. If, on the other hand, the treatise happens to expose the theoretically beneficial effects of free trade, and it is published during a time of heated national controversy over economic policy between protectionists and free traders, his work will immediately acquire a deep political coloration, both with respect to fellow economists and the body politic at large. A text, or an argument in general, can be strictly confined to the sector of economics, while at the same time being a political act. In this way, the essentially economic texts analysed here, although they may never mention the word politics, can be treated as components in the discourse on Japan's foreign policy.

These two ways of understanding politics are also meaningful in another sense. Japan in the 1950s and 1960s, as a small country integrated with the hegemonic system of the United States, guarded by suspicious Asian neighbours hurt in the Pacific War, was not in a position to act conspicuously in the political sector. As the political sector was fraught with difficulties, emphasis on economics was a means of obfuscating aspects of reality that inhibited action. In this way, a space was created where self-confidence could be built, constructive thinking could proceed, and nebulous dreams like the Pacific Age could be imagined (see Korhonen 1990: 33-6). It will be seen in the study how, in places where politics or other non-economic factors are brought into the picture, thinking on regional integration tends to come to a halt, while in places where they are deliberately shut out, it can proceed.

This points to the idea of an intellectual horizon (Palonen 1985). The concept is a spatial one in the sense that it depicts discussion going on inside a space with a limited number of possibilities for action. The space has its own logic defining the properties and relationships of the actors inside it, as well as the possible kinds of actions presented to them. On a purely abstract level, a multitude of possible courses of action could always be constructed, but in practical situations most of them lay, so to speak, beyond the horizon. They are not perceived as anything real or realistic, if there is an awareness of them at all, and they do not feature in the discussion. When discussion as a process evolves with changes in the material world, the intellectual horizon of what is understood as possible also shifts, opening to new visions. The speed of the process is not constant. Some periods are more hectic than others, and the appearance of a new horizon tends to have the nature of a jump into a qualitatively new stage (see Kierkegaard 1982: 122-31).

The purpose of this study has not been to test some theory against data, but to find the path that a historical process of discussion has taken. Theory has been used in places where appropriate as a way of aiding textual analysis. Methodological theory has been used in defining research methods, economic theory has been used in understanding some of the thought patterns of Japanese economists; theory of integration has been employed in analysing the concepts of integration used by the discussants, and theory in international politics has been used in setting Japan into a global perspective. The central emphasis of the study has, however, been the interpretation of a set of historical texts.

What this has meant in practice is that I have worked both backwards and forwards in time, starting with central texts by Kojima Kiyoshi from the middle of the 1960s, as well as sideways into the texts of other economists, other disciplines and ways of thinking, searching for new texts to satisfy my curiosity. As the number of possible sources in this kind of approach is in principle infinite, I had to restrict them to specific research material of manageable size. The amount of material was determined by two main factors: the borders were pushed outwards by my will to grasp adequately the basic structures and categories of Japanese thinking within the specific historical setting in which it took place, but were limited by my ability to read and comprehend Japanese. The problem was actually more apparent than real; in a community of fairly like-minded discussants there is actually not much variation between different texts – especially in the case of basic rhetorical categories – and in a situation like this, the value of each additional text diminishes geometrically. The problem of qualitative textual analysis is not the number of texts, but their selection. When presenting the results of the analysis only very little material can actually be used, there being no sense in presenting similar arguments over and over again.

Consequently, the material in this study was decided as follows: on the basis of a preliminary survey of literature conducted in the library of the Faculty of Law at the University of Tokyo and the utilization of two bibliographies, *The Pacific Community Concept* by the Japan Center for International Exchange (1982) and Iwasaki Ikuo's *Japan and Southeast Asia* (1983), the core of the material was decided to be the published texts of Kojima Kiyoshi, Okita Saburo, and Miki Takeo from the 1950s and 1960s. In collecting this material I was greatly aided by much material found in the library of the Japan Economic Research Center (JERC), which played an important part during the 1960s in organizing discussion of regional integration by sponsoring seminars and conferences. The Diet library and the library of the Institute of Developing Economies were also utilized. As a rule, I chose texts that were of a general nature, excluding texts that treated Japan's relationship with specific countries such as the United States or Thailand. The second part of the study, integration, was made with this material, and on the basis of common references it was considered sufficient.

The principal 'defect' of this material was that it left so much unsaid, only hinting at things which were supposed to be known to contemporary readers, while they certainly were not known to me. Okita might mention that he had participated in an international conference in Bandung in 1955, or Kojima might mention that the Kennedy Round negotiations of the General Agreement on Tariffs and Trade (GATT) were under way when he was formulating his PAFTA proposal. General information on such events and processes could be found from other sources, but be that as it may, if nothing more specific was said it was difficult to infer much from those references. Often there were no such references. Although it is legitimate to use various *ex silentio* type of deductions in historical research, the approach is far from unproblematic and I decided to be strictly bound by the texts. I have utilized those references where possible, but apart from some theoretical insights, few interesting conclusions could be drawn.

There were also certain curiosities in the ideational world of the Japanese discussants, such as recurring references to Japan's smallness, even though during the 1960s Japan had again become a considerable industrial power. There was an intense preoccupation with economic matters accompanied by dislike of military or political matters, equally intense interest in growth and economic development, and emotionally very-highly-charged relationships with both the Asian and the Euro–American nations. Discussion related to integration was clearly not only about international economic integration as such, but involved a psychologically deep process of reinterpretation regarding Japan and her place in the world. The total post-war situation of Japan seemed to be involved. This pointed to the possibility of fruitfully using the rhetorical method. With it, the thinness of analysis when trying to tie the texts directly to material reality could be avoided, because the general rhetorical categories could be used as a mediating link between the texts and reality. At the same time, the rhetorical method allowed for deepening the analysis, as fresh nuances could be discerned from the texts, and the changing of Japanese horizons could be uncovered more clearly. A more thorough presentation of the methodology used has been presented in Korhonen (1992).

To find out about postwar social themes of discussion, two main general interest magazines, *Sekai* and *Chuo Koron* were utilized. These are publications where a multitude of social, political and economic topics are continuously debated. The discussants tend to be various professionals, including economists and other social scientists, government officials, business people, political commentators, and journalists. From them, relevant articles of the 1940s and 1950s were selected. To these were added two government plans, which were often referred to in the texts, namely the Plan for Reconstructing the Postwar Japanese Economy published in 1946 (Gaimushō 1990) and Ikeda's Plan for Doubling National Income (Keizai shingikai 1960). Akamatsu Kaname and his theory of the flying geese pattern of development were also often referred to. Information obtained in this way was then combined with information regarding the principal events and processes of Japan's post-war period obtained from statistics and existing studies of Japan's political and economic history. This is the material with which the first part of the analysis, themes, was made.

Japanese discussion on the idea of Pacific integration is analysed mainly from the point of view of deliberative rhetoric (Aristotle 1959: I.III.1–9, Barthes 1990), specifically, as ways of trying to influence the future Japanese foreign policy in the field of economic communication with the rest of the countries of the world. In this sense, and only in this sense, a common ground is established between the strictly scientific studies of professional academic researchers, bureaucratic committee reports, and more popular publications, so that they can be read as parts of the same process of discussion.

The social situation in Aristotle's treatment of rhetoric was that of a speaker trying to convince his or her audience. As understood here, the new rhetoric, which has been emerging since the 1960s, constructs the situation as a social process of interactive communication where the purpose is to arrive at psychologically, intellectually, and emotionally acceptable social truths (Summa 1989: 89–100; Rowland 1987). An individual is understood as part of a larger epistemic community, following its rules and practices of argumentation, while building up his own arguments in order to acquire the attention and acceptance of the audience.

The Japanese economists and others involved in the dialogue on Japan's economic policy were certainly trying to influence, or 'elicit or increase the adherence of the members of an audience' to their theses (Perelman 1982: 9). They were trying to influence the general way of thinking regarding Japan's economic policies, and this purpose largely determined their audience. This can be defined as being the general educated segment of the population of Japan, which was interested in Japan's foreign economic relations and policies. In other words, they were mostly writing for each other, especially the political and bureaucratic decision-making elite of Japan to which they also tended to belong, or with which they at least had connections in the roles of experts and advisers. The size of the intended audience varies, some committee reports being written mainly for the government and upper levels of bureaucracy, some more popular articles or books being written for a wider audience not composed only of experts, but except for matters such as style, this variation causes no essential difference in the subject matter of the texts. It is only at the later stages of discussion from 1965 onwards that there emerges an important distinction between texts written for a Japanese audience, and texts written in English for an international audience. The influence of audiences on texts will be pointed out in the analysis, as appropriate, but it is not the main point of interest.

The main point of interest is the set of rhetorical categories used by Japanese discussants in formulating and defending their claims regarding the pros and cons of integration. One particular category is 'themes' as analysed in Chapter 2. Themes are understood in the same way that Stephen Toulmin used the concept of warrant in his theory of argumentation (1983: 98–106). The themes are implicit parts of arguments. They are things that everybody in a community knows and accepts, and therefore there is no need to discuss them explicitly. They form the basic common ground between discussants, guaranteeing that they understand each other, and legitimizing their arguments in the particular social context. A wide consensus about these ideas existed among Japanese economists. Some themes may logically conflict with each other, but they have to be understood as a blend. Different writers at different times placed different emphasis, but as a general entity they formed the common ground over which argumentation proceeded.

There are also other categories. The most important of these is the structuring of reality by creating liaisons and dissociations between various phenomena (Perelman 1982: 48–52, 81). In arguing, a skilful speaker chooses as his points of departure only theses that are accepted by his audience. The arguments usually take the form of a simple demonstration, in order to prove the truth of the conclusion from the premises, while actually what is happening is that the speaker is trying to transfer to his conclusion the adherence the audience accords to the premises. We are looking here at argumentation from an angle other than the themes discussed above. The themes are usually implicit parts of argumentation, voiced only when necessary, and have to be known in order for us to be able to step into the same ideational space as the discussants. Here, analysing the structuring of reality, we are looking at the explicit arguments: which kinds of things are placed in conjunction with each other, and which kinds of things are kept separate; what is given presence by being brought into consciousness, and what is left out; what evaluations – prestigious, good, moral, beneficial, wise, etc. – are attached to what kinds of phenomena.

The most important of these kinds of liaisons is the creation of ingroups and outgroups (Palonen 1987:113). The structuring of reality through the use of ingroups and outgroups is by no means unique to Japan, but according to sociological literature and linguistic practice, the Japanese may be even more prone to this kind of practice than any other peoples (see, e.g., Nakane 1985). Thus, groups are formed, e.g., between economists and others such as politicians, and a corresponding distinction is maintained between economic and other matters. Another important division is made between the Japanese and other peoples, and, similarly, between Japan and other countries. A third is the use of geographical classifications. It is as if Japanese writers were constantly holding world geoeconomical and geopolitical maps in their minds while writing. The world is defined in various ways, into superpowers and others, Asian countries and others, Euro-American countries and others, dynamically-growing countries and others, etc., with subdivisions within these groupings. Various criteria are used, and with them Japan is sometimes placed into one group, sometimes into another, with obvious implications favouring proposals for or against integration.

Closely connected with this are the kinds of things that are allowed to be present to us during argumentation. Singling out certain things for our attention is one way of making them more real and important in relation to other things (Perelman 1982: 35). Presence acts directly on our sensibilities. Its use is more important in evoking realities distant from the ideational world of which we have direct experience, but it is also frequently used in emphasizing and amplifying the familiar. The requirement of presence is the reason why texts that skilfully use examples are more easily comprehensible than those that do not. For instance, the material development of societies can be made present to us by naming familiar things like private cars, refrigerators, and other concrete things. Academic discussion also uses other types of illustrations, such as the presentation of statistical tables. For instance, Chapter 2, pages 38–49, of this study is based on the presentation of such tables, in order to familiarize ourselves, not only with the numerical facts faced by Japanese economists, but also with the principal style of making such things present in their discussion.

Prestige is one of the values attached to things to make them more acceptable to us (Perelman 1982: 94–5). Prestige as a property of the authority writers use in backing their claims, and the method for creating prestige for themselves is most important in this connection. The authorities usually cited by the discussants are other economists, like Akamatsu Kaname, whose prestige in Japan hardly needs defending. Other authorities are foreign economists who publish in

English, like Gunnar Myrdal and Wilhelm Röpke. Their prestige is mainly derived from their international fame, although their foreignness may also be a factor, among other reasons because they possess experience of regions with which the Japanese are not familiar.

More interesting are the ways of increasing the prestige of the writers themselves. Important here is the recurring theme of economism. As the presence of the economic outlook is kept constantly in our minds, it also elevates the position of the economists as the most appropriate interpreters of this reality. This method is, in places, heightened by explicit criticism of other professions or disciplines.

Another method is to present evidence witnessed with one's own eyes. The number of Japanese travelling abroad was infinitesimal until the mid-1960s, and travelling writers among them being even fewer, the inclusion of eyewitness accounts was a sure way of increasing not only the presence of arguments, but also the authoritativeness of the writer. One reason was the competence derived from that experience, another, the fact of the trip itself, implying that the person was not ordinary.

A third method is the use of academic and scientific jargon as a special case of prestigious argumentation. The use of this method is familiar to all academics as the adoption of an academic pose (Mills 1970: 240) in the form of shovelling spadefuls of abstract concepts, unfamiliar words, and prestigious names into long and obscure sentences. In Japanese discussion there is a continuum of scientific argumentation, especially numerical and statistical, on one end, and arguments based on feelings, on the other. The latter type of argument can sometimes be effective because it appeals directly to the emotional sensibilities of the audience, like the use of lively examples, without recourse to the cooler use of intellect. In economics, however, there is a preference for numerical arguments and scientific accuracy. Some writers, especially professional economists, take care of the use of language and the accuracy of numerics, as that is one of the principal points on which their competence as experts is based. Some writers are more lax in this, but usually even they try to present some sort of numerics, even of dubious value, to give their arguments a more prestigious appearance.

As a fourth method of increasing their prestige, the discussants without exception argue from the viewpoint of Japan's national interest, presenting themselves as competent and willing to enhance the good of Japan. One of the contexts for such a discussion was the wider debate on opening Japan to the international economic community, a debate between nationalists and internationalists. As the advocates of integration tended to be internationalists, they all the more had to appear as enlightened nationalists. It was around this core of nationalistic outlook that other arguments, like the common good of Asia, or the whole world, or large temporal vistas towards the future, could be employed.

There is one principle which I tried to apply as strictly as possible during my reading and analysis. It is one of the central methodological principles of historical analysis (Palonen 1987: 84–9, 95–116), namely the avoidance of *ex post* wisdom. In means simply refraining from naïve criticism of texts in the light of later historical developments. A historical text should be placed as fully as possible into the original context, trying to identify the problem areas to which the author of the text himself tried to find solutions. The writing of a text can be thought to constitute a political act, while, in turn, politics is an activity where the results have a tendency to get out of control of the intiators and espousers (Palonen 1987: 186). The idea is presented in more concrete terms by Sakamoto Yoshikazu who observed that, just as Great Britain advocated peace and free trade during the nineteenth century, ending up with a colossal colonial structure with England at its apex, Japan in a similar 'fit of absent-mindedness' built up a neo-colonial structure in the Western Pacific during the period of rapid growth and expansion of trade (Sakamoto Y. 1978: 10). Concepts like neo-colonialism and economic imperialism became fashionable in the study of international relations during the 1970s, bringing with them accusations of Japanese domination of other Pacific countries (Sakamoto Y. 1978; see also Halliday and McCormack 1973; Galtung 1989; Steven 1990), but they were not a part of the theoretical framework of Japanese economists during the 1950s or 1960s. At that time the economists were not thinking in terms of domination, but in terms of development. Their position could be described as enlightened nationalism, pursuing Japanese national interests, while limiting those interests by trying to assist the development of other Asian countries even though it meant creating economic competitors for Japan. They considered themselves to be acting morally, trying to construct a system that would bring peace, prosperity, and happiness to a maximum number of people, while guaranteeing the well-being of the Japanese. If they erred in terms of their own ideational framework, it might have been in perceiving the margin between Japan and the developing Asian countries as narrower than it actually turned out to be. It is in the sense of refraining from naïve criticism of the texts by using criteria not immanent in them that *ex post* wisdom has been avoided as far as possible in the study.

To conclude this introduction, the study analyses Japan's attempt to approach the international system after regaining independence in 1952. During this period a discussion on regional integration in Asia hesitatingly started. With the establishment of the European Economic Community in 1958 it increased, but it took until 1962 before Japanese discussion on the matter began to intensify. During the years 1962–5 a debate emerged between an Asian and a Pacific orientation for Japan in the search for suitable partners in a scheme of regional integration. The Pacific as a new horizon began to dawn on the Japanese at that time. The horizon was opened wide by Kojima Kiyoshi's PAFTA proposal in 1965, by which Japan came to be defined as a Pacific rather than an Asian country. After 1965 a boom of future studies appeared in Japan, and when Miki Takeo tied their rhetoric with the PAFTA proposal in 1967, the horizon of the Pacific century opened. In 1968 there was convened a conference in Tokyo where economists from Pacific countries discussed the proposal. Although the time was not yet seen ripe for the creation of a free trade area, the idea of Pacific co-operation was considered fascinating, and further conferences followed. In the final chapter is described the ensuing institutional process of Pacific integration, which gained momentum during the 1980s and 1990s.

2 Themes

In this chapter we shall discuss five general themes, namely (1) Japan as a small country, (2) economism, (3) growth, (4) development, and (5) Japan's relationship with Asia, which appear as an undercurrent in the post-war discussion of Japanese economists. They will be treated as the basic rhetorical categories upon which more specific discussion of Japan's integration was based. They are constructs where the economic sector appears dominant, and consequently Japanese society appears to a considerable extent to be non-political.

Post-war Japanese themes could be constructed differently, such that the society would appear as highly politicized. Sakamoto Yoshikazu's *Gunshuku no seijigaku* (1985) and Hidaka Rokuro's *Sengo shisō wo kangaeru* (1987) are good examples of such constructs. In them, the political sector is emphasized, and within this frame various political themes are constructed, such as Japan's democratization, rearmament, participation in the Cold War, pollution and social hardships, corruption in Japanese politics, Third World exploitation, world peace, and Japan's potential as a neutral, pacifying actor in the international system. This approach in general emphasizes Japanese pacifistic and leftist critique of the government, which has a long history and a vast body of literature dating from pre-war days (Bamba and Howes 1980). These themes were very important in the social discussion of post-war Japan as seen, e.g., in the 30 years of public opinion polls conducted by the Asahi shimbun since 1946 (Asahi shimbunsha 1976).

The themes of the economists as constructed here have much in common with the above, especially if contrasted with the Japanese extreme political right (Axelbank 1977; Dubro and Kaplan 1987). Their discussion has also included democratization, anti-militarism, peace, and betterment of the conditions in the developing countries. However, the economists tended to be conservative, more or less connected with the government, supporting the relationship with the United States, and looking at things from an exclusively economic angle. Because of this, different matters are emphasized and components are weighted differently from the discussion in the political sector. For instance, pacifism and anti-militarism are subsumed under the idea of economism, not separate from, or opposed to it.

The themes the economists constructed here continue up to the end of the 1960s. Economic themes appearing later during the 1970s, such as Japan as a great economic power, or the heated discussion surrounding the supply of Japan's industrial resources, will not be dealt with. Both themes are emphasized by, e.g., Bert Edström, but as he himself acknowledges, during the 1950s and 1960s Japan could rely on an abundant supply of raw materials from the international market (1988: 47), and consequently during that time Japan's poverty of resources appeared only as an attribute of Japan as a small country, not as a special theme of discussion. As Amaya Naohiro argues, emphasis was placed on resources after the supply was threatened following the panics in connection with the soy bean dispute with the United States and the Oil Crisis in 1973 (1975: 211–2).

To contemporary readers it should be pointed out that during the 1960s Japan was not yet generally referred to as a great power, economic or otherwise. Usually she was understood as a small country. This theme centres on the effect the defeat in the Pacific War had on Japanese society, economy, and international standing, when Japan came to be viewed as a small country inside the international system led by the United States, and economically backward with respect to the Euro–American countries. In the early post-war years Japan was stricken by poverty, hunger, and economic hardships in general, and faced an uncertain future under the whims and changing political objectives of the occupying powers. That period lasted formally until the end of the Occupation in 1952, but psychologically until the beginning of the 1970s. The immediate post-war situation created a feeling of inferiority, and a grave lack of self-respect, which flowed into the general theme of Japan as a small, weak country. At later stages, during the 1950s, the theme is gradually transformed into the idea of Japan's harmlessness as a small country.

The second theme is that of economism, in the sense of preoccupation with economic matters, both in national and international affairs. The theme became especially salient among the Japanese economists, but was by no means limited to them. The roots of the theme are the requirements of reconstruction after the war, the general psychological reaction against the excessive militarism of the 1930s and wartime, and the change in Japan's leading elites as the soldiers were disgraced, allowing economists to rise to prominence as planners for the future. During the 1950s and 1960s this theme also underwent a transformation. As the military was not able to return to a position of significant influence in Japanese society, and as it turned out to be difficult to rule the country with rhetoric related to political issues, economism appeared as the common social denominator around which a national consensus could be built during the 1960s.

The third theme is economic growth. During the 1950s and 1960s Japan was able to attain a rate of growth far exceeding that of any other nation of the time. In addition to increased resources as constituents of national power, this also produced a certain sense of success as Japan, according to economic criteria, became the shining success story of the post-war world. These were the criteria of the Japanese themselves, as through economism they had elevated economic values to the highest position among national values. Success in fulfilling these tended in its turn to increase the power of economism as the right method of interpreting the world. These were also the criteria of much international discussion, centring on organizations like the General Agreement on Tariffs and Trade (GATT), the Organization for Economic Co-operation and Development (OECD), and the United Nations, which declared the 1960s a 'decade of development', understood mainly as economic growth. In this field Japan became a model country, praised both nationally and internationally. This in its turn created a new optimistic theme of economic growth in Japanese discussion, gathering strength from the beginning of the 1960s onwards. On this ground a new national self-esteem could be built. The period presents a sort of battle of themes, where the optimistic theme of economic success begins to overcome the pessimistically-coloured theme of Japan's smallness.

The fourth theme is development. In discussing all these themes, emphasis is on the way Japanese economists used them, but this theme tended to be their prerogative. Under this theme is discussed the theory of the flying geese pattern of development as proposed by Akamatsu Kaname. Although the details of the theory are not very well known internationally, the influence of Akamatsu among Japanese economists has been considerable. The perspective is on long-term changes in the industrial structure of Japan and corresponding changes in her relations with the international system. All social theories, even historical ones like that of Akamatsu, tend to be future oriented in the sense that a likely course of development can be deduced therefrom, which in turn influences the policy alternatives the discussants tend to perceive as viable. The relevance of this to the Japanese discussion of integration is obvious.

The fifth theme centres on post-war political and economic processes in Asia, and their significance to Japan. Japan's colonial and military legacy with the other Asian countries complicated her relationship with the area during the post-war period. It was further complicated by the processes during which a number of new East and Southeast Asian countries gained independence, creating a totally new regional environment for Japan. The Japanese had considerable trouble coming to grips conceptually with the situation. Their troubles were further heightened by the ideological division of the region due to the intensifying Cold War, which cut Japan off from a large share of her traditional trading relationships. The near ending of trade with China was an especially serious blow both in an economic and a psychological sense, and in geoeconomical terms placed Japan in a highly unnatural situation. The situation in Asia, and Japan's relationship to it, helped to push Japan towards a new foreign policy horizon.

A SMALL COUNTRY

The theory of hegemonic change has been recently much discussed in international politics (see, e.g., Keohane and Nye 1977; Gilpin 1984; Kennedy 1989; Nye 1990). According to this approach, the post-Second World War international system has been characterized by the hegemonic position of the United States. The United States emerged from the war as the predominant economic and military power in the world. Among the great powers, it was the only one to become richer and stronger during the war. At the end of the war more than half of the total manufacturing production took place in the United States; for several years after the war it supplied one-third of the world's exports, and owned half of the world's shipping. It had the largest military fleet and the largest air force, with which it could effectively project global power, and until 1948 it had a monopoly on atomic bombs. It also had the image of ineffable superiority over any other country. The image was reinforced by corresponding pleas from a multitude of weaker countries for economic help and military support. Consequently, the United States assumed world leadership, dominating the making of new rules of conduct for international communication, the setting up of new organizations, and policy making within these organizations. Some of them were economic, such as GATT, or the International Monetary Fund (IMF), based on the 1944 Bretton Woods agreement and the ideology of global free trade; some were military, such as the North Atlantic Treaty Organization (NATO), the Southeast Asia Treaty Organization (SEATO), or bilateral military agreements, such as the one created between the United States and Japan in 1952. At the end of the 1940s the position of the United States was challenged by the Soviet Union and the socialist countries under its leadership, a confrontation which became known as the Cold War, and which increased the influence of the United States over its allies and other countries it controlled.

Japan was adopted into this system as a defeated, occupied enemy nation. The occupation of Japan lasted from 1945 to 1952, during which period it was subjected to a variety of deep-reaching American influences, including an abrupt policy shift in 1947–8 – the 'reverse course'. While regaining formal independence Japan was tied to the United States as an ally in the Cold War. The lesser countries in a hegemonic system are often divided into two classes: 'supporters' and 'small countries'. Supporters are understood as middle-level powers, bearing part of the costs and responsibilities of the system, as well as sharing some power and prestige with the hegemonic country. Small countries are often pejoratively called 'free riders'. They do not have much power or prestige in the system, while they also tend to try to escape from the costs and responsibilities. They adapt to the system, use it according to their national interests, while paying as little as possible for the system's maintenance (Lake 1983; Inoguchi 1986). According to this view, while all countries try to benefit from the system and get their share out of it, long-term costs tend to devolve to the more powerful members. The practices of the small countries are to an extent tolerated as long as they remain insignificant actors. On the other hand, their smallness and weakness puts them in danger of being crushed in a military confrontation, because they are unimportant from the point of view of the total system.

Any abstract definition of the concept of a small country presents difficulties. There are so many different criteria that can be used as the basis for classification. The material criteria often used are area, population, military capability, economic capability or the size of the gross national product (GNP), but unless a country is small according to all of them, the results of such classifications often prove meaningless (Momose 1990: 2). The problem is especially pronounced in the case of Japan, which even after the war was clearly a big country in terms of population, and became gradually stronger also in economic and military terms from the 1950s onwards. However, the question here does not relate to the material attributes of Japan as such, but rather the Japanese people's *psychological* feelings of weakness, and a perceived lack of influence in the international system. This lack is not total, but rather means that the foreign policy alternatives of the country are limited (comp. Väyrynen 1988: 26–37).

It was with this kind of status of a small country that Japan entered the hegemonic system of the United States, as an occupied and controlled country. She had no means of defending herself. She had a backward, inefficient economy, and an impoverished population. From 1952 onwards Japan began to move to the status of a supporter, first in a military sense with the conclusion of the United States–Japan Security Treaty. It was a slow process, especially in a psychological sense. The initial post-war image of Japan as a small country tended to linger on, and it was still an important theme of discussion even at the end of the 1960s. During that decade Japan was still to an extent shielded from international politics by the protection of the United States, being thus able to concentrate on economic matters (Shibusawa 1984: 23–5). As Edström shows, images of Japan as a big power began to circulate after the beginning of the 1960s, but the image of Japan as a small country was still common even during the 1970s (Inoguchi 1988: passim). Here the interpretation of Inoguchi will be adopted, according to which Japan during the 1970s moved from the role of a small country to that of a supporter (1987: 104–9). Similar arguments have also been made by Nakamura (1987: 106–7) and Yasutomo (1986: 21) in the sense that political considerations became more explicit in Japanese foreign policy at the time, and by Lincoln (1988) in the sense that from the point of view of industrial development Japan became a 'mature' economy at that time.

The decisive beginning of the change seems to have been in 1969 when a difficult trade dispute began over Japanese exports of textiles to the United States, constituting an event when, for the first time in post-war history, the two countries publicly disagreed on an important issue, Japan decisively saying 'no' to the United States (Emmerson 1976: 373–6; Destler *et al.* 1979). In the same year the United States also agreed to return Okinawa, last of the Japanese territories occupied by the United States. The change was triggered when Richard Nixon, who became president in 1968, began to phase downwards the international position of the United States with the 1969 Guam doctrine, followed by the New Economic Program in 1971, and the Sino–US *rapprochement* from 1971. In Japan these were called 'Nixon shocks', followed by the 'Oil shock' in 1973, and various anti-Japanese hostilities in ASEAN countries from 1972 (Nakamura 1987: 218–34; Shibusawa 1984: 62–85). These events forced Japanese people to reinterpret Japan's position in the international system, signifying that their country had become a big power in the international system. Also, in the literature of the time, Japan came to be considered as such, beginning with Herman Kahn's *The Emerging Japanese Superstate* (1970).

However, up to that time Japan was usually depicted as a small country. The small country theme involved four main components, namely, Japanese geography, fall in rank, subjection to forced foreign influences, and lack of influence. Kojima Kiyoshi presents in his *Japan and a Pacific Free Trade Area*, whose preface was dated August 1969, the following description of Japan:

> Japan is a small country, with a high population density and an unfavourable resource endowment.
>
> (Kojima 1971: 9)

The reference regarding Japan's smallness at the time, as made by Kojima, was mainly geographic. The term 'small' referred to the size of the Japanese islands, which were also seen to be poor in terms of raw materials and other resources, considering the high population density prevalent on the islands. The size of the land mass of Japan – before the return of Okinawa – was 369,662 square kilometres, while her population was about 100 million. In terms of population or industrial capacity Japan was a big country, but even at the end of the 1960s there was still a tendency to emphasize, in certain situations, Japan's smallness using geography.

The expression 'Japan is a small country' was fixed. It was the expression around which Japanese self-understanding centred after the Second World War, and at its peak as *the* description of Japan it contained a collection of sensitive connotations. The explicitly geographical sense in which Kojima used it was only a pale echo of a glorious past, but implicitly it still carried undertones of earlier usage.

The world in which the Japanese were used to orienting themselves before and during the Second World War was shattered by defeat in the war. Both at home and abroad Japan had been understood as a great power. Swedish geopolitical theoretician Rudolf Kjellén had elevated Japan to the 'nobility' of countries together with Austro-Hungary, Italy, France, Germany, England, the United States, and Russia in his *Die Großmächte der Gegenwart* in 1914. In the subsequent editions of the book by the German Karl Haushofer Japan was always placed on a similar high rank (see, e.g., Kjellén and Haushofer 1935). Between the world wars, geographical arguments relating to the small land mass of the Japanese home islands were normally used to explain Japanese expansion to overseas territories (Haushofer 1923; Hindmarsh 1936; Iriye 1972; Myers and Peattie 1984). The process ended in the attempt to create the *Dai Tōa Kyōeiken*, the Greater East Asian Co-prosperity Sphere (Elsbree 1953; Jones 1954; Lebra 1975; Ienaga 1978), a regional economic and political grouping in East and Southeast Asia that would have been controlled by Japan.

When Japan was defeated in the Second World War, she dropped down this high international rank, and was confined to the narrow home islands with a population of about 80 million, and subjected to various foreign influences. The fall can be seen for instance in the way the official name of Japan, a very important national symbol, changed after the war. In the pre-war constitution the name of Japan had been *Dai Nippon Teikoku*, Greater Japanese Empire, but in the new constitution of 1946 the name was changed to *Nippon-koku*, Japanese State, where the characters meaning great and emperor were dropped. In this way Japan was symbolically made smaller.

There were other similar changes. Already in the last stages of the war Japan had lost the capability to define herself geographically. In 1945 that capability had shifted to the Allied nations. On 14 July Winston Churchill, Harry Truman and Josef Stalin agreed in Potsdam on a common policy towards Japan. In addition to rooting out militarism and pushing through democratic reforms, they decided to deprive Japan of all of her overseas possessions acquired by arms, and limit the land area of Japan to the four main islands of Hokkaido, Honshu, Shikoku and Kyushu, as well as some smaller islands to be decided later by the Allied Powers. The Soviet Union declared war on Japan on 8 August, and proposed to the United States that Soviet troops would like to occupy Japan from the north as far as the middle of Hokkaido, in addition to taking control of Manchukuo, Northern Korea, Southern Sakhalin, and the Kurile Islands. At that time the Americans still expected the occupation of Japan to be difficult, and they planned that the Soviet Union should occupy not only the whole of Hokkaido, but the northern part of Honshu, called Tohoku, as well (Masamura 1987: 19–28).

Had the American plan been carried out, it would have made Japan a divided country, similar to the two Germanys and the two Koreas created after the war. However, dispute had broken out in Germany between the occupying American and Soviet forces, and the Americans in the end decided to take the occupation of the Japanese main islands into their own hands. Japan under the American occupation was divided into two areas of differing status: Okinawa and the rest of the Ryukyu Islands, along with the Ogasawara Islands south of Tokyo, were under direct US military government control, while the remaining area was placed under indirect military rule.

Japan had also become a poor country. In addition to the atomic bombs dropped on Hiroshima and Nagasaki, bombing with conventional explosives and incendiary bombs had levelled most major cities, including Tokyo and Osaka, as well as most industrial sites. In addition to the dead and wounded, material losses in the industrial base of the country were considerable. There was damage due to bombing, and damage due to wartime conditions. Equipment for civilian production had been systematically turned to military uses, and much of the machinery had become run down due to lack of repairs. Ten years' worth of national wealth had disappeared in one stroke. Many people were in danger of starvation, especially during the winter of 1945–6. The rice crop was only two-thirds of a normal year, and at the same time the means of acquiring income had grown more difficult. There were not enough jobs. Production had fallen for the lack of factories, machines, materials, and energy. The disbanding of military forces turned 7.61 million troops into civilians, the ending of military production made 4 million people unemployed, and 1.5 million people were repatriated from abroad. Under these conditions the number of people living on very meagre incomes was large, and the problem persisted long into the 1950s (Nakamura 1987: 14–22).

The occupation of Japan is usually divided into two periods. The first period is marked by a reformist zeal on the part of the Americans, up to the point where Japan in certain respects began to resemble a gigantic social laboratory for the testing of ideal liberal democracy. During this time Japan was punished as a wrong-doer to be educated in new ways to prevent it from ever again posing a threat to other countries. From about 1947, when the 'Chilly War'

(Yoshitsu 1983: 2) of the immediate post-war period began to evolve into the Cold War, there emerged a 'reverse course' in the policies of the Occupation. At first, reforms were carried out less effectively, or their implementation was halted, and eventually the course was reversed completely. The emphasis of the Occupation shifted towards economic rehabilitation and rearmament for building Japan up as an ally in the struggle against the feared spread of communism. The tension between these opposing policies left deep marks in the Japanese social system.

During the first period, in co-operation with Japanese institutions, the Supreme Commander for the Allied Powers (SCAP) initiated several reforms of Japanese political, economic, agricultural, educational, and labour systems. The thoroughness of the early wave of reforms was caused by what Edwin Reischauer has called the 'devil theory of history' (1984: 279). According to his view, the Japanese leaders since the early 1930s had been engaged in a conspiracy to wage aggressive war. The opportunity of the leaders to do this had been enhanced by several factors in Japanese society itself, such as its 'feudalistic nature', militaristic values, reactionary political system, and huge financial combines. The Occupation set out to eradicate militarism from Japan by placing former members of the Japanese leadership on trial, dissolving the military services, purging over 200,000 persons from public office, breaking up some of the financial combines, and instigating various democratic reforms regarding the political and economic systems, landholdings, and education (Baerwald 1959; Yamamura 1967; Ward and Sakamoto 1987).

The Constitution of Japan was rewritten. Article 9 of the new Constitution was the most revolutionary in contents, and eventually it became an important symbol of the new Japan. Article 9 states:

> Aspiring sincerely to an international peace based on justice and order, the Japanese people forever renounce war as a sovereign right of the nation and the threat or use of force as means of settling international disputes.
>
> In order to accomplish the aim of the preceding paragraph, land, sea, and air forces, as well as other war potential, will never be maintained. The right of belligerency of the state will not be recognized.

Article 9 is without doubt the greatest example of the reformist spirit of the Occupation. It is still in force today, having great influence in the conduct of Japanese foreign policy, although the article has been surrounded by dispute ever since it was drafted.

After the 'reverse course' set in, there were attempts to abolish Article 9, and to proceed with Japan's rearmament, using an interpretation of the article according to which it does not preclude self-defence. The article was, however, accepted by the Japanese people and by several influential politicians, thus making its removal from the Constitution impossible. Continuous dispute around Article 9 has helped to make its contents well known among all Japanese, and it has become an important national symbol. It has also been one of the main factors in creating a strong feeling about a complete change in the nature of Japan. With Article 9 it eventually began to look as though Japan had shed militarism forever. In essence she had become a morally good country.

The Occupation period has been called by Sakamoto Yoshikazu 'the second opening of Japan' (1987b: 3), comparing it with the first opening of the country in the middle of the nineteenth century. During both periods Western culture was brought into Japan on a large scale. The difference between the periods lies in the fact that during the Meiji period Western culture was brought into Japan on the initiative of, and under the control of, the Japanese themselves, but that was not the case during the Occupation. As Sakamoto describes it, the Occupation was such a total enterprise that the borderline separating the country from outside vanished, and outside powers superimposed their authority within Japan as they pleased. In these circumstances it is not so important that many of the reforms instituted greatly benefited and strengthened Japan; the essential thing was the manner in which the reforms were carried out. It was the exact opposite to the situation that had prevailed before and during the war, when Japan penetrated into her colonies and the Greater East Asian Co-prosperity Sphere. This time it was Japan that was placed in a weak position. Japan was redefined, restructured, and reformed by foreign powers. They could even change their policies in the middle of the programme just as they pleased, and the Japanese were always compelled to yield. Although they were not necessarily hostile to Japan and its people, these foreign authorities, wielding their power for six-and-a-half years, created a strong feeling of subjugation in Japan, which is clearly discernible in the public discussion of the period.

A typical opening line in articles published in general interest magazines was the following:

On 19 December last year, a letter was forwarded from General MacArthur to Prime Minister Yoshida.

(Minobe 1949)

The contents of the message are not important; what is important is the simple presentation of the command. There is a foreign authority taking the initiative, while the Japanese side responds and obeys. The structure of the sentence reflects this situation. The sentence is made dramatic by the presentation of the exact date at the beginning, followed by the comma as a pause before the revelation of the main message, emphasis on the letter as a form of one-way communication perfectly suitable for commands, and the order of the two men.

The order of the leader and the follower is almost always the same, leading being the foreigner's responsibility, following, the Japanese part. The foreign authority is not necessarily American. There are authors who refrain from treating the Americans in this way, but have in their place another foreign authority, e.g., the United Nations, or its Asian organization, the Economic Commission for Asia and the Far East (ECAFE) (e.g., Okita 1950).

However, usually the United States is depicted in this role. Authors evaluating what the Occupation brought to Japan see a constant flow of influences: demilitarization, democratization, the 'reverse course', economic reform, forced economic independence, and the Cold War. Also, in the future, the only way to re-enter international society seems to be the road of dependence as a subordinate partner of the United States (Kobayashi 1951).

Shimizu Ikutaro presents the situation from another angle. His problem is how the other people of the world – which boils down to the people of the United States – view the Japanese. According to an American public opinion survey, the results of which Shimizu had happened to see, the Japanese were not popular. They were placed in the group of least liked nations, in the same class with Philippinos, Koreans, Chinese, Indians, and Turks. His principal point is the following:

Because of the loss of the war Japan has again come to stand below the Western countries. There was a time when she could keep her shoulders level with them, but now she has fallen to a low and dark place without a bottom in sight. The Japanese have, again, become Asians.

(Shimizu 1951)

Without dwelling on the matter of how impolite this kind of lamentation might have been to other Asians, we may note that the word 'Asians' in the quotation does not have any prestige attached. At the time it rather had the image of backwardness, ignorance, poverty, and being unwanted. It is noteworthy that Shimizu makes the conclusion that Japan is being placed at the bottom of the international ranking scale on the basis of one single survey. Perhaps it shows how great the extent to which foreign, especially American, opinions could sway Japanese self-esteem, and how weak and shattered that self-esteem had become.

In texts published during the latter half of the 1940s a deep sense of insecurity is displayed. Some of the fear is centred on new military technology, e.g., mass bombing capability, especially the atomic bomb, of whose destructive capacity the Japanese had received ample evidence. The seeming ease of the destruction of whole cities by solitary planes carrying single bombs, accompanied by the difficulty of defence against this kind of warfare, produced a revelation that whole nations could be wiped out at a whim. Even the devastation of the whole world began to look possible. That called for a new way of thinking regarding peace and the conduct of international politics, resulting in a multitude of pacifistic and idealistic articles. They also emerged as a reaction to such ideas having been suppressed during wartime, and they were, in general, in line with the explicit reformist objectives of the early Occupation. There emerged a discussion on world peace, centring on the concept of a world state, and a reliance on the United Nations (e.g., Yokota 1946).

The destruction of the world and Japan did not materialize during the 1940s, but the intensification of the Cold War from 1947 onwards, and the civil war in China generated misgivings about the future. The fears rose to a new fervour at the beginning of the Korean War in 1950 when the concept of a Third World War entered the discussion. Fear of the war escalating and embroiling Japanese territory was considerable (Sekiguchi 1950; Serita *et al.* 1951). The Asian area, including Japan, was depicted as a playground for the competing influences of the United States, Great Britain, and the Soviet Union. Some placed their hopes for peace in Asia on the benevolence of these great powers (Kuno 1950), some were more pessimistic as to the outcome (Sugi 1950). Because of this situation, there was among the Japanese people a tendency to turn inwards to try to forget the frightening outer world (Royama 1951).

The world of politics was a place where occupied Japan was

merely a spectator, without much possibility of influencing the events taking place around her. A more practical worry was the state of the Japanese economy. During the latter half of the 1940s there hardly appeared an article on the Japanese economy which did not contain the word *mondai*, meaning 'problem'. It was very often placed in the title of the article, but the opening sections were also a favourite place. In place of *mondai* other favourite words were *konran* (chaos), and *kiki* (crisis) (e.g., Yamaguchi 1946; Karashima 1948; Nagata 1948; Royama 1948; Itagaki 1949; Arisawa *et al.* 1951). The discussion centred on the terrible situation in Japan, the tone of some articles appearing to be on the verge of hysteria. There was lament over poverty, inflation, unemployment, lack of food, lack of capital, and lack of raw materials. Also, in the field of economics, insecurity surfaced over the wishes of the victors and their plans for the future status of Japan. There was a profound sense of material dependence on the United States, understandable if one considers the figures for Japan's international trade in 1946: 96 per cent of imports came from the United States, and 70 per cent of exports went there. The situation hurt the Japanese economy, which seemed to be in a process of contraction, unable to compete with the vast and efficient American economy (Okita 1947). Some writers took this to mean the eventual colonization of Japan, and when the early American plans became known for stripping both Germany and Japan of any industrial capacity that would enable military recovery in the future, making them in effect agricultural countries, fears about the future grew. Expressions like *saigo no uta*, 'the swan song of Japan' (Nagata 1948) were used, although in 1948 the situation was no longer that serious, with production rising, and the American attitude towards Japan's deindustrialization changing. On the other hand, belief in Japan's abilities to survive alone without the support of the United States was not necessarily great; even as late as 1951 expressions like *kuenai Nihon* (Ryu 1951), literally, 'Japan that cannot eat', were used in arguments *against* the economic independence of Japan (see also Tsuchiya 1951).

Public discussion at the end of the 1940s and at the beginning of the 1950s portrayed Japan in the role of a receiver of foreign influences. Japan was depicted as a small, low-ranking and powerless country, a spectator rather than an actor in the international system. The days of the Empire were past. Nor did there seem to be in the future any possibility of ever becoming a great power again. That horizon was closed for the Japan of the immediate post-war years. In his study of Japanese culture and literature also of later periods,

Kato Norihiro (1985) finds that although Japan became prosperous and economically strong again, she psychologically tended to remain 'in the shadow of America' (*Amerika no kage*), the United States continuing to exert a powerful, alternately restrictive and approving influence on Japan.

The concept of smallness, however, also contains the image of harmlessness. After years of demilitarization and reforms aimed at creating a peaceful Japan, it indeed began to look like Japan would no longer pose any threat to her neighbours. Consequently, the image of a small and unthreatening Japan began to emerge. It was often accompanied by an idealistic idea of the development of a peaceful world, centring on the United Nations system, where the use of force would gradually diminish. In addition, there was deep reluctance about being drawn into the structure of the Cold War as a participant. There was emphasis on the necessity of good conduct for Japan, reformed and demilitarized as she was, not only for her own good, but also for the good of the whole world. Japan should behave like a good citizen in an orderly society. In this limited sense, the image of Japan as a participant, rather than a mere spectator, remained in Japanese discussion.

One of the most explicit advocates of this type of thinking was Okita Saburo. His ideas centred on the expression, *Ajia keizai no hatten ni kōken suru* (Okita 1950), meaning 'to make contributions to the economic development of Asia'. The idea was vague, as Japan lacked the means with which to make a contribution. The idea did not have the connotation of leading, but rather that of *serving* the Asian countries in their development. In this way, a peaceful Asia which would not harbour feelings of enmity against Japan would be helped to come into being.

In the following year, when the Korean War boom stimulated the Japanese economy to develop rapidly, another economist, Arisawa Hiromi, advocated the idea of again starting up investments in other Asian countries. The idea was to make contributions to their development, but also to help Japanese trade with those countries. Referring to investments, he describes the situation with an interesting argument:

> Modern Japan has been reborn and changed, and because this is only a type of commercial activity, would they not accept it?
>
> (Arisawa *et al.* 1951: 67)

Japan had become a new country. She was no longer the old imperialistic Japan, and therefore the other Asian countries might be willing to welcome Japanese investments again. Reborn Japan, as a small country, was no longer dangerous to anybody. She would engage only in peaceful activities, like commerce. This opened the way for reforming relations with other Asian countries, and this could be done most easily in the economic field.

ECONOMISM

Economism, the distinctly Japanese style of concentrating on economic matters both in national and international affairs, has frequently been referred to by both Japanese and foreign analysts. Referring to this as the predominant attitude in Japan since the Second World War, Okita Saburo states as follows:

> Let us concentrate on rebuilding our own economy and not become involved too much in others' affairs.
>
> (Okita 1965: 7)

Okita's idea refers to the narrowing of Japan's foreign political horizons in a post-war situation where efforts were being concentrated on reconstructing Japan's own economy, while putting far less emphasis on international pursuits. This attitude can be regarded as a consequence of Japan's international position as a small country, the military and political sectors being severely restricted.

Some authors tend to place the emergence of Japanese economism at the beginning of the 1960s, a result of Ikeda Hayato's rise to the position of prime minister, and the consequent change in the political climate. The Ikeda government adopted a low posture in politics, trying to avoid ideological controversies, emphasizing instead economic growth as a unifying goal for the whole nation (Shibusawa 1984: 22–5). Edström, too, emphasizes Japan's economic growth in this connection, although he claims that the use of the concept of economism is only an *ex post facto* rationalization for Japan's economic success (1988: 69). As an analytical concept economism no doubt occurred later than Japan's rapid growth, but as a theme it is older, and separate from growth as such.

Economism has also been put forward as a long-term historical dilemma faced by Japan: the necessity to find markets for exports and imports, manifest since she became an industrialized state (Allen 1962). This was heightened by Japan's post-war political and military weakness (Nish 1975).

For our purposes, however, Okita's interpretation of the origins of 'economism' is the most relevant. Our emphasis is thus on Japan's internal political situation, with Ikeda's contribution as the crowning of this theme.

Economism as a way of thinking had already begun to develop at the late stages of the Pacific War, as a reaction to the militaristic ideology prevalent at the time. Both Kojima Kiyoshi and Okita Saburo, when interviewed in Tokyo in the autumn of 1991 concerning the origins of the idea of Pacific integration, started by referring to the Pacific War and condemning the militaristic policies of the time as harmful and contrary to the interests of Japan. Both of them emphasized how, after the defeat, economists took the lead in the reconstruction of Japan. They became the 'brains of Japan', as Okita expressed it, and guided the country to its present prosperity. Okita's statement expresses only professional pride, but the central importance of the economists has also been emphasized by researchers (e.g., Zahl 1973: 142–9).

Criticism of the military has been a consistent theme in the writings of those Japanese economists who were already active during wartime. For instance, Okita was working as a young researcher in the Bureau of General Affairs in the Ministry of Greater East Asia. In this capacity, he had access to confidential information on Japan's internal and external supply of resources. He discovered – as did others at the time – that Japan was fighting a war without a hope of winning. Japan was highly dependent on the import of both industrial raw materials and food, while by 1943 Allied submarine warfare had already more or less cut transportation routes from Southeast Asia. In 1944 connections with the continent across the Sea of Japan became threatened as well. Okita relates in his memoirs an anecdote told during the last stages of the war, which perhaps accurately displays the mood of the time among silent dissidents:

> A poor warrior wanted to buy a splendid suit of armour but had no money, so he cut down on the amount of food he ate and little by little saved enough to buy a fine suit of armour. A war broke out and courageously he left to fight, but because his body had become so weak from his years of semi-starvation, he could not bear the weight of his armour and was soon slain by the enemy.
>
> (Okita 1983: 26)

The war had been a mismanaged affair – especially economically – and it ended in disaster. This showed that Japan could not wage a long-term war on a large scale with any hope of winning. Japan's industry was dependent on the import of raw materials, the population was equally dependent on imports of food, and both the population and industry were concentrated in a few centres along the narrow coastline. Already during the Second World War transportation routes could be cut and the centres of production destroyed, incapacitating Japan. Subsequent improvements in war technology have made this even easier. One of the lessons learned by the Japanese economists during the war was that Japan's welfare and prosperity could not be secured through military means. Japanese economism started as a rejection of militaristic thinking, and it has tended to bear this mark ever since.

The importance of an economic orientation as the basis for promoting Japan's welfare would have been the conclusion drawn even without the reforms of the Occupation. In this sense, the reforms emphasized the lesson, not least because of the changes in the Japanese elite. The military was removed from its former position, and prevented from returning. The new elite was formed by conservative politicians, an economic bureaucracy, and the economic community (Tsuneishi 1966; Thayer 1969; Zahl 1973; Watanuki 1977; Johnson 1986; Uchida 1987; Otake 1987). Intellectuals with an economic background were needed as consultants for the bureaucracy and the government, and to plan for reconstruction.

The basic lines of Japan's post-war reconstruction can be found in a report of the Ministry of Foreign Affairs Special Survey Committee, which was published in September 1946. Work for the report had already begun in 1945, when Okita Saburo, with his mentor Taira Teizo, began to secretly organize a study group to plan for Japan's economic rehabilitation in light of the knowledge that the war would be lost. The first meeting of the group was scheduled to take place on 16 August 1945, and as the war happened to end on the 15th, the group was able to start working openly without delay. Later it acquired an official status as the Committee of the Ministry of Foreign Affairs (Okita 1983: 27–9). The committee was mainly composed of professional economists, and as Okita acted as one of the secretaries, much of the actual text was compiled or written by him.

The report is replete with praise of economics and economic thinking. Setting out from the experiences of the recent war, the committee clearly sees that economic capability determined the war's outcome, and expects economic problems to become even more important in future international politics and diplomacy. As a consequence of technological breakthroughs – such as long-range bombers and atomic bombs – a major task of international politics will be to prevent the destruction of the human race. In the idealistic climate of the post-war world the committee expects that international co-operation as a process towards a more harmonious and peaceful world, leading eventually perhaps to a world federal state, will reduce the importance of the individual state as an independent entity. In general, the new post-war world will see more interest expressed in the welfare of the people than previously evidenced (Gaimushō tokubetsu chōsa iinkai 1990: 146).

Because world trends and the lessons of the war are understood in these terms, Japan as a nation must understand thoroughly the workings of the new world. The committee takes up the problem of education, stating that the Japanese people do not understand economics well enough, and declares: 'Economic education has to be spread to all segments of the nation, so that economics can be made the avocation of all citizens' (Gaimushō tokubetsu chōsa iinkai 1990: 261). The committee proposes that education in economics for all teachers should start at once. The sense of urgency was heightened by the situation in 1946, and by the country's extremely insecure future prospects. A full-scale concentration on economic activity seemed to be the only way to save the nation from continued misery, or even starvation, which might lead to a large-scale diminution of the population. At the same time, as the world had changed qualitatively, economic activity seemed to be the way to succeed in the new world, provided that reconstruction was allowed by the occupying powers.

The primacy of economism was transformed into a style of national politics during the so-called Yoshida years. Yoshida Shigeru was the prime minister of Japan during 1946–7 and again during 1948–54. As Prime Minister, he was acceptable to the Occupation forces because, during his career as a bureaucrat in the Foreign Ministry, he had been a critic of the military since the 1930s. In 1945 he had been arrested by the military police for being at the centre of a high ranking group of officials advocating a negotiated peace (Reischauer 1984: 302–3; Storry 1968: 254–5). During the 1970s his political style came to be referred to as the Yoshida doctrine by political scientists, but economists do not often use this term.

Nakamura Takafusa has termed Japan's foreign political course charted during the Yoshida years as *kyōhei naki fukoku*, 'a rich country without a strong army', (1986: 212). The expression is patterned after the Meiji slogan *fukoku kyōhei*, which meant 'a rich country with a strong army'. In the new post-war situation the builders of a new Japan dropped the goal of a strong military from their plans, and concentrated solely on the economy. The slogan in use at the time was *senzen*, or 'pre-war'. More precisely, a consensus developed around the idea of quickly regaining the pre-war level of economic well-being (Nakamura 1986: 211). The goal was widely accepted by the planners and the population at large, but did not yet contain the idea of rapid growth, which was a later phenomenon.

Yoshida's first government had been responsible for the final drafting of the new Constitution, as well as pushing it through the Diet. During the debate Yoshida had denounced even Japan's right of self-defence (Yoshida 1961: 140; Momoi 1977: 342). Throughout his political career he defended Article 9 of the Constitution. On the other hand, Yoshida was a strongly anti-communist conservative, who strove to lock Japan into a close political and military alliance with the United States. In spite of this, his government opposed American demands for rearmament during the Reverse Course, although it did agree in 1950 to set up a 75,000 man strong National Police Reserve (NPR) after the outbreak of hostilities on the Korean peninsula. Despite its name the NPR was a fighting force. Its military capabilities were improved in 1951, and in 1954 it was transformed into the tri-service Self-Defence Force. Although Yoshida was politically responsible for starting Japan's rearmament, he was reportedly reluctant to increase defence spending. However, as setting up the Self Defence Force was one of the conditions imposed by the Americans for concluding the Peace Treaty and the Mutual Security Treaty, it had to be done (Yoshitsu 1983: 60–5; Momoi 1977: 345).

It seems that Yoshida wanted to ensure the military security of Japan in a way that was heavily dependent on the direct involvement of the United States. In the Cold War situation Japan's educated population, industrial potential, and strategic location would be enough to make the defence of Japan vital to the strategic interests of the United States. In exchange for military protection Japan should politically orient herself towards the United States, and support its position in international affairs. A Japanese military force capable of countering the threat of the Soviet Union and China would unnecessarily divert capital from the economy, and impede recovery. Yoshida's opposition to rearmament was relative, not absolute, guided by the rule that recovery must precede rearmament. His goal was the smallest and cheapest military force possible under the circumstances, commensurate with the economic situation in Japan. He seems also to have been wary of the possible rebirth of the military elite as a determining force in Japanese politics, should the military have been strengthened too much (Yoshitsu 1983: 39–40, 51). As a politician too, Yoshida did not want to support the cause of remilitarization, which was unpopular in Japan at the time (Yoshida 1961: 191–2). In this sense, the legacy of the Yoshida years was the *kyōhei naki fukoku* orientation of Japanese politics, the primacy of economics.

Although adopting the economic goal of reconstructing the Japanese economy to the pre-war level can be said to have constituted a consensus at the time, the Yoshida years also produced grave ideological and political controversies. The other legacy of the Yoshida doctrine was dependence on the United States. The controversy revolved around the concepts of *zenmenkōwa* and *katamenkōwa*. The first expression meant 'overall peace', making peace with all of the countries Japan had fought against in the Second World War, including the Soviet Union and the People's Republic of China, while *katamenkōwa*, 'one-sided peace', meant leaving the socialist countries out (Masamura 1987: 321–44). In the end, because of heavy pressure from the United States, the latter option was chosen. The San Francisco Peace Treaty was signed on 8 September 1951. On that same day the United States concluded the Mutual Security Treaty with Japan. Both treaties came into force on 28 April 1952.

The Japanese Left, which favoured 'overall peace' opposed both the Peace Treaty and the Security Treaty, and led anti-government and anti-American demonstrations after Japan regained independence. The strong presence of US troops had been accepted as long as the country was formally occupied, but now many could no longer tolerate them. In the following years the problem of the American troops and bases became a cause for severe agitation, as revealed in newspapers, periodicals, books and movies. These depicted the bad behaviour and the demoralizing influence of American soldiers (Storry 1968: 259–60). No popular consensus could be created on political matters.

The situation continued during the 1950s, heightened occasionally by scandals like the Bikini incident in 1954, when a Japanese fishing vessel was contaminated by radioactive fallout from an American nuclear test on Bikini atoll. On the other hand, the right wing at times adopted terror tactics, as when the extreme right murdered Asanuma Inejiro, Secretary General of the Japan Socialist Party. The situation culminated in the riots of 1960 over the extension of the Security Treaty. Prime Minister Kishi Nobusuke's government negotiated an extension to the Security Treaty with the United

States with revisions, including the ending of the right of the US to use troops to squash domestic disturbances. As the controversy was over terminating or extending the treaty, however, the process led to several weeks of massive demonstrations and fighting in the streets. Students and mostly left-wing demonstrators were on one side, the police and right-wing hoodlums on the other. The whole society became polarized over the question, and Kishi was forced to resign at the beginning of July (Storry 1968: 274–6).

After Kishi, the style of Japanese political rhetoric changed under the new prime minister, Ikeda Hayato. The new idea introduced was the doubling of Japanese incomes, i.e., an economic topic. It was Kishi himself who had in 1959 ordered the Economic Planning Agency to draft a plan for doubling the scale of the economy in ten years. The official largely responsible for the actual compilation of the plan was Okita Saburo, at that time head of the general planning section of the economic planning agency. At first about 240 government officials and academics were mobilized for committee work and planning, among them Kojima Kiyoshi and Akamatsu Kaname, and eventually the number of people participating reached 2,000 (Okita 1983: 78–9). This may indicate how much emphasis had already been placed on the new idea by Kishi's government.

The new government was formed in July 1960 by Ikeda, who had started his political career as a protégé of Yoshida. He adopted the Income-doubling Plan, *Kokumin shotoku baizō keikaku*, as his public political platform. It became known as the Ikeda Plan. The main impact of the plan was psychological. Chalmers Johnson has called the plan a calmative (1986: 252), because it was so strong in creating a national feeling of self-confidence and optimism, and pulling together a national consensus towards achieving the economic goal of rapid growth (see also Nakamura 1987: 80–1).

The plan introduced a new political vocabulary. A distinctive feature of the plan was frequent use of the word *seichō*, 'growth'. The concept of growth had not been in the centre of economic thinking in pre-war times, nor for a long time in the post-war period, but around the change of the decade it rose to pre-eminence, not only in Japan but also in other parts of the world. In the Ikeda Plan the word is used frequently, either alone or in various combinations, like *keizai seichō*, economic growth; *seichōritsu*, growth rate; *seichōryoku*, growth power; and *seichō katei*, growth process. A heightened positive, even euphoric, feeling is created by the equally frequent use of the words *kō* and *takai*, meaning high. They are used either alone, or in combinations with growth, like *takai seichō* and *koosei-*

chō, high growth; *kōdoseichō*, high level growth; and *takai seichō-ritsu*, high growth rate (Keizai shingikai 1960). The effect can even be called hypnotic, the words high and growth being repeated over and over, page after page. The way the words are displayed above is an exaggerated illustration, but the general impression is similar.

High growth was in a sense a revolutionary goal in the economic policy of Japan. Post-war economic planning had thus far searched for stability and reconstruction of the economy, rather than growth *per se*. If one looks, e.g., to the vocabulary used in the White Papers, *Keizai hakusho*, published by the Economic Planning Agency during the 1950s, the important word was *antei*, stability. It appeared, e.g., in the expression *antei shita hatten*, stable development, but also the expression *antei tekina seichō*, stable growth, was used. Words connoting speed were often used negatively, as in the too rapid development of the Japanese economy, which was leading to inflation, balance of payment problems, and overheating of the economy. The speed of growth of the Japanese economy was naturally noted and commented upon, especially as the decade was drawing to a close and rapid growth began to look more like a permanent characteristic of the Japanese economy, rather than a transient phenomenon, but it was in the Ikeda Plan that a definite shift towards using high speed growth as a goal began (Keizai kigakuchō 1955–9).

Another important word was *kokumin shotoku*, as used also in the title of the plan. In English texts it is usually translated as national income, but an equally correct alternative translation would be citizens' income. It is a concrete concept, and easy to grasp by anyone who receives income, i.e., almost all Japanese citizens. It was accompanied by another concrete word, *baizō*, doubling (see Okita 1983: 78). It was as easy to grasp as income, and it displayed very concrete, simple, and plain optimism, assuring the people that the strong economic performance of the 1950s would continue if everybody worked hard.

The claims of the Ikeda Plan were well grounded. It could point out that the national income of Japan was now 2.4 times higher than ten years ago, or 1.5 times higher than five years ago, and no signs of the end of high growth were in sight. The Japanese demographic structure was ideal for production. The well-educated children of the baby boom of the immediate post-war years were on the verge of entering working life, while the birth rate had fallen, with a consequent drop in the rate of population increase. The worst features of post-war under-employment had disappeared, and the productivity of the working population was rising. The Japanese economic structure was changing rapidly in a modern and efficient direction. The amount of trade in the world economy was expected to continue growing, creating enough leeway for Japan to expand its exports. The Western industrialized countries would continue importing if Japan liberalized its own import restrictions enough, the developing countries were indeed developing and could buy more Japanese goods, and as the Cold War was in a period of thaw the prospects for increasing trade with the socialist countries also looked promising.

The Ikeda Plan was reassuringly optimistic in its contents, and was also effectively propagated in society. No doubt timing was important, as well as the fact that the plan offered a new rhetorical agenda in place of the deadlocked one of security policy. There was a clearly discernible change in the mood of the nation, which Nakamura, e.g., has expressed as 'from the season of politics to the season of economics' (1986: 252). This is not to say that the political and ideological divisions inside Japan disappeared. They moved, however, from the centre of national consciousness to the periphery, economic topics taking the central place in popular discourse.

The change was fast. For instance, in the elections held in November 1960, the Liberal-Democratic Party's campaign slogan was Ikeda's new policy, *gekkyū nibai*, i.e., doubling the monthly salary in ten years. It would have meant a growth rate of about 7 per cent per annum. The other parties, including the Socialist Party, followed the lead, trying to make better offers than the government by devising plans to achieve economic growth of, e.g., 8 or 10 per cent per annum. The Liberal-Democrats lost a few seats, reflecting the recent political disturbances surrounding the security treaty, but were nevertheless able to secure a clear majority for themselves. Their success, together with the general style of the election campaign itself, helped to seal the change in the topics of Japanese political rhetoric. At the time society in general was suffering from what has been called 'confrontational fatigue' (Shibusawa 1984: 23).

The effect on the economists themselves – due to the change in the mood of the time – seems to have been even more profound. For example, Okita comments on the elections in the following way: 'Japanese politics have at last become to some extent modern, and this is really wonderful' (1960: 2). The earlier style of Japanese politics during Kishi's tenure, which had included ideological quarrelling and rioting in the streets, is seen as old-fashioned, while the new style of politics, where all parties concentrate on economics, becomes worthy of being evaluated as modern. A similar interpretation of international politics is made:

> The Cold War between the United States and the Soviet Union has recently turned into a competition for economic growth, and into a competition in development assistance – or in other words growth assistance – to developing countries.
>
> (Okita 1960: 2)

The Cold War between the United States and the Soviet Union – something that Japan is not really seen to be engaged in – appears to be changing. Even the superpowers seem to be modernizing their politics, and the Cold War seems to be receding. In the new world economics would replace the old military and political means as the method of competition. Not only Japan, but the whole world seems to be heading towards a more peaceful and better future. Economic principles seem to permeate thinking throughout the world, becoming general principles at the beginning of the 1960s. Economic growth is seen to have become the main focus of the time, which all countries strive for, and by which all countries are evaluated.

Economism became a general way of thinking in Japan at the beginning of the 1960s. Its meaning had at that time already shifted considerably. It began as a rejection of wartime militarism, but at the end of the 1950s, as the military was not able to return to a significant position of influence, the 'enemy' of economism shifted to politics, understood as ideological quarrelling and other similar unproductive activities. At the same time, economism renewed its positive goal, shifting from reconstruction to rapid economic growth. Economic growth became both the goal of the country, and the lens through which other phenomena were evaluated, national and international alike. This shift was naturally strongest among economists, as the theme tended to elevate their position all the higher. The economists could picture themselves at the focal point of time, in the centre of the action, where they had both the possibility and the responsibility to interpret the world more accurately than any competing groups.

GROWTH

Growth was a central theme of discussion in Japan during the 1960s. Not limited to Japan, the theme was being discussed all over the globe at the time, but in Japan its importance was especially pronounced. This section is based on statistical presentations of the growth of the Japanese economy up to the end of the 1960s, and on comparative international statistics on the state of the world economy during the post-war period. The contents of the theme of growth are presented, and the numerical style of argumentation preferred by economists is introduced. These kinds of statistics are essential for understanding Japanese thought categories, especially in relation to the theme of growth in Japan during the 1960s. However, textual examples of the theme of growth are not presented in this chapter, as some have already been presented in connection with the theme of economism, and others will be presented in connection with analysis of the discussion on integration.

It was during the 1950s that a new method of scoring the achievements of states became widespread, i.e., the compiling of comparative statistics on national income and per capita income by national governments, and by such international bodies as the United Nations, the General Agreement on Tariffs and Trade (GATT), and the Organization for Economic Co-operation and Development (OECD). Consequently, the international standing of a country became increasingly affected by the extent to which it was able to achieve economic development. This led to a new kind of economic competition, which in turn became a force hastening the development of many countries (Hirschman 1960: 10). A country where this effect was particularly strong was Japan.

Growth was not a new phenomenon in Japan. Throughout its modern history Japan had been able to attain comparatively high rates of growth (Maddison 1982). Since the Meiji restoration of 1868 up to the Russo-Japanese War in 1904–5 Japan had exploited its natural resources for exports, and with these revenues built up an infrastructure, including ports and railways, and established industries, such as textile and munitions factories (Allen 1962). During the second phase from the Russo-Japanese War until the Great Depression in 1929 the Japanese economy grew on average at a real annual rate of 3.5 per cent of GNP. Cotton textiles and finished textile products became the big export earners. This was the period when Japan definitely became an industrialized nation. The 1930s form the third phase. When most other industrialized countries were suffering from stagnating economies after the Great Depression, whose effects were heightened by the emergence of economic blocks around the world, the Japanese economy was expanding at an average annual rate of over 5 per cent. It was an extremely high rate for a period before the Second World War. During this phase, in response to the military ambitions prevalent in Japan, chemical, metal, and machinery industries, and large industrial units in general, came to dominate the economic scene. These were added to the existing strong textile base, making Japan a fairly-advanced industrialized country (Patrick and Rosovsky 1976: 8–9).

In the pessimistic aftermath of the Second World War trust in the economy had waned. When Japan again became a sovereign nation in 1952, it was still weak and poor. However, the effects of the Korean War had already begun to reverse the sorry state of the Japanese economy by starting a world wide boom. The Japanese economy was also aided by the special procurements for the US military forces (Kosai 1986: 72–3).

The original goal of attaining the pre-war levels of production and standard of living was achieved during the 1950s – and quietly forgotten. Nakamura has calculated when this happened in various fields of economic activity. His results are presented in Table 2.1.

Table 2.1 Years when pre-war (1934–6) levels of economic activity were attained and doubled

	Attained	*Doubled*
Industrial production	1951	1957
Real GNP	1951	1959
Real GNP per capita	1953	1962
Real total consumption	1951	1960
Real consumption per capita	1953	1964
Real capital investment	1951	1956
Real exports	1957	1963
Real imports	1956	1961
Real productivity per worker	1951	1962

Source: Nakamura 1986: 212

The effect of the Korean war-boom can be seen to have helped already in 1951 to achieve the goal in several fields, such as industrial production, gross national product, total consumption, and capital investment. The per capita figures follow with a lag of two years, because of a larger population than before the war. We should note here that although Japan also experienced a baby boom after the war it never attained the levels of population growth of other Asian countries. The figure for developing countries was well above 2 per cent per annum for the 1950–60 period, while the Japanese figure of 1.1 per cent was comparable with the rather modest level of 0.9 per cent for the West European countries. Even for North America the figure was higher, i.e., 1.8 per cent (UN 1964: 20).

The figures in Table 2.1 also show how Japan's economic structure had changed when compared with pre-war time. Japan had become far less dependent on foreign trade, as seen in the way the figures for trade lag behind the other figures during the 1950s. Because of general democratization, land reform, labour organization, and other reforms Japan created a huge domestic market, which in pace with its rising affluence could absorb most of the products of Japanese industry. Japan's industrial structure had moved a long way from light industry towards heavy industry, such as metals, chemicals and machinery, enabling it to export more value added products, while its imports tended to concentrate on primary products, especially energy, food, and industrial raw materials (Allen 1965; Boltho 1975; Krause and Sekiguchi 1976). The right-hand column is also important. There we can see how the speed of growth continued, doubling

Table 2.2 Per capita gross domestic product by major regions

Region	Amount in 1960 dollars		
	1950	*1955*	*1960*
All market economies	451	520	558
Developed market economies	1,080	1,277	1,410
North America	2,340	2,645	2,718
Western Europe (WE)	655	805	946
EEC	672	872	1,068
EFTA	941	1,090	1,229
Other WE	232	282	322
Japan	193	278	418
Oceania and South Africa	800	872	948
Developing market economies	105	119	130
Latin America	252	277	300
Africa	93	104	113
Far East	69	78	85
West Asia	164	189	214
Others	319	377	472

Source: United Nations 1964: 21

Note: EEC = European Economic Community
EFTA = European Free Trade Association

thc lcvcls of economic activity in a little less than ten years, giving substance to the optimistic claims made in the Ikeda Plan.

Table 2.2 prcscnts the state of economic development of the markct economies, and Japan's place among them, during the 1950s. The table shows that during the 1950s the riches of the world were clearly concentrated on the North American continent, in the United States and Canada. The middle income countries of the time – outsidc of the 'centrally-planned economies' as the expression went in UN parlance – were situated in Western Europe, as well as in the former British dominions including South Africa, Australia and New Zealand. The rest of the world was poor. Here the highest group in 1950 was composed of the Latin American countries, and countries belonging to the heterogeneous group of 'Others', principally, numerous island territories in various oceans. Japan was clearly below this group in 1950, but had in 1955 already attained the average level of the Latin American countries, and was continuing to rise.

The poorest areas of the world during the 1950s were Africa and, especially, the Far East; this term was at the time understood to include the area ranging from Pakistan in the west to the Koreas in the east. This was the area proximate to Japan abounding in poverty, as well as colonial and ideological warfare. In long term statistics Asia's situation was even graver. During the 100 years from 1860 to 1960 this region's share of world income had fallen from 33 per cent to 11.2 per cent. The fall had been especially conspicuous in the southern parts of the region, comprising what are nowadays called the South and Southeast Asian countries, the figures falling from 11.8 to 2.6 per cent, although the share of world population had stayed the same, at 23 per cent. From the point of view of economic development, this region in the vicinity of Japan was thus seen as the most hopeless of all of the regions of the world (Higgins 1968: 4–5).

In terms of its industrial structure or educational level Japan could thus be counted among the developed market economies during the 1960s, but in terms of its living standards – as far as can be expressed by the figure of GDP per capita – it could well be counted among the developing countries. In 1960 Japan had risen somewhat above that level, being, however, still far below Western European figures. The North American level was inconceivably high in comparison with Japan.

Another international statistical comparison, that of gross domestic product (GDP) of major regions during the same period, clarifies Japan's position on the economic map of the world.

Table 2.3 Gross domestic product by major regions

| | Amount in billions of 1960 dollars | | |
	1950	1955	1960
All market economies	732	920	1,090
Developed market economies	622	782	920
North America	389	480	540
Western Europe (WE)	199	255	314
EEC	104	141	181
EFTA	80	95	110
Other WE	15	19	24
Japan	16	25	39
Oceania and South Africa	18	22	27
Developing market economies	110	138	170
Latin American republics	39	49	61
Africa	18	22	27
Far East	45	56	68
West Asia	7	9	11
Others	1	2	2

Source: United Nations 1964: 19; figures rounded by the author

Note: EEC = European Economic Community
EFTA = European Free Trade Association

Table 2.3 shows that most of the accountable production taking place in the capitalistic part of the world occurred in the developed market economies. The percentage remained at about 85 throughout the 1950s. The enormous productive capacity of the United States is conspicuous. In 1950 it accounted for 53 per cent of production, and even in 1960 the share had fallen to just barely below 50 per cent. The share of the whole of Western Europe was only a half of this. Japan appears only as a small and unimportant economy, on a par with such regions as the small non-integrated European economies, or South Africa, Australia and New Zealand combined. Its share of production of the market economies in 1950, 1955, and 1960 was only 2.2, 2.7, and 3.6 per cent, respectively. However, Japan was clearly a member of the industrialized countries, although its per capita share might have been low, as can be seen from the fact that its total production equalled roughly that of the whole of Africa excluding the Republic of South Africa, or that it produced roughly half of that of the rest of the Far Eastern countries.

Table 2.3 also gives a rough estimate of how fast the production in Japan rose in comparison with other regions. A still clearer picture of the growth dynamics of the capitalist world can be obtained from Table 2.4.

Table 2.4 Average annual compound rate of growth of gross domestic product by major regions (%)

	1950–60	1950–55	1955–60
All market economics	4.1	4.7	3.5
Developed market economies	4.0	4.7	3.3
North America	3.3	4.3	2.4
Western Europe (WE)	4.7	5.0	4.3
EEC	5.6	6.2	5.1
EFTA	3.2	3.4	3.0
Other WE	4.9	5.5	4.2
Japan	9.3	9.0	9.5
Oceania and South Africa	4.1	4.1	4.1
Developing market economies	4.4	4.6	4.3
Latin America	4.6	4.8	4.5
Africa	4.1	4.3	3.9
Far East	4.2	4.3	4.1
West Asia	5.2	5.6	4.7
Others	6.2	5.6	6.8

Source: United Nations 1964: 19

Note: EEC = European Economic Community
       EFTA = European Free Trade Association

In general, the growth of GDP was brisk in all regions, reflecting the reconstruction of war-torn economies, the construction of newly-independent economies, and the overall increase in world trade. However, growth was clearly becoming slower during the latter half of the 1950s. Still, in a world historical perspective, even the figure of 3.5 represents a very high number, reflecting the generally positive climate for economic activity. It has been estimated that long-term growth rates for Europe and North America were 2.7 per cent for the period 1870–1913, and 1.3 per cent for 1913–50. These figures show clearly how different the post-Second World War world was quantitatively, and even qualitatively, from earlier periods of world economic history (Nakamura 1987: 54). There were some regions where performance was poorer than the average, especially North America and the European Free Trade Association (EFTA). That was only natural as these were already the richest areas of the world, starting thus from higher levels, which in addition had suffered the least damage during the war, making large-scale reconstruction

unnecessary. As a consequence of their slower growth the abnormally high position these countries had occupied after the war was
beginning to erode, especially affecting the position of the United
States and Great Britain.

There were regions that were doing better than the average.
Among the major regions of the developing world, growth was
highest in West Asia, reflecting the increased use of oil all over the
world as the basic source of energy in industry and transportation.
Among developed countries, the countries that in 1958 formed the
European Economic Community (EEC) chalked up impressive figures, reflecting in part post-war reconstruction and the Korean War
boom, and in part the benefits of the economic integration process
taking place among these countries. It was especially the development of the EEC that seemed to make possible the re-emergence
of Europe as an important actor on the world scene.

In growth terms, however, Japan was in a class of her own. Japan
was growing doubly faster than the world average, and in addition
increased its rate of growth during the latter half of the 1950s, when
all other major regions were forced to slow down. It was this average
annual rate of growth that explains the rapid rise of Japan with
respect to the rest of the world. This was clearly the field where
Japan could outshine all of its competitors, which became in its turn
an additional reason why so much emphasis was placed on growth
as a phenomenon in Japan. At the beginning of the 1960s Japan's
economic success began to be noticed abroad and praise began to
be poured on the country. One of the first and most influential
examples was a series of articles on Japan in *The Economist*, which
were later collected into a book entitled *Consider Japan*
(Correspondents of *The Economist* 1963).

The beginning of the 1960s was a time of optimism and economism all over the world. For instance, the United Nations General
Assembly through its resolution 1710 (XVI) designated the 1960s
as the United Nations Development Decade. The resolution was
aimed especially at the developing countries. Growth was expected
to alleviate economic hardships, and to diminish inequalities both
within and between societies. The objective was to be attained
through planning, each country setting its own target, but all of
them striving for at least a 5 per cent minimum annual growth rate
in national income by the end of the decade (United Nations 1964:
25). These hopes were, like those of the Japanese, based on the
generally good economic performance of the 1950s, and rapid eco-

nomic development was expected in Latin America, Africa, and Asia.

At the same time, the industrialized countries were also beginning to discuss growth in the same terms. For instance, the OECD aimed at achieving a 50 per cent increase in the GNP of its member countries by the end of the decade, meaning, on average, an annual growth rate of 4.2 per cent. The goal was thus set a little lower than that of the developing countries, but was set explicitly on growth. Earlier, during the latter half of the 1950s, after the goal of post-war reconstruction was achieved, the governments of the OECD countries had become preoccupied with the problem of economic stability, but this was now changed on a global scale, so much so that the United Nations could simply proclaim as Okita: 'Economic growth has now become a central objective everywhere in the world' (United Nations 1964: 25). An optimistic, even euphoric wave of enthusiasm for economic growth seems to have swept through the world at the beginning of the 1960s.

Seen in this light, Japan was not at all alone in its plans for economic growth. The Japanese dreams of growth appear wilder than those of the other countries, but actually they were rather cautious. The doubling of incomes in ten years would have required an average annual growth rate of 7.2 per cent, which was indeed a higher rate than in the plans of the United Nations or the OECD. However, in light of the statistics of the 1950s, the latter organizations planned for an increase in the growth rates of respective countries, while the Japanese planned only for a slower rate of growth than the 9.3 per cent they had already achieved.

The government of Ikeda Hayato, and after 1964 the government of Sato Eisaku, had no trouble in fulfilling the objective of the Income Doubling Plan. Actually, during the 1960s the figures were even higher. Japanese statistics, as well as those of the OECD countries in general, and those compiled by the GATT, are usually based on gross national product (GNP), rather than gross domestic product (GDP) which the United Nations normally uses. The former refers to the total worth of all goods and services produced in a country, usually in a single year, while from the latter figure the effect of foreign investment has been removed, and it thus tends to be smaller. Using the former in evaluating the performance of the Japanese economy during the 1960s, Table 2.5 shows the results:

Table 2.5 Growth and structure of gross national product in Japan between 1955 and 1969

| | Annual rate of growth (%) | | |
	1955–61	*1961–65*	*1965–69*
At constant (1965) prices			
Gross national product	10.7	8.6	12.5
Private consumption	8.1	8.9	9.1
Fixed capital formation	20.4	9.9	17.4
Exports	12.3	16.7	16.0
Imports	19.0	9.9	15.3
At current prices			
Gross national product	14.2	13.6	17.2
Private consumption	10.6	15.4	14.3
Fixed capital formation	24.5	11.3	21.2
Exports	11.3	17.7	17.7
Imports	16.0	9.8	17.0

Source: GATT 1971: 4

Growth did indeed slow somewhat at the beginning of the 1960s, but again attained a terrific speed at the end of the decade, 12.5 per cent at constant prices, and the stupendous 17.2 per cent in current prices. The former figure may be more important in describing the real state of the economy, but the latter figure undoubtedly is more important politically; not only because it is larger, but also because it is directly felt as a numerically steep rise in salaries and other income.

As can also be seen in Table 2.5, private consumption rose rapidly during the whole period, following closely the rise of GNP. It made the life of Japanese citizens better, at least in economic terms. However, at the same time its share of total GNP diminished from over 60 per cent in 1955 to 50 per cent in 1969, caused by the even more rapid pace of industrial development. This also reflected a change towards a more capital intensive direction in Japan's industrial structure. For instance, in the latter half of the decade the annual rate of growth of industrial machinery production was 23.7 per cent in current prices. This trend also led to a slowly rising dependence on international trade, both in exports and imports, but overall dependence still remained rather low. The ratio of exports and imports of goods and services to GNP in some industrialized countries in 1968, in current prices, was as follows: the Netherlands 42.9 for both, Belgium 38.2 and 38.6, the United Kingdom 20.1 and 21.1, the Federal Republic of Germany 22.9 and 19.5, Italy 18.2 and 15.8, France 13.7

and 13.8 per cent, and Spain 11.4 and 10.0, respectively. Only for the United States with its 5.0 and 5.2 per cent were the figures considerably lower than for Japan (GATT 1971: 5).

From such statistics, growth appears as a smooth process. However, rapid growth in Japan was actually a series of shorter boom periods, punctuated by periods of slower growth. During the latter periods the figures for growth fell drastically, often to levels near the world average. Up to 1970 there were altogether six boom periods: the Korean War boom in 1951, an unnamed boom caused by a rapid rise in investments in 1953, Jimmu boom in 1956–7, Iwato boom in 1959–61, a softer unnamed expansion in 1963, and the Izanami boom in 1967–9. The Japanese names of the boom periods were coined by Japanese journalists, who referred to these periods of dynamism as the most remarkable since the legendary days of Japanese history. Jimmu was the first Japanese Emperor, supposed to have ascended the throne in 660 BC. After his name was used, still older names had to be found, and Iwato was the name of the cave in which the Sun Goddess Amaterasu Omikami (the great-great-great grandmother of Jimmu) lived for a while in seclusion. Izanami was a goddess, who in marriage with her brother Izanagi (out of whose left eye Amaterasu Omikami was born) gave birth to the islands of Japan (Nakamura 1987: 53; 1986: 246–7; Papinot 1976). The naming of the boom periods with nationalistic names was a part of the reconstruction of the Japanese spirit.

The development of the Japanese balance of payments was not an unqualified success until the middle of the 1960s. The growth of the Japanese economy was basically dependent on imports. Imports of raw materials and technology, both in the form of machinery and licences, were essential. During the 1950s the boom periods invariably led to a worsening balance of payments. The situation was difficult to remedy by increasing exports, because the strength of internal demand tended to channel goods into national markets, so that there simply were not enough goods to export. The progressive deterioration of the trade account culminated in 1961, with an overall balance-of-payments deficit of US $950 million. In such a situation the government was forced to impose tight money measures, curbing internal demand as well as imports. It led both to a relative and an absolute growth of exports, correcting the balance of payments. That in turn allowed the easing of monetary tightness, leading eventually into a new boom period. In other words, as Japan tried to achieve maximum economic activity, it expanded production facilities, but before long always ran up against the limit of its ability to import.

This limit was reached at the growth rate of approximately 10 per cent (Nakamura 1987: 51–4; GATT 1971: 5–6).

During the 1960s the pattern began, however, to change. In 1965 Japan already had a surplus of US $1,900 million on the current account, and a smaller surplus of US $400 million in the balance of payments as a whole – although during the next year the figures again entered the red. From 1967 onwards the balance of payments remained in the black, and foreign currency reserves began an upward spiral, which in 1970 amounted to US $2,000 million. This favourable situation lasted until the Oil Crisis hit Japan in 1973. The change was caused mainly by the alteration in Japan's industrial structure. It moved continuously towards more value added industries, especially heavy and chemical industries. In 1950 about half of Japan's exports consisted of textiles, but in 1955 the figure had already dropped to 37 per cent, and in 1975 it was only 5 per cent. Steel's share of exports had risen to 34 per cent in 1960, but after that even its share began to diminish, falling eventually to 10 per cent. Machinery and transport equipment, especially ships and automobiles, replaced steel as the leading exports. This reduced Japan's need to import such goods as industrial machinery, or expensive consumer goods like cars. Post-war Japan rebuilt itself as a processing trading nation, shifting continuously towards the export of highly-processed, high-value-added goods, and this enabled Japan to gain better prices for its exports. Japanese labour productivity also grew apace. The annual average rate of growth of productivity was 8.8 per cent during 1955–60, 5.5 during 1961–5, and 15 per cent during 1965–9. This kept Japanese goods competitive even though salaries shot upwards. A cycle of virtuous cumulative causation developed, consisting of rising salaries increasing internal demand, which facilitated fast expansion of production. It kept Japanese factories modern and efficient, and sharply increased labour productivity, which in turn facilitated increases in salaries. During the same period world demand for manufactured goods also rose continuously and rapidly, pushing prices up. The prices of raw materials rose on the average much more slowly. The production of crude oil, especially in the Middle East, grew rapidly from the early 1950s on, being virtually in a perpetual state of market excess, so that an adequate supply level could be taken for granted, and prices were either stable or falling. Also the prices of other primary products, particularly iron ore, were quite steady. Since the 1950s about half of Japan's imports comprised raw materials and fuels, about 30 per cent food, while machinery and other manufactured goods represented in most years less than 20 per cent of imports Nakamura 1987: 54–63; GATT 1971: 6–13). Thus, Japan was in the middle of two favourable cycles, and her terms of trade were continuously improving during the period of high growth.

During the 1950s and 1960s Japan experienced a rare period in its history. During those twenty years Japan was quite effectively shielded from major, harmful international events and influences. The higher than average growth enabled Japan to surpass in the size of her economy most other industrialized countries, even Great Britain and the Federal Republic of Germany, becoming in 1967 the second largest economy in the Western World, as the term went. It was only at the end of the 1960s that serious trouble began to surface again, both nationally and internationally. A period of national anti-American disturbances, similar to those of 1959–60, erupted at the end of the 1960s over the negotiations with the United States for the return of Okinawa (Emmerson 1976: 153–99). At the same time, increasing environmental pollution began to cause criticism of the single-minded rush for economic growth, and as Edström argues, public support for growth waned at the turn of the decade (1988: 69–70). Growth began to pass away as a social theme of discussion.

However, during the period under study it was a strong theme. Japan lived on its own terms peacefully, and relatively complacently in the middle of a world that seemed to be growing more prosperous all the time. According to the economic terms of that world, Japan was doing very well, being a model country: peaceful and successful.

DEVELOPMENT

Development as a theme in the discussion of Japanese economists is distinct from growth, as such. Growth relates more to the quantitative changes in the productive capacity of a country, but the concept of development refers more to the qualitative changes in the productive structure of the country. Both growth and development have direct relevance to the changes in the relations among members of the international system, but the importance of development is even more pronounced than that of growth. The rapid growth during the 1960s became much like a sugar coating for Japan's longer term history of industrial development, providing food for epideictic rhetoric and allowing the rebuilding of self-respect, and the theoretically sophisticated economists especially treated development as the really important matter.

Development as a theme in the discussion of Japanese economists is an old one. It has deep roots in the Japanese national experience of being the only Asian country able to develop its industrial structure to the point where it could challenge the nations of Europe, North America, and Russia/Soviet Union. The challenge as understood here was not primarily a military one, but an economic one, in the sense that Japan was roughly from the Russo–Japanese War onwards able to compete successfully with those countries in international trade, although only in limited fields. In a word, Japan was able to succeed at their own game.

This historical experience was crystallized into an economic theory by Akamatsu Kaname. The basic ideas of his theory were already conceived before the Second World War at Nagoya Kōshō (Akamatsu 1932), although he continued refining them until the 1960s. In foreign countries, Akamatsu is only known among experts in economic theory (Kojima 1975: 230–1; 1977: 165–6; Rapp 1975; Allen 1975; Penrose 1975), but in Japan his influence has been tremendous, and he is still being debated. His theoretical insights have guided or inspired many of the economists who took part in Japan's economic reconstruction, and have carried Japanese economic thinking further during the post-war time, as seen, e.g., in the impressive list of articles appearing in the book honouring his memory (Monkasei 1975).

Akamatsu also had a direct impact on the discussion of integration in the Pacific. His name surfaced in international discussion in 1985, when Okita Saburo in his presentation at the fourth Pacific Economic Co-operation Conference (PECC) drew heavily on Akamatsu's theories (Okita 1985; see also Okita 1975). His strongest impact has, however, been made through his most important pupil, Kojima Kiyoshi (Akamatsu 1975d: 65–6), who became a professor of economics at Hitotsubashi University. Kojima in his turn has not hesitated to acknowledge his intellectual debt to Akamatsu, calling him *onshi*, honoured teacher (1962f: 6), and exclaiming that the originality of his scientific achievement is a source of pride before the whole world (1958: 215).

In his youth Akamatsu studied Marxist economics and philosophy, and after becoming critical of the Marxian approach went to Germany to study Hegelian philosophy (Akamatsu 1975d; Korhonen 1994). The world view of a continuous process of development through struggle towards ever higher levels of perfection, inherent in these philosophical systems, is an integral part of the writings of Akamatsu, too. At the centre of Akamatsu's thinking is *gankō keitai hatten ron*, the theory of the flying geese pattern of development.

The flying geese pattern is a general principle of development, which refers to a situation where less advanced countries adopt the industries of advanced countries, and start to pursue them along the road of development. The idea arises from the image of all of the countries which take part in development forming a group, which advances towards one goal, that of higher levels of technological sophistication. The grouping is one-dimensional, in the sense that the single goal of industrial development is the constituent criterion of the grouping.

Countries are divided into two subgroups, *senshinkoku* and *kōshinkoku*. The first concept refers to the leading industrial countries as 'countries that advance in front'; the second concept refers to the developing countries as 'countries that advance behind'. Countries are thus divided into leaders and followers. There is also a middle category, *shinkōkoku*, or 'newly-rising countries'. During the 1950s this category was more or less reserved for Japan alone. Also the expression, 'less advanced or newly-rising country' was used to describe the position of Japan (Kojima 1958).

The term *kōshinkoku* had the connotation of a backward country. At the beginning of the 1960s, in accordance with the spirit of the United Nations Development Decade, it was abolished, and new terms, such as *sangyō hattenkoku*, literally, 'countries that are developing industries', or *hatten tojōkoku*, 'countries that are on the road of development', were adopted. This reflected the change in the concepts as used in world English discussions, led by the United Nations. The loaded expression 'backward' was replaced first by 'underdeveloped' (Myrdal 1964: 11), and later by 'developing' and 'less developed' (Higgins 1968: 30–1). In his English texts published at the beginning of the 1960s Akamatsu prefers the terms 'advanced' and 'less advanced' countries (1975b; 1975c), which similarly connote movement, as do the terms *senshinkoku* and *kōshinkoku*.

Although a variety of new terms appeared at the beginning of the 1960s, the basic idea did not change. In development, the group of countries moves forward in an orderly fashion: there are the leaders, the most advanced industrialized countries, followed by other industrialized countries in the order of their level of industrial sophistication, followed in turn by the less-advanced countries according to their respective levels of development. There is a simple hierarchy. However, just like the position of the geese in their formation is not fixed for any length of time, the relative position of the countries changes over time. The leaders tire, moving backwards in the formation, giving their place to other countries; some stronger follower countries advance faster than others, moving to positions nearer the vertex of the formation. It is thus a group with a competitive relationship between its members, but there is a general consensus about the direction of the group, namely, the technical development of industries. The theory does not concern politico-ideological divisions among countries, but concentrates solely on the process of advancing industrialization within the countries.

A *kōshinkoku* enters the first stage of development by importing strange, interesting, or merely useful goods from industrialized countries. The manner in which this 'seduction' is carried out, whether by a forced opening of trade as in many cases, or by the temptation of economic profit, is of no importance here: international communication begins. Imports increase gradually, as consumer demand picks up, until the limit of possible international exchange is reached. In Japan this pattern was evident in consumer goods like white sugar, tobacco, clocks, plate glass, soap, and other curios imported in small quantities ever since the first contacts with the Western countries; but it was after the forced opening of Japan's ports in 1854 that large quantities of goods began to be imported. Important among them were items like woollen goods, cotton yarn and cotton cloth. They were not strange things, but as they were produced by modern factories, their price was very attractive (Akamatsu 1959: 514).

As a rule, this process will not be easy in a less-advanced country, especially when the amount of imported foreign goods swells. The import of cheap factory-made goods destroys handicraft industries existing in the less-advanced country, driving handicraftsmen out of work, into poverty and starvation. This process has been the same in all Asian countries – in Japan, India, China, and elsewhere. Trade with an advanced country is a terrible shock to the whole culture of a less-advanced country. The effect is often heightened because the advanced countries are usually able to subjugate the less-developed countries militarily, or can at least control them politically (Akamatsu 1975c: 3–5).

However, in the long run, it is impossible to maintain permanent structures of domination. The workings of capitalism itself eventually destroy the structure. Little by little industrial production begins in the *kōshinkoku*. The less-advanced countries have by definition at least one, or often all three of the following economically beneficial conditions: low wages, cheap raw materials obtainable locally, and a market within a short distance. Wages may have been lower already before communication with the advanced countries began; after the harmful effects of trade and political measures have destroyed the traditional economic structure of the country, they certainly are lower. Raw materials are in abundance, because that has been the direction in which the stronger industrial countries have developed the local economy, by intensifying agriculture, opening mines, and so on. There is also a market for cheap industrial goods, as the population has grown accustomed to them. Akamatsu maintains that the initial import of foreign goods is a necessary prerequisite for a relatively rapid jump towards development, because it creates a market for such goods – perhaps on the strength of the goods themselves, or perhaps accompanied by bits and pieces of foreign culture, which change the values and ways of life of the people. Industrial production may start with local capital, as happened in Japan, which avoided colonization; but it may also start with foreign capital. In search of larger profits Western European capital built up industries in colonies in North America as well as in Asian countries such as India, even in defiance of the overall colonial policies of the home countries.

If development is to continue, a shift towards national capital and national political organization becomes necessary before long. This is what happened when the North American colonies formed the United States of America and declared their independence in 1776, and the same happened during the wave of decolonization after the Second World War. Native capital has to be accumulated, and its use has to be determined by native industrial policies. Because the market has already been created, local production is in the advantageous position of having a definite goal in sight – namely that of overcoming imports from foreign countries, by whatever means. Offering cheaper prices is the most basic means; better quality, if obtainable, is another (Akamatsu 1959: 515).

It will often be necessary for the state to apply protective measures, such as the use of tariff policies, or import restrictions. Economic nationalism, often a by-product of the struggle for independence, may be very beneficial for the follower country – if protective measures are used only in cases where the native industry is healthy, and merely needs time to be able to achieve a scale large enough to compete with foreign manufactures. However, if local industry fails to develop efficiently, economic nationalism may impoverish the economy. Although difficult to carry out in the short run, in the long run it would be far more beneficial to drop protection, and simply let imports destroy the inefficient industry. If the industry were still desirable from a national point of view, it could then be given a fresh start (Akamatsu 1975c: 6). To create strong local industries, a measure of competition with the more efficient advanced countries is needed; otherwise, the local entrepreneurs may become uncompetitive in too easy conditions. Akamatsu uses vivid figurative language to describe this period, talking about a 'death struggle' (*shikatsu no tōsō*) between the imported and locally-produced items, requiring the local entrepreneurs to 'pour out their hearts' blood' (*shinketsu wo susugi*) into copying foreign goods, and inventing new ones so as to win the upper hand over imports.

The expansion of local production does not mean the end of the need to import. Quite the opposite. To facilitate expansion of the means of production, technology and capital have to be imported. If raw materials cannot be produced locally in sufficient quantity or quality they too will have to be imported. For instance, to produce cotton yarn and cotton cloth in Japan in the late nineteenth century, spinning and weaving machines had to be imported, and because cotton produced in Japan was both expensive and insufficient, raw cotton also had to be imported. Thus this kind of development tends to increase overall international trade, even though strict measures against some product categories might be adopted in individual countries. Then, at some point in the process of development, there is a qualitative jump: local production 'rises suddenly to power' (*bokkō*), and the rate of increase of imports turns downwards. At this stage, this holds true only for finished consumer products; imports of machinery and raw materials still tend to increase. This phase, when local industry strengthens into an economically-viable position in the local market, is the second stage of the flying geese pattern of development (Akamatsu 1959: 515).

The third stage is reached when national production increases still further so that exports can be started. Imports diminish in absolute terms, until a point is reached where the volume of exports exceeds that of imports for a given category of consumer goods. This situation improves the developing country's overall balance of payments. Exports enable more imports, such as capital goods, for continued expansion of production. Also new consumer goods can now be afforded, and they introduce new industries into the developing country (Akamatsu 1959: 515).

This three-stage development of import, production, and export as sketched out here is the basic structure of the flying geese pattern of development.

As a rule, it is not possible to attain the same level of sophistication as the leading countries in one stroke. The normal course leads first to crude products, and only later to more sophisticated ones. A long time is needed. Accordingly, there usually will be a phase when crude products are exported, while more expensive sophisticated products are imported.

The picture becomes more complicated when capital goods enter the flying geese pattern. As the general level of technology in the follower country advances, it becomes possible to produce capital goods there. However, to build spinning and weaving machines in Japan, higher-level machines with which to produce ordinary machines had to be imported. During the early twentieth century, imports of spinning and weaving machines diminished; eventually they became an export item. This is an even more important change in the industrial structure of the country, and not only because different categories of products are added into the industrial base of the country. It has wider repercussions in society. The production of the means of production turns the originally imported industry into a local one. It pushes roots deep down into local soil. The process starts with the importation of foreign things, a negation (*hitei*) of the original culture of the country. This then becomes negated by local production, by a negation of the negation (*hitei no hitei*), thus effecting a return to oneself (*jiko kanki*) (Akamatsu 1945: 313).

Akamatsu's terminology is that of Hegelian dialectics, but his point is important. As a foreign culture digs deep roots into the country through work, the imported culture becomes an essential part of national self-understanding, and of the international image of the country. In the inter-war period, the image of Japan was of a country exporting various consumer goods, such as toys, at 'sensationally low prices' (Röpke 1959: 191); that of the world's strongest textile exporting country (Hindmarsh 1936: 133–42), and a country producing extremely sophisticated textile machinery, such as the Toyoda loom (Hindmarsh 1936: 174–5). In post-war Japan a similar national and international image came to be built around the production of ships, consumer electronics, passenger cars and machine tools. Cusumano's treatise on the development of Japan's automobile industry is instructive in this regard (Cusumano 1985). A similar mode of production leads to a similar social structure and life-style. This cultural process tends to increase the group aspect of the flying geese formation, making countries increasingly similar to each other, the more they approach the vertex of the formation. Portions of the indigenous culture would, however, be combined with the imported ones; these various mixes mean that countries never end up exactly the same.

Because the countries in the flying geese formation differ in their level of development, there is a considerable time-lag in the pattern of development. For instance, when Japan was completing the pattern for its cotton textile industry at the turn of the century, India was climbing to the second stage of increasing local production, while China was still at the first stage of increasing imports. At the same time, the relationship between Japan and Great Britain, which had been the leading country, was changing. Not only had British exports to Japan diminished considerably, but also in the international market Japanese textiles were eroding the position of Great Britain. Japanese success in the field of textiles would not, however, be unqualified with respect to the future, because India was already beginning to resist imports. Eventually India was expected to begin to compete in the international markets with Japan, and after some time it could be expected to displace Japan from the leading position, only to be displaced later by China or some other country. At the same time, Japan would be competing with Great Britain in the export of other consumer goods, as well as capital goods like spinning machinery, and thus the industrial development of the whole group would go on (Akamatsu 1959: 517).

Development would before long lead to the fourth stage of the flying geese pattern. Export of industrial goods from the follower countries to the leading countries would begin. An example was the beginning of exports of cheap textiles from Japan, India and Hong Kong to Great Britain before the Second World War. This stage harkens theoretically back to David Ricardo's theory of comparative advantage (Ricardo 1987). At first on the level of crude products it becomes profitable to import from less-advanced countries; with the passage of time the phenomenon may extend to more refined products as well. When the process continues, little by little the advanced countries have to abandon the production of ordinary consumer goods, and concentrate on producing capital goods or devising new types of consumer goods. During periods of world economic history when trade is comparatively free, and the flying geese pattern can work effectively, the international division of labour moves forward rapidly. During periods of protectionism the pace is slower, but the process itself cannot be extinguished (Akamatsu 1959: 517).

The theory of the flying geese pattern of development is constructed on a philosophical premise, which Akamatsu calls 'synthetic dialectics', by which he means:

All beings become possible through opposition to other beings, and this opposition can be divided into homogeneous opposition and heterogeneous opposition. Homogeneous opposition constitutes a substitutional relationship which mutually repulses and opposes, while heterogeneous opposition constitutes a complementary relationship which mutually attracts and implements.

(Akamatsu 1975b: 26)

We have thus far discussed only certain product categories. Generally, in individual countries development causes qualitative changes in the industrial structure, but on the global scale this is only quantitative change. In world economic history there have also been periods of global qualitative changes, where the forces of homogeneous and heterogeneous opposition can be seen in play.

The idea starts from the homogeneous nature of the world economy. We have countries A and B, which both engage in agriculture and handicraft production, and are in this sense homogeneous. Homogeneous opposition means that they are in a direct competitive relationship with each other, like England and France during the age of mercantilism in Europe. War between the countries is a possible outcome of the situation.

Following this there occurs an industrial revolution in country A. It begins to produce textiles industrially, and eventually to export them. It may need to buy raw materials from country B, and in that case increased revenues enable country B to import textiles from country A. Modern international trade related to industrial production begins. In terms of the stages of industrial development the countries now differ qualitatively, and the total economic system has reached the stage of heterogenization. Heterogeneous opposition means that the less-advanced country in this situation is easily subjugated economically, as well as politically and militarily. The opposition may lead to wars of subjugation or liberation. However, economically the countries attract each other, and especially at the beginning the relationship enables both of the countries to grow and develop rapidly.

Before long, country B also develops a textile industry, and the two countries again become homogeneous. The situation again may lead to a conflict between the established and the newly-risen industrial power. Because of their combined increased production of textiles, countries A and B draw agricultural country C into international trade, selling raw materials and buying industrial products. Their relationship with country C is heterogeneous, but sooner or later country C is also expected to start a textile industry, and move towards a homogeneous relationship with A and B.

Eventually there will be another qualitative leap in the world economy. It may start in country A if it is able to preserve its dynamism, or it may happen in B or C if either of them overcomes country A in innovative dynamism. One of the countries turns in a new direction, like heavy metal processing or chemicals, creating a higher level of heterogenization. The process goes on, and more and more countries are recruited into the formation from the lower end. Countries compete with each other and overcome each other, sometimes through the quantitative process of increasing the efficiency and quantity of production, sometimes through qualitative changes in the mode and categories of production.

The theory of Akamatsu Kaname is dynamic and deterministic. We are not here interested in its accuracy as an economic theory (see Minami 1986: 234–8; Kojima 1961a: 23–36; Rapp 1975). The importance of the theory of the flying geese pattern of development lies in the way it portrays the global economic system, and Japan's place in it. The theory is dynamic in the sense that it describes a continuous movement in the global economic system, denying the possibility of any lasting stability in it.

Countries overcome each other, but no country is ever able to achieve anything but temporal advantages over its rivals, as long as it succeeds in escaping its pursuers, but before long it is bound to tire. It is not possible to create a durable international division of labour, and thus the system is insecure for any country. As Akamatsu wrote while a student of philosophy in Heidelberg, 'when a process of perfection has been concluded (*eine Vollendung vollendet ist*), immediately a new process begins. Reality moves eternally forward from conclusion to conclusion' (Akamatsu 1975a: 58).

Each country is different, with its own special combination of advantages and drawbacks. The ability to develop is influenced by various factors: the kind of productive base a country has, or the industrial, trade, educational, and social policies adopted by the country, etc. Moreover, the relative importance of different factors changes over time. The flying geese pattern of development will not happen in the same way in all countries; the process of industrialization will not necessarily be completed in all of them; and logically there will always be only a few positions open at the vertex or near it. However, as there is no time limit, many countries will be successful sooner or later.

Even though nothing certain can be said about the performance of any given country, the total group will move deterministically forward to ever higher stages of industrial development. Thus, the theory is both deterministic and optimistic, in the same sense which Hegel displayed in his *Vorlesungen über die Philosophie der Geschichte* (1980). In Akamatsu's sense the historical development of the spirit of industrialism will inevitably proceed through struggle and periods of stagnation towards increasingly higher levels of perfection. This deterministic optimism of Akamatsu is similar to other offshoots of Hegelianism, like Marxism, which depicts the historical progress of humankind from feudalism through the bourgeois society to communism, or that of Kierkegaard in the case of individuals, where the individual can proceed, guided by dread, to spiritually higher stages of the aesthetic, the ethical, and the religious (Kierkegaard 1980; 1982).

An interesting point concerns the implications of the theory related to the conditions of countries in different positions in the formation. Adapting a long-term perspective, the flying geese theory is not a theory of domination. Hegelian philosophy is teleologically directed towards freedom, in the sense that 'the Spirit is free, and the striving of the world spirit in world history is to realize this essence, to reach this privilege' (Hegel 1970: 401). Although it is difficult to interpret what Hegel himself understood this to mean at the level of real nations and real human beings, there was clearly an emancipating interest in his philosophy, which a more practically inclined thinker like Akamatsu connects directly with the material world. In Akamatsu's sense, development will, in the long run, bring freedom and well-being for the world as a whole, even though rivalries will always remain between specific actors. As the weak always have fairly good chances of becoming stronger as the homogenization of the world economy spreads through development, the grip of any dominating power is bound to loosen eventually.

However, in shorter and more practical temporal perspectives, such as those of a single lifetime, there are various threats against the development of any one country. Seen from the vantage point of a country in the middle of the formation, like Japan, there are two kinds of threats. One type of threat emanates from the more advanced, leading countries. They are always tempted to use non-economic means to retain control of the system. They may suppress the rising country militarily, whip up local conflicts by divide-and-rule policies, devise new rules of international conduct in their favour, or limit access to their markets. A crucial point is the degree of national autonomy that the less-advanced country is able to hold over its own affairs. If that degree is considerable, the threat from the more-advanced countries diminishes. By definition, the follower country will always have at least two things in its favour: a comparative advantage based on cheaper wages, and the clear goal of absorbing an existing and well-proven industrial culture.

There is a dialectical paradox at work here. The more a follower country can become influenced by foreign culture during the early phases of communication, the more independent it will later become.

Japanese history is a suitable example of this. It fits the theory perfectly – and indeed, the theory is based on it. During pre-modern times, when China and Korea were the leading countries and Japan the follower, development had been rapid during periods when culture was imported from these countries. A new wave of development occurred during the sixteenth century, when communication with Europe began – first with the Portuguese and later with Dutch traders; but during the seventeenth century Japan, like the other East Asian countries, adopted a defensive policy of seclusion. Although they continued to develop according to national indicators, there was relative stagnation with respect to Western European countries. After the first forced opening of Japan in the mid-nineteenth century, followed by an eager absorption of Western culture, Japan became rapidly both stronger and more independent, eventually a great colonial power with its own empire in East Asia. The only difference in Japan's policy compared with those of China and Korea was that Japan rapidly started an all-out importation of foreign culture as a national policy, while for a long time both Chinese and Koreans tended to regard Japan as a traitor to East Asia's time-honoured Confucian culture. However, although they imported culture, the Japanese guarded their national autonomy with diplomatic manoeuvres, and later by military might. After ultranationalism set in during the 1930s, Japan started again to become relatively weaker, and the period ended with the total destruction of Japan's former greatness. Then, during the post-war period, after the second opening of Japan and the absorption of massive cultural influences from the United States, the new leading country of the world system, Japan again became strong and successful.

Thus, with respect to the advanced countries, the most successful strategy for a follower country is close communication with them, to facilitate the import of appropriate bits of their culture. This must be combined with carefully planned policies for trade and other forms of international communication, always keeping in mind the protection of national autonomy. This strategy should guarantee, with a fairly high degree of certainty, catching up with the more advanced countries. As Okita observes (1975: 146), the theory of the flying geese pattern of development is most useful for the follower countries, because it describes a clear national goal, as well as the practical steps to attain it. The practicability of the theory in the sense of making it psychologically more acceptable is strengthened by the deterministic optimism it displays. Observed from below, the leading countries are seen to be in the most troublesome position, constantly in need of refining their products, and having to try to make qualitative leaps into new modes of production without the help of existing examples.

The situation of an advanced or relatively advanced country with respect to the followers is the reverse. Strong competitors are bound to emerge from the latter. For some time one can attempt to control them and use them for one's own benefit, as Japan did with other Asian countries before and during the Second World War. Akamatsu, writing during the war, was sceptical about Japan's possibilities for making it alone (1945: 301–2). In the post-war situation, when Japan had become a small country without a strong military, this method was seen to be non-existent, but the re-emergence of a comparatively free trading system under the leadership of the United States allayed these worries. In that situation, the best solution for Japan was to run as fast as possible along the road of development, before the pursuing Asian countries could catch up.

In the long run, dominance does not work in favour of the dominant. The closer the relationship between the dominant and the dominated, the easier the flow of culture between them. Thus, in the long run any country is fighting a losing battle in trying to preserve the production of any important category of export commodities. The only solution is continuous upgrading of existing products, plus the introduction of new ones.

The deterministic nature of this theory may in part explain Japan's post-war industrial policy, for instance, the relative ease – compared with most other industrialized nations – with which the Japanese designated certain industries as sunrise industries, which received special support from the state, and some others as sunset industries, from which this support was phased out. The former category included, e.g., metal and chemical industries, and shipbuilding during the 1950s, cars during the 1960s, and computers and telecommunications equipment during the 1980s. The latter category included coal-mining during the 1950s, textiles during the 1960s, and basic metal and chemical industries during the 1970s (see, e.g., Johnson 1986; Woronoff 1985; 1986).

At first sight, Akamatsu's theory bears some resemblance to the ideas of another economic historian, W. W. Rostow, especially to his theory of the stages of economic growth (1961). In this connection, Rostow is widely known as the originator of the concept of the 'take-off' of growth (Higgins 1968: 174–87). Japanese economists discussing the theory of the flying geese pattern of development in an international context do not as a rule, however, compare Akamatsu with Rostow. Usually they compare his theory with Robert Vernon's product cycle theory (Minami 1986: 234–8; Kojima 1975; Shinohara 1982: 63–4, 71–2), emphasizing that Akamatsu clearly preceded Vernon. Vernon's theory simply states that technical innovations tend to happen in advanced countries, but under conditions of international trade the comparative advantage of production eventually shifts to less-advanced countries with lower production costs. From a managerial point of view, products thus tend to have a cycle, being profitable only for a while, and this international structure has to be taken into consideration in investment plans (Vernon 1966). This is indeed a restatement of Akamatsu's theory from another angle.

The problem with Rostow seems to lie in the fact that his central point of interest, growth, was misplaced. From a Japanese point of view, what was important in industrialization was not growth as such, but upward change in the productive structure of a developing country. Rostow was also relatively uninterested in trade, while it was exactly international free trade that formed the basis of the theory of the flying geese pattern of development. Similarly, judging by the names of foreign theoreticians of development theory appearing in Kojima's works, although he knew of Rostow's work, he seems to have valued, above all, authors who emphasize the importance of international trade as a prerequisite for development, like Jan Tinbergen (1958), Ragnar Nurkse (1959), and Albert O. Hirschman (1960). The most important theoreticians in this sense were Wilhelm Röpke and Gunnar Myrdal, whose theories will be treated in Chapter 3, pages 94–102.

On the other hand, the theory of the flying geese pattern of development seems to be diametrically opposed to another variety of development theory, namely, the theory of structural imperialism, operating with the concepts of metropole and satellite (Frank 1967), or centre and periphery (Galtung 1971; 1980: 107–39). The theory basically states that under conditions of apparent free trade the industrialized countries are able to dominate and exploit the less developed countries. The dominant countries have all the 'good cards' at their disposal. They not only have a stronger industrial base but also various structural means of guaranteeing that the gap between the dominant and the dominated does not close, but rather widens. This is the theoretical approach through which perhaps the majority of political scientists learned their international economics during the 1970s, and on into the 1980s. During the 1980s, however, the phenomenal economic performance, especially of several East and Southeast Asian countries, seemed to defy the implications of the theory, and interesting debate on the issue ensued, exemplified by Mommsen and Osterhammel (1986), and Appelbaum and Henderson (1992).

The theories are opposite, but not necessarily diametrically so. The connecting idea between them is the value placed on the degree of national autonomy. Akamatsu emphasizes that besides being able to export, it is also necessary to have a nationalistic psychological attitude, national control of capital, and national initial protection of industries to achieve enough strength to compete in the international marketplace. The approach of structural imperialism emphasizes a similar notion with the concept of self-reliance (Galtung 1976; 1980: 393–413; Galtung *et al.* 1980). The argument can be connected with the theory of Akamatsu, especially in the form of open autonomy (Galtung 1980: 403; Korhonen 1990: 160–70), as opening to interaction with other actors after assuring that it would not harm one's essential self. In this sense, the main difference is that Akamatsu tends to be fairly optimistic about the outcome of such situations, while the structuralists tend to expound the enormity of the problems and hazards on the road of development. A sort of middle position has been taken by, e.g., Senghaas (1985), especially concerning the export-led development of small Scandinavian states like Finland.

ASIA

Asia as a theme in Japanese discourse was a special one. Japan had shared close geographical and historical ties with the area, but most of them had been cut at the end of the Pacific War. At the same time both Asia and Japan changed drastically. Japan was – as Sakamoto put it – 'forced out of Asia', as Japan's relations with the newly-independent Asian nations were severed through the defeat and American occupation, one result being to heighten the pre-war aspirations of the Japanese to 'leave Asia and enter the West'

(Sakamoto Y. 1987b: 48). In contrast to such former European colonial powers as Britain, France, the Netherlands, and Belgium, which had to face anti-colonial struggles after the war, discuss publicly the question of granting independence to their former colonies, and even after that continued political, economic and cultural ties with most of them, Japan was simply cut off from communication with her former colonies with the onset of the Occupation. There was no need for any special discussion, even less for any policy measures, and consequently, the former colonies tended to disappear from the Japanese mental map of Asia (Sakamoto Y. 1978: 7).

A related observation has been made about the Southeast Asian countries. Japan had not had much communication with that region before the war, as it had been the domain of other colonial powers. The only heavy involvement was during wartime. For several years after the war there was no reason to try to approach the newly-independent countries, except through the narrow channel of trade. It is indicative of the situation that extensive study of these countries did not start before the 1960s. Even after that, little interest was expressed among the population at large, or even the elite, in learning anything about these countries (Khamchoo 1986: 290–5). Sakamoto speaks about 'epistemological de-Asianization' in this connection (1978: 9).

Asian countries became clearly visible in the Japanese mental world map only among a few experts and other involved people. There was one country that was clearly visible, namely China, but China was caught up first in the Civil War, and later in the Cold War. Japan could not start to recreate a working relationship with her until the 1970s. The opposite side of the situation was that Asian perceptions of Japan tended to be heavily coloured by images of the war, and because of the low level of intercommunication these images tended to remain unchanged for decades.

The Asia theme, as understood here, thus means that although Japan was geographically, historically, and ethnically an Asian country that needed to create an economic and political relationship with the area, she had great difficulty in doing so. Especially during the 1950s, Japan had to explore almost unknown terrain, overcome hostility at various levels, and do this utilizing quite confused conceptions of what constituted Asia. During the post-war period Japan was defined as an Asian country, as argued in pages 24–8, but this definition most of all referred to Japan's international rank. Japan of the immediate post-war years did not have a relationship with

Asia. It had to be created through a long and tedious process. This made Asia an important theme of discussion, although confined mainly to the level of experts. In the following, the theme will be taken up from three angles, namely, the severing of Japan's relations with China, the difficulty of relating to other Asian countries, and the redirecting of Japan's trade from Asia towards the advanced industrialized countries.

The two most important phenomena in the international political arena in Asia after the Second World War were the emergence of a number of newly-independent countries, and the ideological division of these countries into mutually hostile socialist and capitalist camps. Also the group of non-aligned countries emerged. In terms of economics, however, the practical division was between two kinds of countries: countries accepting the rules of the Western international trading system, and the socialist countries that withdrew from it. In part they withdrew of their own accord, in part because they were excluded from it, as it suited the Cold War strategy of the United States.

For Japan, the emergence of an Asian Cold War meant a thorough change in the basic orientation of its Asian relations, because it cut off the traditional relationship with China. In pre-modern East Asia, China had for thousands of years been the *central country*, as its name, transcribed *Zhongguo* in modern Chinese, *Chūgoku* in Japanese, implies. A multitude of cultural influences, including written language, either emerged from there, or as in the case of Buddhism, was transmitted through China to Japan. Especially during the 1930s Japan's trade began to concentrate on what came to be called the Yen Block of Japan, composed of China, Manchukuo, Japan, and its colonies. Japan's trade with this area expanded with its increasing military control of the area, and with the gradual exclusion of Japan from other markets controlled by the Western European countries and the United States. Important raw materials, such as iron ore, coal, raw cotton, as well as soy beans, rice, sugar, and other foodstuffs were obtained from China, and various industrial products, such as textiles, sundries and machinery were exported there. Before the outbreak of the Second World War, already over 50 per cent of Japanese exports went to the area (Nakamura 1987: 5).

During the immediate post-war period the perceived importance of China did not diminish, but rather grew. As a result of the loss of the war, the relative weights of Japan and China were seen to have become reversed. China was seen to be moving into the position of Asia's great power, with the help of the United States and Soviet Union, while Japan had become a small country, which would be controlled by China (Gaimushō tokubetsu chōsa iinkai 1990: 150; Karashima 1948). China was the country most often mentioned in the plan for the post-war reconstruction of the Japanese economy, either alone, or with other Asian countries or regions. What is notable here is that China is usually specifically mentioned, whereas this is often thought to be unnecessary with respect to other countries. The following examples illustrate this:

China and all Asian countries . . .
China and the southern direction . . .
The whole region, beginning with China and India . . .
China, Korea, and all other countries . . .

Usually deemed sufficient as designations for the rest of the Asian countries were expressions like 'all countries' (*shokoku*), 'southern direction' (*nampō*), or 'whole region' (*kakuchi*). The other countries sometimes referred to in a similar vein were India and Korea, as in the third and fourth examples, but the place they occupied in the Japanese mental map of Asia was nothing compared to China.

After the war, it was thought that the countries in the Sinic cultural area would continue to hold the central place in Japan's trading relations, as had already been the case for a decade, but that was not to be. With the defeat, Japan's external trade fell to drastically low levels. This situation lasted until the end of the 1940s. Most of the remaining trade came to be conducted with the United States, mainly as the importing of food and other daily necessities to Japan. In 1946, 96 per cent of imports came from the United States, and 70 per cent of exports went there (Okita 1947: 15). During the following years the situation did not change much in terms of volume, although the direction of trade began to change somewhat. In 1948, 78 per cent of imports were still coming from the USA, at that time including industrial raw materials, and 27 per cent of exports went there. Forty-nine per cent of exports went to the whole of Asia, but only 15 per cent of imports came from there. The most alarming fact was that trade with the countries nearest to Japan – called the *kinrin shokoku*, meaning Korea, China, Taiwan and Hong Kong – did not pick up as hoped for. Exports to this area amounted to only 15 per cent, and imports a meagre 5 per cent (Okita 1950: 48). Thus the area that had traditionally been the most important to Japan, and was geographically the nearest to it, was quite effectively separated from Japan at the end of the 1940s.

The civil war in China naturally had much to do with this. After it ended, Japanese hopes for re-establishing trade with China rose again. The Japanese leadership, including Prime Minister Yoshida, strongly favoured the establishment of diplomatic relations with the communist government, but that was not allowed by the United States, which pressed Japan to deal only with the Nationalist government on Taiwan. The situation was called the 'zero-minus' option by the Japanese, as it implied that there was nothing to be gained from Taiwan that could not have been achieved otherwise, and everything to be lost regarding mainland China. As this matter became one of the principal points in the US–Japan negotiations about the peace treaty, the Japanese had no other recourse but to yield (Yoshitsu 1983: 67–83). Trade with the People's Republic of China did not end completely, but its volume remained low, subject to wild fluctuations caused by changes in the political climate, and it took until 1972 before relations between the two countries were normalized (Newby 1988: 5–6).

In a similar way Japan's relations were limited also with regard to the two Koreas. It took twenty years until diplomatic relations could be normalized with South Korea in 1965, and relations were extremely strained during this period (Emmerson 1976: 262–6). As in the case of the two Chinas, normalizing diplomatic relations with South Korea created difficulties with North Korea, with which diplomatic relations were established in 1973.

The Asia with which Japan began to create a relationship after regaining independence was composed of the newly-independent countries in southeastern Asia, and Thailand. The emergence of new countries in the area had much to do with the Japanese themselves. By embarking on the Pacific War they brought destruction to the colonial empires of Great Britain, France, the Netherlands, and the United States, and by losing the war they also effected the destruction of their own colonial empire (see, e.g., Elsbree 1953; Jones 1954; Hoyt 1986; Sasaki 1989). This fact is, however, hardly touched upon in the post-war Japanese discussion analysed in this study. The particulars of Japan's actions were for the most part quietly forgotten, or rather, they formed a sort of taboo that was hardly touched upon directly. They belonged to Japan's military past, and had no place in the discussions of the new Japan. The only common explicit reference to the wartime experience was that hostility existed towards Japan, and that it should be alleviated by doing friendly deeds. Otherwise discussion proceeded from the blank situation that the new countries simply existed.

The area presented other problems, too. It was poor, and torn by ideological, racial, religious, and other tensions usually associated with new states (Calvert 1986). The states were led by inexperienced nationalistic governments, which were trying to engage in nation building. The area did not form any kind of unity, but still it had to be discussed using unifying concepts, such as 'Asia' or 'Southeast Asia'. The situation was confusing with respect to Japan's practical relationship with the area. In view of Japan's limited economic capabilities even at the beginning of the 1960s, the area was too large and undifferentiated.

Part of the Japanese confusion about the concept of Asia resulted from the fact that the geographical concept of Asia is a European invention. It is historically unsuitable for the Japanese as a means of constructing a meaningful political, economic, or cultural entity. Some Japanese writers, such as Oki Hiroshi, have complained about the matter:

> When viewed by Europeans and Americans, all Oriental countries east of Turkey are subsumed under the concept of Asia, but as seen with the eyes of the Japanese who live in the Far East, the numerous countries west of Afghanistan and Iran are as a matter of fact very different from Japan. Even countries like Pakistan and India differ considerably in terms of race, social structure, and culture from the countries of the Far East. It feels extremely difficult to treat this multitude as one unit.

> (Oki 1965: 72)

We may point out in passing that the Far East was another curious European concept that Oki did not, however, criticize. If we were to speculate about the naming of geographical areas, in making the Japanese position clear, we could say that the Japanese might have felt most comfortable with a conceptual map of Asia where China (i.e., the mainland, Taiwan, Hong Kong and Macaco) and Korea would form 'Near Asia', the stretch of countries from Indochina to the Indonesian archipelago 'Central Asia', and the Indian subcontinent 'Far Asia'. Siberia might form 'North Asia' if it was included, but after hundreds of years of Russian domination it could as well be included in Europe. If also the regions called 'Middle East' and 'Mediterranean' were included there, it would make Europe, like Asia, a similarly amorphous concept.

In early post-war Japanese discussion the concept of Asia usually included all eastern, southeastern and southern Asian countries (see, e.g., Karashima 1948; Okita 1950; Kuno 1950), but from 1950 onwards the Japanese horizon on Asia began to turn towards the Southeast Asian countries (see Sugi 1950; Arisawa *et al.* 1951; Okita 1956a; 1956b). During this process the concept of Asia began to be interchangeable with Southeast Asia defined, as Oki did, as the region east of Pakistan. Usually the socialist countries were left out of the concept of Asia, or rather they had only a peripheral place in it in the sense that they were hardly included in the discussion. This was the situation during most of the 1960s. In addition, the area often appeared as an undifferentiated mass of poor and politically unstable countries, too vast in terms of meaningful policies towards it. It was only at the end of the 1960s and during the 1970s, after the creation of the Association of Southeast Asian Nations (ASEAN) in 1967, the emergence of the Asian Newly Industrialized Economies (NIEs) of South Korea, Taiwan, Hong Kong and Singapore, and after normalizing relations with the People's Republic of China, that a conceptually meaningful geoeconomic area started to emerge in the vicinity of Japan.

On a material level, a comparable situation prevailed also in Japan's trading relationships. The geographical distribution of Japan's foreign trade developed during the 1950s and 1960s as shown in Table 2.6.

When reading Table 2.6, we have to keep in mind that from 1955 to 1970 Japanese trade was growing rapidly, just like the economy in general, from about US $2,000 million in 1955 to US $19,300 million in 1970. The average annual rate of growth was over 16 per cent. Thus any increases in the percentages mean rapid increases in volume, while decreases in percentages do not necessarily mean any decrease in volume, but only a slower rise.

The United States was throughout this period Japan's principal trading partner. Both in exports and in imports it was the most important country, and its significance especially as a destination for exports increased rapidly throughout the period. In imports, its significance rose until 1961, but started to decline slowly thereafter. Of other developed countries in the Pacific region, Canada and Australia were also important; not so much as export destinations, resulting, among other factors, from their relatively small populations, but as sources of raw materials. Japan's total imports during the 1950s and 1960s grew faster than those of any other industrialized country, the rise being particularly dramatic in primary products. At the end of the 1960s Japan became the world's largest market for raw materials, fuels, and a number of important foodstuffs. Japan imported, e.g., large amounts of soy beans, feed grains,

Table 2.6 Geographical distribution of Japan's trade; percentage shares in total Japanese exports (E) and imports (I)

		1955	1961	1969
Developed areas	E	42.2	47.9	55.9
	I	50.8	60.3	53.1
United States	E	22.7	25.2	31.0
	I	31.3	36.1	27.2
Canada	E	2.3	2.8	3.0
	I	4.4	4.6	4.5
Australia	E	2.7	2.4	3.0
	I	7.2	7.8	8.3
Western Europe	E	9.6	12.9	12.9
	I	6.9	9.6	9.9
Developing areas	E	55.9	49.6	39.3
	I	45.6	36.0	41.3
South and East Asia	E	37.0	32.7	27.8
	I	25.0	16.8	15.8
S. Korea, Taiwan, Hong Kong,	E	12.0	14.4	17.1
Thailand, Singapore	I	7.0	3.7	4.1
Others	E	25.0	18.3	10.7
	I	18.0	13.1	11.7
Middle East	E	5.0	4.9	3.9
	I	8.0	9.1	13.2
Latin America	E	9.0	7.5	5.1
	I	10.0	8.3	7.5
Africa	E	5.0	4.3	2.0
	I	3.0	1.4	3.8
Mainland China	E	1.4	0.4	2.4
	I	3.3	0.5	1.6
USSR	E	–	1.5	1.7
	I	–	2.5	3.1

Source: GATT 1971: 33

and cotton from the United States, wool and iron ore from Australia, and forest products and iron ore from Canada. In this way, the developed Pacific countries, Australia and North America, took the place the countries of the Sinic cultural sphere had occupied before and during the Second World War. They were the principal destination of exports, and the main sources of raw materials.

In addition, the United States was the most important source of Japanese imports of industrial products, followed by Western Europe, which was also the third most important area as a market for Japanese exports. Thus, during the 1950s and the 1960s Japan's total external trade tended to concentrate on the developed countries, away from the developing countries.

There were some exceptions to this trend. Rising imports of crude oil made the Middle East an important supplier of Japan's energy, and in exports Japan's trade with South Korea, Taiwan, Hong Kong, Singapore and Thailand rose rapidly. These rises were, however, offset by the diminishing importance of other Asian countries, both in exports and imports. At the end of the 1960s Southeast Asia took just over a quarter of Japan's exports, and supplied less than a sixth of its imports. Moreover, both figures were diminishing. In terms of trade, Japan was moving away from Asia, just as it was doing in terms of the development of its industrial structure, or living standards.

The importance of Latin America and Africa had been quite small from the start, and was also diminishing. It heightened Japan's declining involvement with the developing countries in general.

Another distinct feature of Table 2.6 is the negligible amount of trade conducted with the socialist countries. In spite of the size of its population, the share of China in both exports and imports was lower than that of even Canada or Australia.

Japan was faithfully following the Cold War strategy of the United States. Japan remained inside the economic empire of the United States, and concentrated on exploiting the economic possibilities the empire opened. During this period, Japan had no reason to try to change the basic lines of foreign policy laid down during the Yoshida years. Japan continued to be politically and militarily dependent on the United States. The United States was also the country to concentrate on in terms of economic matters, both as a trading partner, and as a country to be followed according to the theory of the flying geese pattern of development.

3 Integration

In this chapter we shall examine Japanese discussion on international economic integration. It began gradually during the 1950s, and gathered momentum during the 1960s. The immediate starting point for Japanese discussions was the need to re-enter the world after gaining independence, and economic integration in Europe. International integration proceeded first in the form of the Organization for European Economic Co-operation (OEEC) in 1948, the European Payments Union (EPU), and later as the European Economic Community (EEC) in 1958. Other similar economic organizations, such as the European Free Trade Association (EFTA), the Council for Mutual Economic Assistance (COMECON), the Latin American Free Trade Area (LAFTA), and the Central American Common Market (CACM) contributed, too, as well as other corresponding groupings being discussed throughout the world during that time.

Integration is a theme of the post-Second World War period. During the 1940s the idea centred on global integration, being developed by theoreticians like Mitrany (1943; 1975). The idea was exemplified by the formation of such global international bodies as the United Nations in 1945, together with its special agencies, such as the Food and Agriculture Organization (FAO), World Health Organization (WHO), and the United Nations Educational, Scientific and Cultural Organization (UNESCO). Other similar global organizations were the General Agreement on Tariffs and Trade (GATT) established in 1947, the International Monetary Fund (IMF), and the International Bank for Reconstruction and Development (World Bank). The OEEC also developed in a global direction when it was reorganized in 1961 under a new name, Organization for Economic Co-operation and Development (OECD). Canada and the United States joined it in the same year, and Japan was accepted as the first Asian member in 1964.

Japan thrived during this era of global integration, where the flying geese pattern of development could work in ideal conditions, enjoying high economic growth, rapidly-changing industrial structure, and equally rapid expansion of trade with various partners. Japan was admitted to the IMF and the World Bank after regaining independence in 1952, and to GATT in 1955, although negotiations had been difficult (Shiraishi 1989: 68–72, 91–2). Japan also became a member of the United Nations in 1956. For Japan, these memberships were signs of its re-acceptance into the world community. The economic organizations were also a means of obtaining cheap capital for development, as well as opening up trading relations. The balance of trade was improving gradually, and Japan's development was going rapidly forward, indicating that this system of global integration was of clear benefit. This system enabled Japan to make rapid progress. Japan had no special need to make any drastic changes in the organization of the global system.

The new global discussion of regional integration appearing at the end of the 1950s posed a possible threat to Japanese economic interests. However, because no great hurry was perceived, Europe being no longer so important to Japan's trade, discussion picked up only very slowly, and for many years the number of those involved was small (Shiraishi 1989: 151–2).

The following story of the Japanese discussion unfolds in the 1950s, with Japan trying to approach the global system, and attempting to cope with the mistrust of other countries. In this chapter, the section on pages 87–94 deals with the idea of regional integration in the Asian setting at the beginning of the 1960s; first, on the governmental level of the United Nations Economic Commission for Asia and the Far East (ECAFE), Okita Saburo being involved in this process; and second, on a more academic level through the study project of Kojima Kiyoshi at the Institute of Developing Economies. Pages 94–113 deal with the theoretical concept of integration developed by Kojima during 1962 in connection with a project on the EEC, and the way he structured the international environment of Japan with respect to possibilities of integration, and pages 113–28 analyse the change in Japan during 1963–4, when an active search started for possible partners with which to engage in regional integration. In practice there were only two possible orientations, the Asian one, and the direction of the Pacific advanced countries. Pages 128–33 continue the story of the Asian orientation in 1965, when a new image of a dynamic Asia in the process of development began to emerge, treating in particular the texts of Oki

Hiroshi and Fujii Shigeru. Pages 133–45 analyse the original Pacific Free Trade Area (PAFTA) proposal put forward by Kojima Kiyoshi in 1965, and pages 145–53 deal with the so-called Miki Conception, and with the boom of future studies in Japan, 1966–1967. Foreign Minister Miki Takeo became interested in Kojima's proposal, developing the idea further as a political ideology. The final section (pages 153–66) analyses the texts of the first Pacific Trade and Development Conference held in Tokyo in 1968. It is used both as a way of contrasting Japanese rhetoric with foreign types to clarify its characteristics, and in order to show the initial international reception of Kojima's PAFTA proposal.

RE-ENTERING THE WORLD

After the end of the Pacific War Japan was cut off from most contacts with other countries in the world except the United States, and it was only after regaining independence in 1952 that diplomatic relations began to be opened up. The pre-war exclusion of Japan from global markets was still to an extent continuing, and throughout the 1950s Japan tried to establish friendly and stable relations with other countries. It was even difficult to enter GATT. Since 1948, when GATT was established, the general headquarters of the Occupation sponsored Japan's entry into the organization, but mainly because of opposition from several European countries, that did not succeed. After Japan regained independence in 1952 some trade treaties were automatically renewed with countries like Sweden and Switzerland, which had remained neutral during the war. When diplomatic relations were restored pre-war treaties could be renewed with some countries, such as Finland, Yugoslavia and Thailand, but with most other countries treaties had to be renegotiated. The most important of this kind of bilateral treaty was concluded with the United States in 1953, and in 1954 a treaty with Canada was concluded. Japan acquired a provisional membership of GATT in 1953, but at that time ten GATT countries refused to deal with Japan. Even in 1955 when Japan was accepted as a member with the vote of all of the 34 members of GATT, 14 of the countries, including Great Britain, France, The Netherlands, Belgium, Australia, New Zealand, Brazil and India, declined in practice to negotiate agreements with Japan. This was partly because of distrust dating from wartime, partly because Japan restricted its own imports, and partly because Japanese low-priced products were seen as a threat, as in the pre-war time (Shiraishi 1989: 64–71, 91–2).

The situation in Asia was similar. After 1952, with the establishment of diplomatic relations, foreign travel and participation in international conferences picked up. However, Japanese participation in Asian affairs was still quite limited during the first half of the 1950s. Only after relations were sufficiently restored, or created with the new independent states, could Japan begin attempts for a more active role in Asia during the second half of the decade. The year 1955 can be taken as a turning point, as in that year the Eleventh General Assembly of the ECAFE was held in Tokyo, Japan acting as host for the first time.

During the decade a few individuals took on the responsibility of becoming specialists on Asian affairs, as it took until 1960 for Asia to become the object of systematic research in Japan. Okita Saburo became one of the most prominent of these experts on Asian and world economics. In 1950, when very few Japanese were able to travel abroad, he was sent as a researcher for the Economic Stabilization Board on a five-month economic fact-finding mission to Europe, America, and Asia. He was also a member of the first Japanese delegation to attend the Seventh General Meeting of ECAFE in 1951. In 1952, when Japan became an associate member of the organization, Okita was sent as the sole Japanese representative to the ECAFE Secretariat in Bangkok, where he spent almost two years. After returning to Tokyo at the end of 1953 he continued his work as a senior researcher in the Research Division of the Economic Counselling Board. It was reformed in 1955 into the present Economic Planning Agency, Okita becoming the director of the Research Division. His chief work there was to plan ways of expanding Japanese exports, where his Asian expertise was of good use (Okita 1983: 65–75).

Consequently, Okita's interest in the international economy centred on trade, while the idea of regional economic integration was only of peripheral interest in his writings at the time. For instance, he discusses in his *Tōnan Ajia no hatten riron* (The Development Theory of Southeast Asia) the regional organizations that had sprung up in Europe after the war, such as OEEC and EPU. They were created in order to aid European recovery through harmonizing national plans, increasing international commerce, and aiding countries with balance of payments difficulties. Okita cannot, however, find many possibilities in Asia for similar schemes, which would link Japan with other Asian countries. The principal reason is the mistrust felt by the other Asian countries towards Japan. Japan is, however, seen to be a part of Asia, a little more developed industrially than the other Asian countries, but in many ways so backward that it is essentially in the same boat as them. Okita likens Japan to India, which is also an industrializing poor country, and a somewhat bigger power in the middle of smaller, suspicious neighbours (1956a: 26).

The Asian feelings described here should not be seen as unanimous. In his memoirs, Okita relates instances where the war was not seen as an obstacle in Japanese–Asian relations, and during the 1950s there was a gradual lessening of tensions. Prasad Singh argues for a similar view, according to which Japan's return to communication with other Asian countries was welcomed by some of them, especially from the point of view of using Japan's industrial potential in reviving Asian economies, but there were also opposing views from various countries in various situations. The general atmosphere was that of distrust, of varying intensities (Singh 1966: 7–11, 37). In Okita's thinking, Japan needs to dispel this mistrust, so that some kind of regional structure with a place for Japan might become possible at some time in the future. Japan also needs to enlarge its markets in Asia. The economic development of Asian countries is too slow, and their buying power is rising too slowly with respect to Japan's need for expansion of exports. Both problems can be solved by one method: 'Japan has to cooperate with the Asian countries in development, and make contributions to that effect' (1956a: 27). As Japan proves that it is no longer a dangerous conqueror, but a peaceful country that really assists the development of other Asian countries, eventually goodwill towards Japan would develop.

Peter Drysdale has called Okita the 'intellectual father' of Japan's comprehensive security concept, which he names the 'defenceless-on-all-sides' concept. It stresses maintaining a low defence posture and non-aggressive diplomacy, which are the legacies of Yoshida, but with Okita the concept became widened in a still more economistic direction, with emphasis on constructive international co-operation and foreign aid (Drysdale 1983: viii).

In his texts Okita does not adopt the high posture role of defining the Japanese security concept, but remains in the role of an economic expert. However, in that role throughout the 1950s he continuously points to the importance of Japan making contributions to Asian development. This can be seen as an expression of the theme of economism in Japan's international setting. Okita's goal is to spread economism to the Asian area, ameliorating the dangerous political and military tensions there, and building a stable Asian international system on this foundation. It was a political goal, but conducted in the economic sector, with economic means. It would guarantee Japan's security, allow her to find a place among the Asian countries, and benefit her economy. In this way, the theme of development is extended to the Asian setting as an economic goal for the Asian nations instead of a political goal. Okita points out that this process involves a problem. With the further development of other Asian countries, they will become more serious competitors to Japanese exports. He expects, however, that the general expansion of markets in the area would offset this, leaving room for the Japanese economy to operate (1956a: 19).

In the background of Okita's proposal were two international conferences held in 1955, an Asian–African conference in Bandung, Indonesia in April, and an Asian conference in May in Shimla, India. Okita had participated in both as a representative of Japan, and in both conferences Asian economic co-operation through a regional organization was discussed, promoted especially by India and Japan. Both gatherings came to naught in this respect. There were widespread misgivings about possible Indian and Japanese domination of other countries because their technological level was higher, and because they might be able to grab a lion's share of the economic assistance offered from outside of the region. In April, President Dwight D. Eisenhower had proposed to the Congress of the United States that US $200 million be set aside as economic aid to be allocated multilaterally for Asia. A regional organization should have been set up for this, but this was not to be so. The Bandung Conference was marred by discussions of the Cold War and nonalignment, while the Shimla Conference could not reach agreement on any single important item on the agenda. The Asian countries wanted economic assistance, but they wanted it to remain on a bilateral basis according to the Colombo Plan. It did not seem possible to promote Asian regionalism at the time (Okita 1956a: 22–7; Singh 1966: 7–11).

Okita finds two ways for Japan to make a contribution to Asia. One is to offer Japan's historical experience of development to the other Asian countries as an example, to show how an Asian country can rapidly develop intensive agriculture, various small and medium enterprises, modern industries, a working financial system, and so on. Japan could also provide trained experts in various economic fields for other Asian countries (1956b: 13).

The other method is to give direct assistance, for instance, through the Colombo Plan. The Plan was set up in 1950 in Colombo in the first post-war meeting of the foreign ministers of the British Commonwealth, and later several other Asian non-socialist countries also joined the Plan. If it could be called a regional organization, it was extremely loose. It had a Consultative Committee meeting yearly as a forum for discussion, but no secretariat, and almost all practical activity was strictly on a bilateral basis. Nor was it a plan for Asia's development in any economic sense, but only an aggregate of the bilateral agreements involving foreign aid for South and Southeast Asian countries. In 1951, in view of Britain's economic difficulties, the United States joined the Plan and became the principal donor country. Japan was admitted in 1954, mainly as a donor of technical assistance, although among Asian countries the distinction between donors and recipients was not sharp (Singh 1966: 169–206). Within this structure Okita supports inflow of both private and public foreign capital to the area, without specifying that it should come from Japan; rather, he emphasizes in this connection that Japan is still one of the low income countries of the world (1956a: 27; 1956b: 16), implying that Japan would not be able to do much in this respect.

Another form of assistance was payment of war reparations to some Asian countries. Agreements were concluded with Burma in 1954, with the Philippines in 1956, with Indonesia in 1958, and with South Vietnam in 1959. These payments took the form of capital goods and services. An 85,000 kw power plant and railways were built in Burma. Electrical appliances, buses and trucks were exported, and plans for various assembly plants, such as plants for agricultural machines were implemented. Ships were sent to Indonesia and the Philippines and plans for resource development were developed, and South Vietnam received a 160,000 kw power plant (Oki 1965: 110–24). These were bilateral agreements, and Singh, for example, treats them similarly to ordinary Colombo Plan assistance. They tended to further increase Japanese exports to the area. At the turn of the decade Japan created similar agreements of economic co-operation with other Asian non-socialist countries, and financial assistance also started to enter the picture. However, up to 1965 the total amount of Japanese technical assistance remained low, and among the Colombo Plan countries Japan was not only a donor, but also a recipient country, receiving small amounts of technical assistance from, e.g., India and Pakistan (Singh 1966: 171–2).

This kind of assistance beginning with the reparations payments was in a sense ideal from Okita's point of view, alleviating Asian bad feelings towards Japan, assisting the Asian countries economically, and promoting Japanese exports; its amount was just not enough to have much effect on the Asian situation (1958: 104). Even by 1955 Japan still did not have formal trading treaties with most Asian countries; it was only during the latter half of the 1950s that the situation began to change in Japan's favour (Shiraishi 1989: 66–7). The immediate problems for Japan at the time were the negative Asian attitude towards Japan and the necessity for trade expansion, but any schemes of regional integration were merely a vague concern for the future.

The publications of Kojima Kiyoshi deal with similar matters. His 1956 *Kōeki jōken* (The Terms of Trade) deals with international trade in general, as a theoretical discussion on the concept of the terms of trade. The work is mainly historical in the sense of that it examins the historical trading experiences of Great Britain and Japan, both maritime trading nations, with global trading relationships. The perspective is on globalism, not regionalism, and integration as a concept is not a point of interest in the study.

In his *Nihon bōeki to keizai hatten* (Japan's Trade and Economic Development) in 1958 Kojima continues a similar discussion of global trade, together with the idea of development, drawing on the ideas of Akamatsu Kaname. Kojima stays on a very abstract level in this study, hardly specifying any markets or trading partners. The perspective usually used is that of a lone country (*ikkoku*) engaged in economic communication with an unspecified outer world. The perspective is well suited to the international situation of the 1950s, the principles of free trade, and GATT, which were based on universalism in trading values all over the globe. At this time Japan was only moving in the direction of global economic integration, and the characterization as a lone country suited Japan well.

Kojima is, however, quite optimistic about the situation, especially in the light of Japan's recent success in economic development. Kojima is even baffled by Japan's rapid development, as it was becoming difficult to handle within the conceptual framework of Akamatsu. He points out that the theory works well up to the Russo–Japanese War, but already during the 1930s new elements were being introduced into the pattern of change of the Japanese economy. His problem is chiefly that Akamatsu had distinguished clearly between periods of structural change and stable growth, but what was curious about the 1930s, and especially about the ongoing 1950s, is that change and growth no longer fit into this kind of beautiful pattern. They seem to be happening simultaneously, or so fast that it has become impossible to differentiate between periods

(1958: 308–9, 318–19). This does not mean in any sense a refutation of the theory of the flying geese pattern of development, but is a way of pointing out how dynamic the Japanese economy had become.

Relying on his knowledge as an economic historian Kojima displays a strong sense of reliance on the continuation of the growth of the Japanese economy, despite recent worries (1957–8) about imports greatly exceeding exports, or the amount of foreign loans rising very fast. Both processes are driving the Japanese economy forward qualitatively, and raising the efficiency of production. In this way Japan is becoming continually more fit for the global trading system, enabling it to phase down its own trade restrictions. Kojima is clearly an economic optimist, and it is exactly Japan's economic growth and development, in light of the flying geese pattern of development, on which this optimism is based.

However, in 1958 Kojima perceives Japan only as a relatively strong country. The attribute given to Japan in the study is 'middle advancing country' (*chūshinkoku*), as well as 'follower or newly-rising country' (*kōshinkoku naishi shinkōkoku*), which has a similar meaning. Japan is situated between the Euro–American and the Asian countries, having common characteristics with both of the groups, but as a unit is different from both of them.

The year 1960 presents a watershed in the way that Japan's position in the world is perceived. Ikeda's Income Doubling Plan and the debate surrounding it seem to be the direct cause of this. The general change of vocabulary can also be seen in the texts of Kojima; for instance, even the title of his *Keizai seichō to Nihon bōeki* (Economic Growth and Japan's Trade) in 1960 displays the word 'growth', and stability is no longer a worry for him as in the previous study. Economic growth and the accompanying idea of dynamism became the new attributes of Japan. The strength of these attributes provided arguments for a new opening of the Japanese economy, so that Japan could be better accepted as a participant in global economic integration.

Kojima always stays cool and academic in his texts, using deliberative rhetoric, but Okita engages also in epideictic rhetoric, freely displaying feelings of pride and satisfaction. For instance, in his *Nihon keizai no shōrai* (The Future of Japan's Economy) published in December 1960, Okita reminisces about his own post-war career, how he 'set his heart' on becoming an economist during the war, and how he took part in the building of the successful economy of the new Japan. This should not be taken only as indulgence in self-praise, although even that may be part of the reason these reminiscences are included in the book. The Economic Planning Agency, in the wake of the publicity on the Ikeda Plan, attempted to break away from subordination to the Ministry of International Trade and Industry (MITI), and place one of its own men, namely Okita Saburo, into the post of vice-minister of the agency. The attempt did not, however, succeed; MITI placed one of its men in the post, as it had done before (Johnson 1986: 252). It seems that this book may have formed part of Okita's campaign, but it also had other purposes as a publication directed to the general audience.

Okita argues that Japan's future will be as glorious and dynamic as the past decade has been. Okita's audience consists of all kinds of pessimists, who are still suffering from the post-war mental trauma of regarding Japan as a weak and vulnerable country, and who consequently do not rely on the possibilities of the new, economically-dynamic Japan. There are two things on which Okita places his trust in the future, one national, the other international. The national one is the industrious nature of the Japanese people:

> Japan is poor in natural resources, but in terms of intelligence, hard work and vitality the Japanese people lose to nobody in the whole world.
>
> (Okita 1960: 3)

Okita begins by using the old theme of the small and poor Japan, only to contrast it with the theme of the successful new Japan. The good properties of the Japanese guarantee that they can persevere in the struggles of this world. The positive reinforcement is part of the process of building a new economically-optimistic national identity.

The other source of faith in the future is the post-war international free trading system, and what Okita calls the spirit of Bretton Woods:

> The spirit liberated world trade, with the idea of a mutual striving for prosperity. One of the big mistakes of the pre-war time was economic nationalism, when all countries tried to carve out their own spheres of power, erecting trade barriers, and adopting a policy of blockism.
>
> (Okita 1960: 18)

This quotation is built on another contrast, namely on a comparison of global economic policies of post-war and pre-war times. The post-war prosperity is the result of the spirit of Bretton Woods, all countries together contributing to the well-being of all. On the other hand, the spirit and practices of the pre-war time resulted in terrible suffering for all. Thus, Okita here takes sides for global free trade, against both narrow nationalism and regionalism. The argument centres not only on the economic hardships created by that kind of 'blockism', but hints also that the phenomenon was one of the reasons leading to militarism and the Second World War.

Okita does not say directly that losing the war was beneficial to Japan – but he says that at least it was not a minus (Okita 1960: 20–1). Defeat brought with it the various social and economic reforms which became the basis for the Japanese post-war economic miracle. Similar changes towards the well-being of all people happened globally. Former colonies became independent. The will to control economic cycles, and reaching full employment on a global scale, created international organizations like the United Nations, the World Bank, and the IMF. After the period of the Cold War during the 1950s even international politics seemed to have returned to the general post-war trend of increasing peace and well-being, by becoming economistic. In 1959 President Eisenhower visited India, promising the country a large sum of developmental assistance, and in 1960 Chairman Nikita Khrushchev visited the same country, promising a roughly equal amount of assistance. The military race seemed to be shifting towards a developmental aid race. This is highly preferable to Okita. He uses pacifistic arguments about nuclear weapons being able to destroy the whole world, and the big powers wasting terrible amounts of good capital on the production of weapons, when far better uses for the money exist in economic development. International peace, global free trade, and economic development are the corner-stones of the new post-war world, as seen by Okita.

Okita also presents other interesting interpretations of the new situation facing post-war Japan, constructed as persuasive in elevating Japanese self-respect, and in creating optimism for the future. Before the war, nations strove to possess a big land mass to be able to feed their populations, but in the qualitatively different post-war world this is no longer necessary. Quite the opposite to the pre-war situation, the small land mass and the big population of Japan are assets, because they enable the concentration of people and industry. Continuing economic development is already decreasing the birth-rate, leading to a demographically stable population whose standard of living will rise quickly. Like Kojima in his texts, Okita also praises the example of England, the traditional advocate of free trade. Before the war England could feed only 50 per cent of its population with locally-grown food, but during wartime it was able to quickly convert idle land to food production. This is a model that also suits Japan. It should import food from the neighbouring countries with big land masses, where it can be produced more cheaply than in Japan. It would increase trade in the region, and enable the countries to buy more Japanese industrial products (Okita 1960: 39–41).

The same reasoning also holds true for industry. Japan may be dependent on the imports of various kinds of raw materials; in 1960 Japan was importing over 80 per cent of iron ore, almost 100 per cent of raw cotton and wool, practically all of its oil, two-thirds of soy beans and sugar, etc. This was, however, nothing special or alarming. When we look at the world at large, we can see several other countries, for instance in Europe, which are in an identical situation to Japan. There are also many countries that are dependent on the export of raw materials and foodstuffs. They are stuck with their piles of raw materials, only waiting for somebody to be kind enough to buy them (*dareka katte kurereba*); otherwise they will not be able to advance in their own development (Okita 1960: 41, 46–7). Both the content and the grammatical structure of the argument place the Japanese in a position where they can choose, and where others are dependent on them. Countries like Canada and Australia, as well as several South American and Southeast Asian countries, are in this situation. The total argument thus rests on the idea of mutual dependence. As all countries want to grow and develop, they have a mutual interest in keeping the global trading system open. Both the Euro–American countries, which can no longer rely on their colonies, and the raw material producers are in this situation. Within this system Japan can thrive.

As it seemed at the time, the world was full of raw materials. Okita in 1960 sees no end in sight, and much more is expected still to be hidden below the surface of the earth. New supertankers and huge ore carriers had been developed which could supply large factories, while transport costs were diminishing. There was an abundance of energy in the world; in addition to coal and oil, the prospects of using nuclear fission seemed promising, and further in the future there would also be the possibility of nuclear fusion. The human race seemed to be liberated from the limitations of the scarcity of nature. All that was needed was to process the raw materials in factories, trade them, and increase the prosperity of humankind. Okita argues that as development goes on around the world, and world prosperity rises, its buying power also rises. There will be an expanding market for Japanese transistor radios, cameras, toys, art work, household goods, cars, ships, etc. (Okita 1960: 47).

Okita's text is euphoric in its developmental optimism. Naturally, he usually qualifies his statements in a Japanese way, using expressions like 'it would not be a mistake to think so' (*to kangaete machigai nai*), or the volitional forms, which are quite oblique, in the sense that they allow the writer to throw in different ideas without taking an absolute stand on them. However, the general thrust of his arguments is as presented above, euphoric, trying to create similar feelings in his readers. No doubt part of the reason is – apart from his personal political ambitions – that Okita, as one of the architects of the Ikeda Plan, wrote the book to propagate a similar psychological state of mind to that which the plan was attempting to achieve.

Consequently, as he argues for global free trade, Okita is not especially interested in the idea of regional integration. He is not against regional integration taking place in Europe and Latin America after becoming satisfied that they do not represent a return to the pre-war blockism. Asia is taken as a totality, and seen still in 1960 as quite undeveloped. Many of the Asian countries do not have much to sell beyond one or two agricultural products, the area is torn by political divisions, and the newly-independent countries tend to prefer the other of the pre-war evils identified by Okita, economic nationalism, in the sense of concentrating on development on the national scale only. Most of them are also continuing a dependent relationship with their previous colonizers. Thus, no meaningful economic actor can be created out of the region. Trade should be increased; that would benefit both Japan and the Asian countries, but there is no reason to go above that level. In addition, Okita points out that the relative share of Japan's trade with the region has been declining throughout the 1950s, Japan's trade shifting towards the high income countries like the United States, or Western Europe, so that the importance of Asia to Japan seems to be diminishing. He hopes that Japan's trade with the area will pick up in the future, but this was not the situation at the beginning of the 1960s (Okita 1960: 95–9).

At that time there was also a shift in the identification of Japan with other regions of the world. As the general climate of discussion had turned increasingly away from the image of a small Japan towards the optimistic image of a dynamic Japan, Japan's international rank as evaluated by the Japanese had tended to rise. The points of reference were changing accordingly. Comparisons of Japan with the European countries were increasing, and those with the Asian countries diminishing.

One European country that Japan was usually identified with was England, a maritime trading nation, as in the examples above. The countries defeated in the Second World War that were devastated and had to be laboriously reconstructed afterwards were also points of identification. The increasing incomes of the Japanese introduced new consumer goods into everyday life, such as refrigerators, electric washing machines, televisions, and cars. The dietary habits of the Japanese were also changing. All of this was making life in Japan resemble more and more that of the European countries. In Okita's book it is not so much Germany, but Italy which stands out in this sense. Both Italy and Japan had been, so to speak, poor local big powers, but after the loss of big power status both came to experience unprecedented prosperity and growth in economic activity. Okita even made a trip to Italy to study the conditions there (Okita 1960: 47–9), and can thus speak with the authority of an eyewitness.

Okita also points to another important international phenomenon. The rise of Western Europe and Japan has coincided with an unmistakable fall in the international economic position of the United States. Its economic power is visibly waning. After 1958 it began to run deficits in its balance of payments, due to worsening trade balances with Japan and Western Europe, accompanied by increased investment and military spending overseas. In 1960 the Eisenhower Administration asked other countries to lower their tariffs, ease import quotas, and reduce restrictions on trade in general. Advanced countries were also asked to take more responsibility for their defence, and for aid to developing countries. Various 'Buy American' policies were promoted at home. The same measures were continued also during the Kennedy era (Calleo 1982: 9–25; Shiraishi 1989: 120–3). Okita does not blame the American economy for being sluggish, or anything resembling the international quarrels since the 1970s; rather, he is thankful that the United States actively helped the economies of Western Europe and Japan back to their feet, thus purposefully making strong economic competitors of them. As a result, the total world economy is now bigger and more prosperous than ever before. However, as another result, a great change in the international balance of power is taking place:

> Thus far the economy of America has been unquestionably stronger than that of any other country, and America has taken

the lead. However, recently the smooth operation of the international economy has begun to require that all countries take
part in discussions. Also, for Japan it is becoming necessary to
move from discussing only the Japanese economy to preparing
herself for presenting opinions about the operation of the global
economy.

(Okita 1960: 272)

Okita carefully stays only in the economic sphere without mention-
ing any other, but at least in this sphere the world has indeed
changed. The horizon of again taking part in international decision-
making is beginning to open. Okita discusses particularly the American economy, the importance of defending the value of the dollar,
and the importance of helping the global economic system to continue opening, so that President John F. Kennedy's goal – a growth
rate of 5 per cent – could be achieved by the American economy.
His ideas probably refer to the Joint Japan–US Committee on Trade
and Economic Affairs, which was to be set up in January of 1961.
Also during the same year the first meeting of Japanese and American economic ministers took place. Preparations for these events
had obviously been under way when Okita was writing.

   However, it is interesting to note that Okita concentrates only on
the United States. He presents Japan as a supporter of the international position of the United States. He does not treat Japan as
being in any big power position in this context, nor with respect to
the Asian countries. Nor does he think that there is much possibility
of influencing Asia. He points out that even though Japan can
engage in small amounts of aid to Asian countries, including war
reparations payments, in view of the size and needs of the region
the Japanese contribution becomes diluted. It is not of much effect
in the total situation. The main contributions should come from rich
countries, Japan being only on the sidelines in this sense (Okita
1960: 99). Okita reiterates, however, his position of 1956, emphasizing Japan as an example (*zenrei, jitsurei*) for them. Japan is the
most relevant example for the Asian countries, and advances in
development in front of them. In terms of the flying geese theory
this creates the image of Japan as a leader of the Asian countries,
but only in the sense of an example. The image does not contain
the idea of political leadership. Being an example is seen as the
principal contribution Japan can make for the development of
the Asian countries, in addition to buying their foodstuffs and raw
materials.

In his book regarding the future of the Japanese economy, Okita thus reinterprets the position of Japan from fresh angles. He carefully refrains from references to a political big power status for Japan, but in the global economic sphere Japan is presented as a rising power with respect to the United States. This is a move away from the idea of a small and weak Japan. The change comes with the idea of Japan's dynamism, based on the theme of rapid growth during the 1950s and planned-for growth during the 1960s. Consequently, the idea that Japan can again start to influence substantially the world around it, and even has the responsibility to do so, begins to emerge. However, the change does not reach the level where Japan should start diverting considerable amounts of capital from its own development to the Asian countries; in this context Japan continues to be presented as a poor and small country. Still, even here pride is discernible, caused by Japan's economic success, seen in the way Okita presents Japan as a leading example for the Asian countries.

As argued above, during the 1950s regional integration in Asia was not of special concern to either Okita or Kojima, and according to Shiraishi (1989: 151–2) this was also generally true in Japan. Japan's position towards the Asian countries was characterized by the general need to dispel Asian distrust of Japan, as a good thing in itself, and also the desire that Asia could form a better export market for Japan.

REGIONAL CO-OPERATION IN ASIA

Regional economic co-operation in Asia was promoted most of all by ECAFE. Since its establishment in 1947 it had been, however, rather unfruitful. Although ECAFE was primarily an economic United Nations organization, its functioning was nearly paralysed by various political questions. The Cold War and big power rivalry entered into the organization because both the United States and the Soviet Union were non-regional members, and especially during the 1950s their political quarrelling often took up most of the time in meetings. The colonial past tended to enter discussions, as Great Britain, France, and the Netherlands were also non-regional members – as well as Australia and New Zealand – while some Asian countries, notably North Korea, China, and North Vietnam, were not. As Mongolia had no rival regime claiming the status of sole representative for the whole country, it was a member. There was political tension between Japan and some other Asian countries, the image of the Greater East Asian Co-prosperity Sphere being kept alive in discussions. Tension existed also between non-aligned and aligned countries, between India and Pakistan, between Malaysia and Indonesia, between Malaysia and the Philippines, etc. (Singh 1966: 26–52). Consequently, ECAFE was mainly an organization for research and recording, which was conducted by its secretariat in Bangkok.

After the Bandung and Shimla conferences in 1955, Japan, at the instigation of Prime Minister Kishi, attempted to put the idea of regional trade expansion and a proposal for an Asian Development Fund on the agenda in 1957, but only India offered support. Several countries, especially South Korea, Taiwan, the Philippines, Thailand and Pakistan opposed it, partly because Japan and India supported the idea, and in general because they were still not willing to discuss the question of regional planning (Singh 1966: 120–3). Also the United States was not interested, as Kishi asked the United States to supply the funds for the programme (Yasutomo 1983: 27–8).

It was only after the formation of the EEC in 1958 that the atmosphere began to change. India presented a draft for a resolution on economic co-operation in Asia, which was eventually adopted unanimously as the Bangkok Resolution in 1960. The step was not a big one, but it at least meant that regional economic integration now became a legitimate subject of discussion in ECAFE meetings. However, no practical measures could be taken then, and the consensus was already broken in the next meeting in 1961 (Singh 1966: 149–56).

However, encouraged by the Bangkok Resolution, the secretariat in 1961 convened a consultative group of economic experts, which was dubbed in the press the 'Wise Men's' Commission (Yasutomo 1983: 29). Its chairman was K. B. Lal of India, the other two members being Luang Thavil Sethaphanichakan of Thailand, and Okita Saburo of Japan. The report of the group was not published, its circulation being confined to ECAFE member governments, because it became a sensitive political issue. However, its main contents were leaked to the press, and became well known. In an article published in February of 1962, 'Ajia keizai kyōryoku no shomondai' (The problems of Asian economic co-operation) Okita also explained his views. The expert group proposed the establishment of an Organization for Asian Economic Cooperation (OAEC), conceived as an executive agency for taking concrete measures and implementing programmes of action agreed to by member countries. It was to work through a council of ministers who would make policy decisions, assisted by the ECAFE Secretariat, and it was also to have the authority to make decisions binding on member governments. These ideas were clearly too much for most regional member countries at that stage, in view of the political situation (Singh 1966: 158–60).

The goal of the expert group was not a full-fledged free trade area, but entailed the ideas of subregional and sectoral economic integration aimed at economies of scale and expansion of intra-regional trade. Okita emphasizes that in view of the differing levels of development in Asia, the formation of a free trade area, or a common market in the European style, might be harmful for the development of many Asian countries. As industrial development in these countries was mostly new or just being established, there was a danger of their development being harmed by a free flow of industrial products from Japan. The goal was thus only the partial and carefully managed dismantling of trade restrictions, with a heavy emphasis on technical co-operation (Okita 1962: 76–80).

The general tone of Okita's article is that such integration might be good for both Japan and Asia, but with respect to European integration the matter is not pressed. The formation of the EEC and other groupings is in the background, seen as a breech of the spirit of GATT, and as the general reason why the discussion of Asian economic co-operation was needed in the first place, but is evaluated in the following way:

> During the post-war period, schemes for regional co-operation have adopted the idea, at least as their public position [*tatemae*], that a regional grouping acts only as a step towards future global integration.
>
> (Okita 1962: 74)

Okita thinks that at least as long as they keep this position, and there are no other reasons for changing their minds, these regional schemes do not represent a return to pre-war blockism, and are not a threat to Japan. His evaluation of the general situation is similar to the one he made in 1956, but with the use of the word *tatemae* there is a clear shift towards scepticism.

Okita also goes a step further in his article in reinterpreting the international status of Japan. He very carefully points out that just as the United States has a special relationship with Central and South America, and Europe has a special relationship with Africa, as an analogy it is possible to think of a similar relationship between Japan and Southeast Asia in the sense of co-operation (Okita 1962:

74–5). In this roundabout way Japan is now included structurally in the group of advanced countries. This reflects the new rhetoric of the Ikeda period, with its emphasis on Japan's new international status. Okita does not call Japan a big power, which Ikeda himself sometimes did, nor does he use the other famous Ikeda slogan of the 'three pillars', namely Western Europe, the United States, and Japan, which would co-operate in the international system. However, Okita's claim amounts to the same thing.

Too much should not be read into these claims; they should be understood according to the themes of economism and growth. Just as Yasutomo interprets Ikeda's claims, saying that the Japanese still viewed them with humility, and did not equate them with either global political or military power (Yasutomo 1983: 26), Okita's claim is also clearly a very careful one, the content of the claim still centring on technical co-operation.

The opposite side of the coin was that Japan became reinterpreted in these terms in foreign countries. It seems that Ikeda's Japan was more acceptable to many Asian countries than Kishi's Japan. Japanese economic success was noted too, with a corresponding increase in pleas for economic assistance (Yasutomo 1983: 27). In this way, also from the outside, Japan came to be placed in a structural position *vis-à-vis* the developing countries similar to that of Western Europe and the United States.

Japan's economic policies towards the Asian countries changed correspondingly. During the 1950s emphasis had been on war reparations provided as goods and services, but during the Ikeda period aid increasingly meant financial contributions, and the amount began to grow. The rhetorical goal also changed from emphasizing the alleviation of Asian distrust to emphasizing help for Asian development. From 1961 onwards the Ikeda government increased Japanese economic aid to Asian countries and established an Overseas Economic Co-operation Fund, an Asian Productivity Organization, as well as an Overseas Technical Cooperation Agency, including a Youth Volunteer Corps modelled after the American Peace Corps. Planning for the Asian Development Bank also began during this time (Yasutomo 1983: 24–40).

This, however, did not mean support for an Asian trading area. ECAFE held a meeting in Tokyo in March 1962 to discuss the expert group's proposition for OAEC. Japan adopted a hostile attitude towards the issue, espoused by large segments of the government, bureaucracy, private business, and the press. In his analysis of the Japanese debate, Singh finds two types of arguments used: little advantage was seen in concentrating on the Asian market, because Western Europe and North America offered far better prospects, and a commitment to OAEC might have prejudiced Japan's negotiations in Paris for membership in the OECD (Singh 1966: 160–1). These arguments involved both Japan's material benefits and status, and in both senses Japan was in the process of leaving Asia. As the attitudes of other Asian countries, with the possible exception of India, were also hostile to the idea, the prospects for an Asian trading area even in the limited sense of OAEC were non-existent. Although ECAFE continued to have yearly meetings, there was no real progress.

During this period Kojima Kiyoshi also entered the discussion of regional integration in Asia. In 1960, Prime Minister Ikeda had established an institute for Asian economic research. If one wants, one can read even in its name something of the situation of the period. In English it is known as the Institute of Developing Economies, the name implying a global approach, while the Japanese name, *Ajia keizai kenkyū jo* (Asian Economic Research Institute) implies only a concentration on Asia, more suitable for Japan's resources. Both names emphasize economics. It was a government organ for the study of the economic situation of Asian countries, and the possibilities of commerce with them. Kojima Kiyoshi became one of the leading economists associated with the Institute. While most of the publications of the Institute centred on limited and practical questions, such as specific countries or specific trading items, Kojima's task was to provide a general conceptual framework for thinking about Japan's economic relationship with the region.

In Kojima's opinion, Southeast Asia was economically a very backward area facing grave difficulties in the development of its national economies. The products that the area had to offer did not fare well in the international market. They were concentrated in areas where demand was not rising, or was even contracting. The situation led to wild fluctuations in prices, which even in the long term were not rising. In the international market this meant an abundance of raw materials usually with low prices beneficial to the industrialized countries, but hurtful to the Asian countries. Besides tin and other metals, the exports of Southeast Asia consisted mostly of foodstuffs, such as rice and sugar, and agricultural raw materials, such as natural rubber, hemp, and raw cotton. These materials were not needed in the industrialized countries as much as before. The reason was that during and after the war, economic development in the industrialized countries had concentrated on two main fields:

agriculture and synthetic materials. Difficulties of transportation during the war, the collapse of the colonial empires after it, and various programmes of social welfare and full employment led to the expansion of agriculture in the industrialized countries. It caused less need for imports of foodstuffs from the previous colonies. Kojima even claims that, accompanied by rising efficiency, the comparative advantage in agricultural products was moving from the developing to the industrialized countries (Kojima 1961a: 34). Simultaneously, technological innovations in the chemical field, such as the development of synthetic rubber during the war when the areas producing natural rubber were mostly under Japanese occupation, led in the same direction, so that after the war natural rubber was not needed in industry as much as before (Kojima 1961b).

Most of these countries were either densely populated or their population was rising fast. That created an additional problem, forcing the countries to grow and develop to be able to provide the necessities of life for the people. The prospects of development along traditional lines were, however, bleak. Because of a general lack of capital, intensive investment projects in agriculture were not possible, and perhaps not even feasible considering the international commercial situation of these crops. There was only one area where the countries had a natural comparative advantage over the industrialized countries, namely, cheap labour. Thus Kojima comes to the conclusion that a change in the structure of production towards a wide range of light manufactures is the only feasible, or even inevitable (*hitsuzen*) condition for their development. That would also be ideal considering the scarcity of capital in those countries. Small factories for light manufactures could be started with limited capital. However, effective and wide-ranging industrial development is not feasible on the national scale only. It is necessary to be able to use international markets, where the law of comparative advantage can work (Kojima 1961a: 33–7).

Kojima's stress on the inevitability of the situation is inspired by the theory of the flying geese pattern of development, but as a more modern authority he uses Gunnar Myrdal's concept of second-grade international specialization. The concept corresponds to the flying geese pattern, namely, that developing countries start their industrial development using their cheap labour to produce cheaply low quality goods, which are competitive first in the home market, and then in the international markets (Myrdal 1964: 258–9).

In this way Kojima argues forcefully that the countries of Southeast Asia have to start to climb the ladders of development. However, he is worried about the aspect of the flying geese theory which points out that no stable and durable system of international organization can be reached in this way. The theory is beautiful in the sense that it gives hope for any country which wishes to advance from the bottom upwards, but Kojima's Japan of 1961 was already so far advanced on the road to development that the newly-rising competitors were a source of insecurity. Kojima thinks that somehow the principle of a stable and durable international division of labour has to be established in the post-war world. In this light, totally free international trade would be disruptive, however advantageous it would then be from the point of view of global economic efficiency. The flood of cheap labour-intensive products would cause serious trouble in the already industrialized countries where salaries are considerably higher. It would cause either a general reduction of salaries, and a reduction of living standards, or a partial reduction of salaries in the industries affected. Equally undesirable would be large scale unemployment. Financial troubles might even halt economic development in the capital intensive industrialized countries (1961a: 40). Kojima's argument rests on the foundation that unrestricted free trade would shatter the social policies of general welfare and full employment adopted in the industrialized countries as a safeguard against the re-emergence of fascism and similar movements born from the hardships of the 1930s, as well as a way to compete against the ideological influence of the socialist countries. Japan would probably be the country hardest hit, as light manufactures at the beginning of the 1960s still formed about half of its exports. It would imperil the democratization achieved after the war, and the road to prosperity that Japan had travelled ever since.

Kojima identifies the problem as combining the necessary development of the newly-independent poor countries with that of the continuing development of the industrialized nations. As a solution he offers the grouping of countries according to the principles of homogeneity and a similar level of income. Inside of such groupings a mutually-agreed division of labour and balanced growth would take place. This would not mean closed blocks – a similar object of abhorrence for Kojima as for Okita – and the principle of free international trade would still prevail, but the grouping would allow measures of protection for whatever reason against countries outside of the grouping. Thus, his solution in 1961 for the development problem of the Asian countries is increasing co-operation and trade among themselves, while not cutting themselves off from wider international economic communication. Integration is not seen by

Kojima as touching Japan, but limited only to the case of the development problems of the Asian countries.

Up to 1960 regional economic integration was not a special concern either in Asia or in Japan, and, although in that year it became a topic of discussion with the Bangkok Resolution, it was not seen as a pressing immediate concern. Politically, Asia did not represent an area where a regional economic grouping could have been set up. Japan was not in a position where she could have influenced matters much, even if there had been the political will to do so, and there was not. The case of Japan's lack of interest in ECAFE's attempt to forge regional integration in Asia, and Kojima's theoretical discussion both point to the fact that regionalism was not understood as a relevant policy alternative for Japan. With respect to integration, Japan still preferred a globalistic position as represented by GATT.

KOJIMA'S CONCEPT OF INTEGRATION

The concept of regional integration entered Japanese discussion through observing the process of integration taking place in Europe, and not as an abstract idea as such. Study projects were initiated to find out what was happening in Europe, and integration theory entered Japanese discussion through them. One of the projects was connected with the Institute of Developing Economies, involved several economists, and was led by Kojima Kiyoshi. The project was entitled *Sekai keizai to kyōdō ichiba* (The World Economy and Common Market), and publications began to appear in 1962.

Kojima does not seem to have known the works of political scientists of integration like Mitrany (1943), or even Haas's *The Uniting of Europe*, published in 1958. Kojima's theoretical concept of integration was inspired by economic theoreticians, above all by the German Wilhelm Röpke and the Swede Gunnar Myrdal (Kojima 1962a: passim; interview 1991). In his *Beyond the Welfare State*, first published in 1960, Myrdal differentiates between an Old School of Internationalists who advocated classical international free trade policies with minimum state interference in the necessary adjustment processes, even though it would cause unemployment and business losses, and a New School of Internationalists who advocated free trade combined with welfare state policies, both nationally and internationally (Myrdal 1961: 122–6). Myrdal himself is a representative of the latter school, Röpke would represent the former, and Kojima would be situated somewhere between them, while continuing to stand on the theoretical basis provided by Akamatsu.

The principal work of Röpke used by Kojima was *International Order and Economic Integration*, published in 1959. The world view presented in this book is in many respects very similar to the one held by the Japanese economists, although in Röpke's case the initial intellectual shock of war was provided by the trenches of the First World War, making him an anti-militarist and anti-nationalist. The subsequent events, which forced him to emigrate from Germany, and which led to the Second World War, have only reinforced his views, also making him antipolitics, equating politics with 'arbitrariness, emotions and rivalries' (Röpke 1959: 17). Thus, as an economic peace researcher he has come to understand the attainment of peace with decentralization and federalism, both on the national and the international levels, leading to a weakening of the authority of the centralized state both from the inside and the outside.

The ideal country for him is Switzerland, as well as other small industrialized European countries like Sweden and Holland. Because of their smallness they have low political profiles and no inclinations towards military conquest, and are for free trade, as 'islands of economic reason'. He even claims that 'if these small states did not exist, they would have to be invented today' (Röpke 1959: 170). Röpke's argument rests both on the interdependence of states as a guarantee against their becoming belligerent, and on their weakness, making them unable to stir up nationalism and other political passions that might lead to war. He represents economism in the same sense as the Japanese economists studied here, concentrating on the economic sector and using economic rhetoric, but there is a political goal in his activity as a researcher.

Röpke does not argue for the integration of Europe, but rather for its reintegration. He looks romantically upon pre-First World War Europe:

> The author of this book belongs to the generation which in his youth saw the sunset glow of that long and glorious sunny day of the western world, which lasted from the Congress of Vienna until August 1914, and of which those who have only lived in the present arctic night of history can have no adequate conception.
>
> (Röpke 1959: 3)

In Röpke's thinking, the world economy of that time centring on Europe, with free trading Great Britain as its nucleus, was an ideal economic system. It was a system of interdependence and intercommunication, where trade was flowing comparatively freely. Import duties existed, but they were not prohibitive, and quantitative import restrictions hardly existed. The system was multilateral, not based on bilateralism where planned regulation of foreign trade is easy, and it was not restricted to a certain number of participants, making the system open. The international monetary system based on the gold standard made the system, practically, a global payments community, and the basic freedom of international movement of not only goods, but also of capital and human beings was made possible under the system. The whole structure was based on a common spiritual heritage, on the historical, cultural, religious and political unity of Europe developed over 2,500 years, leading to a distinct European way of life and consciousness. Röpke sums up his ideas in the following way:

> This highly desirable state of affairs, as regards the economic integration of Europe, already existed . . . it was integration which required no plans, no planners, no bureaucracy, no conferences, no customs unions, and no High Authorities.
>
> (Röpke 1959: 226)

Consequently, Röpke is sceptical about, or even outright opposed to, the kind of integration taking place in Europe after the war; the process leading to the EEC especially fits this view. It was governed too much by political considerations, being state managed, leading possibly to an ever higher political entity representing closed European nationalism. It was a mirror image of the closed 'totalitarian imperium of Communism' led by Russia, which to him is the worst possible economic and political system (Röpke 1959: 228–30). Röpke is not against regionalism as a first step in loosening the grip of economic nationalism, but regionalism should be open in its character, so that new strong supranational political entities cannot rise up. In observing the EEC, Röpke is especially critical of France, which in his opinion seemed to be too interested in engaging in shows of military might around the world, although its resources were no longer adequate for the task, and which also in its approach towards European integration seemed to be inclined towards furthering political objectives and protectionism rather than open trade (Röpke 1959: 259–69).

Röpke's thinking is heavily Europe-centred; he does not seem to have much knowledge about, nor interest in, other parts of the globe, apart from, naturally, the United States. Nor are the concepts of growth and development much used by him; he is rather trying to build a stable and open system where matters such as the development of poor countries would take care of themselves according to the rules of comparative advantage. His romanticism does not include any advocacy of returning to the days when most of the non-European world was colonized. Development would follow automatically from global free trade, industrialization beginning in the agrarian countries as a response to the economic profitability of first producing simple and coarse consumer goods, then developing towards higher industries. This would destroy some industries in the old industrialized countries. It should not be lamented, because increased demand for capital goods would create new industries there. Even here Röpke mostly has in mind the European agrarian countries, and it is only Japan, a country advanced quite well along this road, that becomes clearly visible beyond the European horizon (Röpke 1959: 187–92).

In spite of this, it is clear how well Röpke's thinking would complement the thinking of Akamatsu. Kojima terms Röpke's approach 'functional', (*kinōteki*) (Kojima 1962a: 56) – although Röpke himself would not have accepted the term (Röpke 1959: 229–31) – as it was based, according to the laws of classical economics, on the natural growth of a community from the basic economic needs of the people. Especially appealing to Kojima was the idea of minimizing the role of the state in integration.

In terms of generational outlook Röpke and Akamatsu have much in common, and in a similar sense, as representatives of a later generation of economists, Kojima also has similarities with Gunnar Myrdal. Myrdal can also be called a peace-researching economist, although the term itself was not yet in use at the end of the 1950s. However, Myrdal does not have an aversion to the political sector as such, and does not argue for any primacy of economics, but tries to attain a combination of the two. Also, as a representative of the New School of Internationalists, relying on the welfare state approach in both national and international situations, the blending of economics and politics comes naturally in his thinking. In his *An International Economy*, first published in 1956, Myrdal defines integration in the following way:

> 'Economic integration' is the realization of the old Western ideal of equality of opportunity . . . economic integration is at bottom not only, and perhaps not even mainly, an economic problem, but also a problem of political science, sociology, and social psychology.
>
> (Myrdal 1964: 11)

Equality of opportunity in societies assumes the emergence of a community with growing social cohesion and solidarity among its members, and with freer social mobility based on the norms of equality and liberty. Thus, Myrdal adds to the basic idea of integration as parts being brought together into a whole, a strong normative element for the realization of classic and basic ideals of democracy. Economic, political and social integration have to be understood together, each supporting the other, and each of them being unattainable without the other. The countries, which Myrdal at the time sees as coming quite near the ideals, are the rich countries of Northwestern Europe, North America, Australia and New Zealand. However, they have done this only on the national scale, and the world at large was still far from attaining that normative goal.

Haas has termed Myrdal a Utopian thinker (Haas 1964: 461–3), and criticizes him for taking the Western capitalist pattern as the norm towards which the underdeveloped world will develop. Haas's main point of critique is that there are strong nationalistic and political forces which will make this kind of development extremely difficult. His critique is, however, irrelevant in this context. It is made from the sector of politics, and only clarifies that Myrdal argues basically from the sector of economics. In this sense he is totally compatible with Röpke, and as he also has similar premises to Akamatsu in terms of the idea of development, his ideas were very easily accepted by a Japanese economist like Kojima.

Just as the theory of the flying geese pattern of development emphasizes moderate nationalism, Myrdal also sees national integration to a certain extent as a prerequisite for international integration. However, because national integration means economic nationalism, the purpose of the welfare state being the guaranteeing of a good life for all of its members, national integration also easily becomes an obstacle to international integration. International integration leads inevitably to the relocation of industry. Because welfare states are committed to full employment and to defending the standard of living of their own citizens, rich nations are bound to start applying brakes on international integration at such a time (Myrdal 1964: 56–65). In this sense, Myrdal is as equally sceptical about Western European integration as Wilhelm Röpke, and similarly regrets the disintegration of the pre-First World War European system. This is where Röpke would have started to demand the dismantling of the state apparatus to let the economic forces have their free play, but Myrdal takes another road.

He points out that in the post-war conditions of expansive economic growth in all countries the effects of international integration would matter less. They could be coped with more easily than during times of stagnation when national autarkic tendencies would inevitably strengthen. There is also a need for moral education in the advanced countries to increase the solidarity of their citizens with those of the poorer countries, so that the concept of a welfare state could be widened into the concept of a 'welfare world' (Myrdal 1964: 324). In addition, there is also the classical argument, which Röpke would have agreed with, that although international integration would cause problems of relocation in the old industrialized countries, in the long run the basic arguments for free trade, increased productivity through development and division of labour, together with expansion of trade, would also bring considerable benefits to the rich countries. Thus, there are ways to counteract the forces of national integration in the rich countries, while preserving and even furthering the achievements already reached.

However, still more important would be what the developing countries themselves would do. A great step had already been taken. At that time a great many of them had already attained political independence, and the process was going forward. Myrdal calls the process the 'Great Awakening'. The resulting challenge would be for them to start national integration. They would need to strengthen themselves to be able to increase their bargaining power with the developed countries, and to set in motion the processes of democratization, social cohesion, and economic development.

A crucial problem would be the development of industrial production in the developing countries, and the ability to market the products. Myrdal uses the concept of second-grade international specialization in this connection, which means that because the developing countries would for a long time have incomplete industrial structures combined with cheap labour, their target should be the production of goods of cheaper and coarser quality. With their price competitiveness, they could undersell these products in the advanced countries, if only those countries would not close their markets. The bigger markets would, however, be in the developing countries themselves. They would soon start to squeeze out some products of the advanced countries from their own markets where price competitiveness, because of the low level of incomes of the people, would be the most effective. Myrdal points out that this is already happening in many developing countries in the production and trade of textiles (Myrdal 1964: 259). As can be seen, these ideas match those of Akamatsu.

There is, however, an important refinement, which brings in the concept of regional integration. Akamatsu's thinking centred on the situation of a lone follower country in economic communication with the international market as a whole, but in the new post-war situation, when there appeared at one stroke a great number of independent states facing a similar developmental situation, Myrdal goes a step further. He suggests that the developing countries form groupings among themselves focused on trade in manufactured goods. In his *Economic Theory and Underdeveloped Regions*, first published in 1957, Myrdal even maintains that any groupings, including political ones which have nothing to do with economics, are considered as good in so far as they increase solidarity among the developing nations (Myrdal 1965: 68–76). They need to defend themselves against attempts at military intervention, as well as against political and economic pressures from the old industrialized nations.

Also, in economic terms, regional integration would be beneficial for the developing nations. They would be in need of larger markets, and for the growth of productivity they would need international competition. In this sense the ideal solution would be to form regional groupings – with protection against competition from the old industrialized nations – while the old industrialized nations should not be allowed to erect protective walls around them (Myrdal 1964: 259–62). In a sense this would create a double standard of morality in international economics, but in another sense it would not. The question is not only about righting the historical inequalities of hundreds of years of exploitation and breaking down the relationships of monopolistic domination. Trade restrictions by the developing countries would represent a wholly different phenomenon with respect to international trade than those of the advanced countries.

For one thing, the exporting of raw materials and agricultural products to the industrialized countries would not change. The industrialized countries would need these products as before, and the industrializing countries would need the exports to earn capital for industrial development. Myrdal points out that this has been the pattern of development in the old industrialized countries, like the coal exports of England during the early phases of its industrialization, or the export of wood products by Sweden and Finland as their basis for being able to develop both wood-processing and other industries. In their industrialization the developing countries would need huge amounts of imports for the building of infrastructure and productive facilities. They would have to import as much as their export earnings would allow, and they would be able to earn all the more the stronger their integration and development became. Thus their import restrictions would not decrease total world trade, but expand it (Myrdal 1964: 288). That would be a process of world-wide cumulative causation which would turn the vicious circle of poverty into a virtuous circle of development.

When assessing the importance to Kojima of Röpke's and Myrdal's theoretical inspiration, we have to keep in mind the content of the Japanese economic debate at the time. As mentioned above, it did not concern regional integration, but centred on the debate on global integration versus nationalism. Since the late 1950s Japan had faced strong demands for the liberalization of its economy. In autumn 1959 the IMF held a meeting in Washington, and in December GATT held a general conference in Tokyo. Both meetings demanded that Japan free the convertibility of its currency and open its domestic market to foreign products and investment. This was the situation when Kishi's cabinet started to plan the opening of the economy, which eventually led to the Ikeda Plan. Foreign pressure continued during the 1960s. The economic ministers of Japan and the United States held their first meeting at the end of 1961, when the Americans asked for faster liberalization. Also Great Britain continued similar demands, and the IMF and GATT continued their pressure. At the same time the Japanese were also debating about applying for membership in the OECD, as the first Asian country to do so. The application was submitted in 1963 and Japan was admitted in the following year. Here was another process that committed Japan, not only to trade liberalization, but also to the removal of controls on capital transactions. The debate between the nationalists and internationalists was extremely heated during this period (Johnson 1986: 263).

One difficulty with Akamatsu's theory is that it is nationalistic, while also being based on the ideas of global free trade. It is open both to a nationalist and an internationalist interpretation. If the distance between the follower and the leading countries is seen to be great and the economic viability of the follower is evaluated pessimistically, the theory gives strong grounds for a self-legitimization of protective measures against foreign countries. Similarly, when the level of the follower country is seen to have risen high and its prospects for development are evaluated optimistically, the theory favours an interpretation of proceeding towards liberalizing trade. This is one of the reasons for the deliberate optimism of the Japanese internationalists, and their re-evaluation of Japan's international rank as being almost on a comparable level with the West European and North American countries.

With the inspirational backing of theoreticians like Röpke and Myrdal, Kojima can place himself on the side of the internationalists. Röpke would support Kojima by his insistence on the primacy of economics, while Myrdal would not accept Röpke's insistence on totally free international trade. Myrdal would inspire him to try to combine national integration with international integration, and to keep an eye on the developmental level of the countries concerned, giving more freedom to the developing countries, and placing more demands on the developed ones. For instance, the form of Kojima's discussion earlier in 1961 regarding the benefits for developing Asian countries if they created a regional grouping of their own was probably inspired by Myrdal.

The first publication of Kojima's research project on integration was *EEC no keizaigaku* (The Economics of the EEC). In this publication Kojima displays fairly enthusiastic interest in the new way of organizing regional economics. For him, the European Economic Community forms the basis for a new way of attaining an international division of labour. Kojima praises the achievements of the EEC, using expressions such as 'wonderful' (*subarashii*), and 'a thing which has to be stared at in wonder' (*dōmoku subeki mono*). The EEC had shown the beneficial effects of integration in various areas, such as the economic growth of its members. According to the statistics he uses, the average economic growth of the EEC countries had been 5.3 per cent in 1959, rising to 7.0 in 1960. The latter figure was no longer far from the Japanese figure. Also the growth figures for the EFTA countries had risen perceptibly, from a low of 3.5 per cent in 1959 to 5.0 per cent in 1960. These figures are compared with those of the USA and Canada, which in 1960 were 2.7 and 2.3 per cent, respectively (Kojima 1962a: 42). Integration had enlarged the economies, increased trade, and strengthened the competitive power of the participating countries, hinting at a revival of Europe as an important actor on the world scene.

It had also given a vast new vision of the world as a whole. European integration shows the road to long-term prosperity for all the countries of the world. Kojima expects that the economic dynamism of the EEC will increase world trade, both between the industrialized countries and the EEC, as well as between the developing countries and the EEC. The good things are the principles of horizontal integration between homogeneous countries on a similar level of income, the physical proximity of the countries, and the creation of a common market (Kojima 1962a: 1).

However, the enormously-important problem which would have to be discussed continually is the harmonious co-ordination of the approach of a common market with that of the global approach. The ideal is the combination of regionalism with globalism. There would be nothing threatening in an outward-looking EEC. This was also the basic criterion Röpke had used in evaluating the EEC. Kojima points out that interest in the EEC is high. Great Britain had applied to the organization in July 1961. This is to him a very positive phenomenon, because Great Britain, with the strongest traditions as a free trade country, with responsibilities to the British Commonwealth, would be an important factor guaranteeing that the EEC develops 'looking outward'. A similar effect would also follow if the small EFTA countries were to join, provided they were considered to be 'islands of free trading economic reason' as Röpke had. Discussion was already going on there, and with the EEC they could form a 'Greater European Common Market'. A similar discussion was going on in the United States about getting at least closer to the EEC, if not joining it outright. At the same time discussion had spread to other parts of the world, both in industrialized and developing nations, of creating similar regional groupings elsewhere (Kojima 1962a: 39–40). Regional integration indeed seemed to be a new and fascinating principle, around which a global movement was gathering.

Discussion had emerged in Japan, too, but Kojima comments that the Japanese tend to feel themselves 'international orphans', fretting restlessly about the matter. It would be quite difficult for Japan to enter such formations, because no partners were perceived as suitable (Kojima 1962a: 40). Kojima speaks ironically about this excessive feeling of confusion, and sets out to find other perspectives on the problem.

He proceeds from the idea that the rationale behind international common markets need not necessarily be their internationalism, but reaching reasonably large economies of scale. He assumes that 50 million people is the minimum size for a single economy or economic grouping in this sense. At the beginning of the 1960s, the United States alone comprised 170 million people, the six countries of the EEC 170 million as well, and the seven countries of EFTA including Great Britain, 70 million. Similar reasoning can also be applied in the case of Japan. The population of Japan was nearly 100 million, and that made it feasible to think of the Japanese economy as a common market of its own (Kojima 1962a: 80). Kojima also points out that Japan's dependence on foreign markets had diminished after the structural changes of its industries. The traditional textile industries were still clearly export industries, exporting a greater part of their production, but the newer Japanese heavy industries were exporting only 10 per cent of their production, 90 per cent being consumed at home. As an advocate of economic optimism, Kojima tries to turn the developing Japanese 'international orphanage' complex upside down with this exercise, arguing that although Japan may still be a small *country*, she is no longer a small *economy*, and thus not in a helpless situation. As an economy Japan is strong enough to handle the international problem of regional integration proceeding under the principles of GATT without any need to panic.

However, the argument also shows that even in Kojima's eyes there are no prospects for regional integration for Japan. He dismisses the idea of integration with the Asian countries on the same grounds as before, saying that it would disrupt the degree of national economic well-being Japan had already attained – just as Myrdal's theory pointed out that the argument would be used in the old industrialized countries. The Japanese argument is only strengthened by the additional fact that Japan's industrial structure still included large sectors which were under-developed. Kojima is, however, becoming interested in the idea of Japan 'educating' or 'rearing' (*sodatete iku*) the Asian countries in their own schemes of integration (Kojima 1962a: 80). The educational process would mean increased economic co-operation, and the argument is essentially similar to the one proposed by Okita.

There was also another logical possibility:

> One hears about the idea of the United States, Canada, Australia, New Zealand and Japan engaging in Pan-Pacific economic integration, but. . .
>
> (Kojima 1962a: 80)

As can be readily seen in the syntax of the sentence, Kojima does not feel any special enthusiasm about the idea. It was being thrown around by journalists at the time (Kojima 1980: 26). The term 'pan', which seems to be somewhat out of place in the 1960s, probably reflects the newness of the idea; it is apparently constructed by using a form of pre-war expression such as Pan-Asia. From the start, Kojima rejects the idea that this grouping could in any way develop into anything resembling the EEC, although the grouping could be used as an approach to expand trade in the region. However, he does not dwell much on the idea, but rather considers it as a thought experiment, nothing else.

Although Kojima regards regional integration as useful for the world economy as a whole, as a solution for the developmental problems of many regions, he does not favour it as a policy alternative for Japan. Regional integration has drawbacks, too. A common market presupposes that the growth of its members is balanced, and this would create problems for a special country (*tokuteikoku*) growing faster than others. This special country would either destroy the balance of the group, or it would be forced to slow down growth to the level of the slower countries. It is clear that Japan is exactly this kind of special country:

> For Japan, which must close the gap with the Euro–American countries, this is a grave problem.
>
> (Kojima 1962a: 81)

The Japanese language has a handy concept, *Ō-Bei*, which neatly lumps together both Europe and America. The concept is not so much geographical, but rather refers to the cultural, political, and economic entity composed of Western Europe and North America. It is this group of countries that currently form the special frame of reference for Japan. It ranks higher than Japan in the economic dimension, but not considerably higher. The race to reach the level of the Euro–American countries is presented as an important national goal. No reasons are given for the emotionally-loaded demand – although the translation does not display the emotion very well – but it can be taken as an expression of a deeply felt desire to rise in the international ranking hierarchy back to the level Japan had occupied before the Second World War. Okita had expressed similar feelings after the beginning of the discussion on the theme of growth in 1960, and the goal was now perceived to be rapidly attainable.

Kojima gives another reason why Japan has to keep on growing fast. Japan has to be able to increase its purchasing power to be able to buy more products from Asian countries, thus helping their development. In this connection Kojima actually advocates decreasing trade between Japan and the United States. Japan should stop importing so many primary products from there, and instead shift to purchases from Asian countries. Simultaneously, Japan should continue liberalizing its trade and allow the import of industrial products from Asian countries. For instance, Hong Kong and India were already exporting light manufactures to the United States, and Kojima would also have liked to include Japan as a market. Japan and the United States could well co-operate in this sense of providing markets for Asian developing countries (Kojima 1962a: 81–2).

In *Amerika, Nihon, Tōnan Ajia sankaku bōeki no kihon rosen* (The Basic Line of American, Japanese and Southeast Asian Trilateral Trade) Kojima develops the idea further. As Japan and the United States are both in need of dismantling trade restrictions, they should engage in an increased mutual trade of industrial products, which would further develop their industrial structures, while the two should also increase trade with the Asian developing countries, importing both raw materials and industrial products from there. Japan would still be too weak to be the principal market for manufactured exports of the Asian countries without experiencing grave difficulties, but if the main thrust of exports went to the United States, Japan could very well participate, especially if its exports to the United States could also be expanded. As Japan's industrial structure was still lagging far behind that of the United States, it would continually need to import large quantities of higher technological products from there, and the Southeast Asian countries would need lower level technological imports, thus constituting an expanding market for both Japan and the United States. This structure could benefit both of the two already industrialized countries, and create room in the world economy for the Asian industrializing countries to develop. This would be beneficial to all, and leave Japan ample leeway to continue its rapid growth (Kojima 1962d).

In later reports regarding the research project on integration, Kojima's enthusiasm for the general concept of regional integration begins to wane. In *Dai ichiji shōhin bōeki to kyōdō ichiba* (Trade of Primary Products and the Common Market) Kojima comments on the EEC that the political objective of creating a third power to stand by the side of the United States and the Soviet Union is understandable, as well as the other political objective of overcoming the compartmentalization of Europe, which had already driven the subcontinent into two big wars during the twentieth century, but that the economic rationale behind the EEC is obscure (Kojima 1962b: 91–2). Kojima seems to be moving towards a Röpkean-style critique of the EEC. Probably the fact that the entry of Great Britain was at the time being opposed by France, also stopping the movement of the other EFTA countries towards the EEC, influenced Kojima's evaluation of the situation. The EEC seemed to be developing towards a trading block, and that was not his preference.

Kojima's revised opinion was that the industrialized countries would be far better served by global free trade than by regional integration. The problems facing the developed and the developing countries are different. The developing countries have to try to establish new, diverse industries for which they need a measure of protection. That could be provided by a regional common market. That would also provide economies of scale, competition on a homogeneous level, and a regional division of labour. The developing countries could arguably benefit from regional integration. On the other hand, the basic problem of the old industrialized countries is redistribution and modernizing an existing industrial base, and in this they need strong international competition. The biggest problem in the developing countries is the lack of income, technology and capital, but if these are provided, development should be relatively fast and easy, as presented in the theory of the flying geese pattern of development. The biggest problem in the developed countries is the existence of old and inefficient industries, some of which should be demolished, some made more efficient. International market forces would take care of this (Kojima 1962b: 101–2). Thus Kojima comes to the conclusion that regional integration would be good for the developing countries, but more or less harmful for the developed countries.

Kojima makes a thought experiment about what regional integration might look like in Asia in *Tōnan Ajia keizai kyōryoku no kōzu* (The Structure of Southeast Asian Economic Co-operation). As the whole region is too big to fit into one grouping, the principle of homogeneity, broadly interpreted, is used in determining viable economic subregions. Far-reaching integration in the style of the EEC is not necessary in Asia, but rather something like a limited customs union or a free trade area. Kojima presents the following list of groupings:

Subregion A: *The Indian Subcontinent Group*
               India, Pakistan, Ceylon, Burma
Subregion B: *The South Asian Group*
               Thailand, Malaya, Singapore, Indonesia, Cambodia,
               Laos, South Vietnam
Subregion C: *The East Asian Group*
               The Philippines, Hong Kong, Taiwan, South Korea
Japan

(Kojima 1962c: 213)

Japan can be thought of as a subregion of its own, as Kojima had already argued before. The rationale behind Subregion A is that the countries form a geographically contiguous area, and are culturally similar. Religiously, the countries are divided, i.e., there is the division between Islam and Hinduism, but it may be only temporary, as these religions had been able to coexist for hundreds of years. All these countries had been British colonies, and in that sense, too, they share a similar culture and history. The way of life and standard of living is similar in all of the countries, and in the latter respect the Indian Subcontinent Group is on the lowest level of all.

Subregion B is also a contiguous area. These are all predominantly agricultural countries. Besides rice as their main crop they produce rubber, sugar, maize, coconuts, bananas, palm oil, coffee, and other similar primary products. The countries are mainly Buddhist or Islamic, but there is not very much religious confrontation. Many Chinese merchants are living in all of the countries. The way of life and standard of living is similar among them, higher than in Subregion A, lower than in Subregion C. Excluding agricultural products, the tin of Malaya and the oil of Indonesia, there are no special raw materials in the area. Thus it is a significant fact that just by exporting agricultural products these countries have been able to raise their standard of living above that of Subregion A. However, there are also problems. Except for Indonesia, they are sparsely populated small countries, and they do not have much capital or educational skills for industrialization. India, at least, is beginning to industrialize. The countries of the South Asian Group are the most backward countries of all, but because of their higher standard of living Kojima still finds their prospects for industrialization good. Fertilization industries should be started, and Singapore, especially, should be developed as a high-level industrial centre.

Subregion C is somewhat of a problem, because Kojima has included the Philippines. His main reason is that in this way he can make the population of the grouping bigger, up to 69 million. Without the Philippines it would be only 44 million, less than the 50 million that had been deemed to be the lowest feasible amount from the point of view of the economies of scale. However, Kojima mentions that the Philippines could just as well be inserted into Subregion B. In reality Thailand, Malaya and the Philippines had already formed a regional grouping in 1961, albeit mainly a political one, namely the Association of Southeast Asia (ASA). This is one indication of how free of actual politics, and how much on purely economic grounds (*jun keizaiteki*) (Kojima 1962c: 214) Kojima wants to stand.

If we think of the culture of the area, the countries excluding the Philippines are all influenced by the Sinic culture. These countries also have the highest level of income and standard of living, which means that in spite of the smallness of their population the three Sinic countries might well succeed in integration. The countries already have industries, and they have the greatest potential for more industrialization. Kojima expects Subregion C to become the industrial centre of Asia. He even calls the countries middle-level advancing countries (*chūshinkoku*), an epithet similar to the one that had been used for Japan until recently. As Japan moves ahead in the flying geese formation, the middle position in the Asian setting becomes vacant, and the countries of the East Asian Group can step in.

A small scheme of regional integration for Japan is contemplated in passing. If Japan should be obliged to engage in regional integration in Asia, Subregion C would be the most natural partner. If Japan were forced for some reason to abandon its solitary road, this group would be the best partner. Although Kojima does not give his reasons for this, they are obvious. With the Philippines excluded and Hong Kong treated as a special case, the remaining countries formed that part of the pre-war Japanese Empire which remained outside the socialist block, and less than 20 years had passed since they had been integral parts of the Japanese economy. This is the place where Kojima could have used the term reintegration, resembling the sense in which the term was used in the European discussion, but as the situation was taboo, it could not be touched on directly.

Kojima goes on to state matter-of-factly that in the present situation integration with Subregion C would mean grave problems for Japan, because Japan's textile industry and other light industries would inevitably suffer damage as a result. He emphasizes again that Japan is in the position of globalism, not in that of regionalism. Japan could supply training, planning, and technical know-how to the countries, and Japan could increase imports of primary products, as well as half-finished products and consumer goods. He once again expressly warns pessimists that nobody in Japan should be afraid of economic development in the neighbourhood; i.e., the process of development means that the fire of increased demand is lit in the developing countries, and their buying power will expand as well (Kojima 1962c ibid. 228).

These ideas are clarified further in Kojima's next major work, *Sekai keizai to Nihon bōeki* (World Economics and Japanese Trade).

The book contains an interesting discussion of world economic trends for the following 20 years. Kojima divides the period into two parts, the first reaching up to 1970, the second up to 1980. He expects the general trend of growth of the world economy to continue. During the first 10-year period until 1970 Kojima expects that the relative share of Great Britain and the United States will fall considerably, and that of Africa, Latin America, and Australia somewhat less. The risers will be Western Europe and Southeast Asia.

During the second phase – where simple extrapolation of present trends does not suffice, and theoretical insights and individual presentiments have a freer play – Kojima expects the share of the United States to fall even more sharply, and the rise of Western Europe to slow down. The rest of the world is expected to start rising fast. All the downward curves of Africa, Latin America and Australia are expected to turn upwards. The already rising curve of Southeast Asia is expected to rise ever more steeply, giving it the most rapid growth rate of all, the success story of the 1970s (Kojima 1962f: 60–1). Japan's growth is also expected to continue briskly.

Kojima's forecast is based on the idea that the abnormally high position of the United States will inevitably continue falling as other regions continue to gather strength, and the same holds true also for Great Britain. Further, Kojima expects the effects of integration in Western Europe to stave off these effects for some time, but in the long run, integration will not be the strongest force at work in the world economy – especially if integration is regional and tends to contain elements of undue protection for old industries. Development will be the strongest force in the world economy. The decisive moment was the attainment of national independence by the former colonies, after which the laws of the flying geese pattern of development, in the Myrdalian sense of cumulative causation, will push development forward with an irresistible force. It is unclear why Kojima considers Southeast Asia to be continuously the most successful of all developing regions, disregarding the fact that in some respects it seemed to be the poorest and the most hopeless of all regions even at the beginning of the 1960s, but at least in the Institute of Developing Economies optimism among researchers for the prospects of Southeast Asia seems to have run high (see also Ebihara 1962).

These expectations for the future place Kojima's ideas about 'educating' Asia into a better perspective. As development is understood to be such a strong force, Asia, especially Southeast Asia, would rise whether Japan did anything or not, but it would be easier if

Japan made a positive contribution. It would be good from the moral and normative standpoint of a developmental internationalist. It would also be in Japan's self-interest to be closely involved with the Asian area as it rose, not the least because positive contributions would create goodwill towards Japan, guaranteeing its future security in the region. Kojima never actually engages in this kind of discussion, being reluctant to broach anything outside of the domain of pure economics, but as presented earlier, the responsibility for contributing to Asia's development is part of the theme of economism.

If we return to the Japanese debate between the nationalists and internationalists, Kojima is naturally worried about some aspects of the rise of Asia, and what it would mean to the salaries and employment of the Japanese. He is, however, confident that through the gradual implementation of theoretically inspired policy measures a middle road could be found in trade liberalization, which would benefit both Asia and Japan (Kojima 1962f: 409–10). From the point of view of an economic historian used to observing long-term trends, the outcome of the Japanese debate between nationalists and internationalists was clear, especially in light of Asia's developmental dynamism. The abolition of restrictions on imports of raw materials and machinery would lower their price, which would help to lower the price of Japanese exports, making them more competitive in the international market. Free imports of capital would speed up the necessary structural changes of Japanese industry. At the same time, liberalization of imports would blunt the edge of the political pressures from abroad, and help Japan remove some of the trade barriers it in turn faced in some of its export markets, such as Europe. This might also contribute to the direction European integration would take with respect to its openness or closedness. In other words, cheap imports would lead to cheap exports, and free imports would lead to free exports, both of which would expand Japanese trade and help to continue the development of its economy (Kojima 1962f: 430–2).

Kojima favours a slow pace in the implementation of liberalization measures, on items starting from the least dangerous from the point of view of employment, namely raw materials, machinery, and capital. After perhaps a decade, the problem of light manufactures from Asian countries would have to be faced directly, and preparations for that should be started (Kojima 1962f: 427). The structural change of Japanese industry, at the time clearly composed of two separate sides, light manufacturing, and heavy and chemical industries, would have to emphasize the latter strongly. Kojima here uses two concepts, 'sunset industries' (*shayō sangyō*) and 'sunrise industries' (*shinkō sangyō*), or literally 'newly-rising industries'. The concept of sunset industries refers to the older industries, which the rise of the general developmental level of the country was leaving behind. They were destined to be, before long, overcome by foreign competition from follower countries whose developmental level they would fit perfectly. They should be gradually phased out of receiving support through the industrial policy of the state, i.e., left to struggle on their own, as the term sadly implies. They would not all go down. Stronger ones would be able to continue developing and stay above the surface, but most of them would inevitably sink. The newly-rising industries are the ones in which the Japanese should put their faith for future prosperity, and on which all of the developmental strength of Japan should be concentrated. That would be Japan's only way of staying a step or two ahead of the pursuing Asian nations, ensuring its own prosperity, and not standing in their way, or blocking their development.

Thus the concept of international economic integration, developed by Kojima during this period, can be stated as follows: The overriding concept is global economic integration, including the ideas of global expansion of trade, and global development. This would bring prosperity for all, and diminish global inequalities. The relative rise would be higher for the less developed nations, so that the follower nations would slowly catch up with the older leading industrialized nations. Implicit in Kojima's thinking is also a process towards a more peaceful world, which the growing prosperity for all could ensure. He is not satisfied with the idea of Akamatsu, according to which development leads to raw competition. Kojima rather likes to see a global structure with some permanence in the division of labour. This could be achieved if the older industrialized nations would be able to continue their development, so that their lead would shorten only slowly. This conflicts a bit with the idea that Japan should continue growing to be able to rapidly attain the level of the Euro–American countries; it is only the smallness, the political and military insignificance of Japan, and Kojima's extensive economism, which prevents this discrepancy from becoming acute. At any rate, the beneficial development of the world in general, and Japan's development in it, would both best be served by global economic integration.

Regional integration is also useful in some situations. Its model is the European integration process; not politically, but the functional development of an economic community over the pre-existing base of a degree of homogeneity between the participants. Historical relations, common culture, feeling of community, a similar level of development and income, etc., are factors constituting such homogeneous communities, the more of them the better. However, nothing prevents attempts at purely economic regional integration even over a shallow, pre-existing homogeneity. This is what has to be done in the case of developing countries, and this is the only case where regional integration can be attempted without misgivings. It can be attempted also among the developed countries, as in Europe, and it has short-term beneficial consequences there, but in the end may prove to be counter-productive.

Japan has no special place in any scheme of regional integration. There are two directions in which Kojima has made small thought experiments: one being the industrialized Pacific nations, the other the non-socialist Sinic East Asian countries. There is not much pre-existing sense of community among the Pacific countries, and while there are historical ties with the Sinic countries, the political tension in the region, Japan's record as a conqueror and colonizer, and the direct competitive relationship these countries have with Japan's still important sunset industries, make that kind of regional scheme unviable. The best solution for Japan is to stand alone, as an economic region of its own, while continuing measures to increase trade in the region. Increasing trilateral trade among Japan, the United States, and the Asian countries would be one method of doing this.

AN ASIAN VS. A PACIFIC ORIENTATION

From 1963 onwards discussion about integration picked up momentum in Japan. It shifted from the question of whether Japan should engage in regional integration or not to the question of the geographic direction of Japan's integration. The 'feelings of loneliness' led to a search for suitable partners in case they might be needed. Only two directions appeared practical, one of these being the Pacific countries, the other the Asian countries, but both of the directions presented various problems.

Nihon Keizai Chōsa Kyōgikai (The Japan Economic Investigating Committee) in 1963 published a report entitled *Taiheiyō keizai kyōryoku no hōkō ni tsuite* (On the Direction of Pacific Economic Co-operation). The document contained the first comprehensive semi-official proposal concerning Japanese economic integration in the Pacific Area. The investigation was essentially a bureaucratic venture along with business representation. The Ministry of International Trade and Industry had the heaviest representation among the committee members, but also other ministries, such as the Ministry of Foreign Affairs, the Ministry of Finance, and the Ministry of Forestry and Fisheries were represented, as well as the Bank of Japan, the Economic Planning Agency, Hitachi, Marubeni, Fuji Bank, and Fuji Seitetsu.

As the title of the report suggests, the committee is investigating the possibilities for Pacific co-operation. They deal quickly with other regions of the world, leaving out of consideration the socialist countries, like China and the Soviet Union (Nihon Keizai Chōsa Kyōgikai 1963: Hashigaki). This exclusion is in a sense absolute; the socialist countries are something that lay completely outside Japan's foreign political objectives.

The rest of the world is divided into two groups, the developed and the developing countries. Of the developing world, the Southeast Asian countries – which, as usual, are not defined – are the most important for Japan, but it suffices the committee to note the special relationship Japan has with the region, namely, giving aid to it. The committee also quickly goes through other ties that Japan has with the Asian countries. There are the important trading relationships, and an emotional relationship not found with other developing regions, but there is nothing else to tie Japan to the region (Nihon Keizai Chōsa Kyōgikai 1963: 1).

It is to the developed world that the committee sees Japan as belonging. This view is qualified by the notion that Japan is poorer than the other industrialized countries in terms of per capita income, which is negated by the notion of Japan's rapid rate of growth, smoothing the situation in the future (Nihon Keizai Chōsa Kyōgikai 1963: 5). The theme of growth is thus tied in with the category of the future, and this special combination is emphasized in connection with the advanced industrialized countries, balancing Japan's otherwise low rank as a relatively poor country. With this calculation Japan can be included in the grouping of advanced countries in places where the topic of discussion is on material well-being. The other way of doing this would be to emphasize the theme of development wherever industrial structure is discussed, as Kojima does.

The developed world, however, presents two worrisome problems for Japan. Japan's trading position is seen to be severely threatened by the internationalization being forced on her economy by outside pressures from the United States, GATT, and the IMF. In the report there is not much trace of the optimism present in the writings of the internationalists; instead, the atmosphere is somewhat panicky. However, the committee emphasizes that in spite of its hazards, increasing global free trade under the auspices of GATT would be a comparatively small difficulty in Japan's situation at the time. It was a known system, with almost twenty years of history behind it, and with clauses providing for a multitude of exceptions, which could be used to diminish the effects of opening Japan's economy. The graver problem was that this kind of global economic integration, which had been the fashion of the immediate post-war period, had given way to regional integration since the end of the 1950s, the movement picking up momentum during the 1960s.

To this movement, a worrisome problem was the development of the EEC. The EEC seemed to be acquiring mythical qualities. Time and again the rapid economic development and growth of the EEC countries are mentioned in the text, and it is called 'a miracle of this century'. As the EEC is perceived as an extremely successful venture, it might also be dangerous. The worry of the committee is that the EEC is attempting to turn itself into a third economic giant on the same scale as the United States and the Soviet Union. It was taking good care of its rank, and seemed to be in the process of becoming a protectionist economic sphere. This would present a serious problem for the Japanese export industry.

An even more dangerous aspect of the EEC is the spread of the idea of regional economic integration. It is discussed and emulated around the world to a frightening degree. This leads to the following analysis: 'The process of the reorganization of the global economic system along the lines of regional economic co-operation and integration, comprising both the developed and the developing countries, seems to be in full bloom' (Nihon Keizai Chōsa Kyōgikai 1963: 2). In Europe the EEC and EFTA, and COMECON, which had been formed by the socialist countries already in 1949, were expanding their scope. In the Americas, the Central American Common Market (CACM) was formed to accompany the South American LAFTA (United Nations 1959). In Asia, Malaya, Thailand, and the Philippines had formed ASA in 1961; and in 1963 the Malaysian Federation was created out of Malaya, Singapore, Sabah and Sarawak. Other former British colonies were also in a tumult, because in 1961 Great Britain had tried to join the EEC, and the countries of the British Commonwealth felt betrayed. India, Pakistan and Ceylon had begun to talk about creating a regional economic grouping of their own. The ideas of Arabian economic integration and an African Common Market were also on the agenda. The discussion that was most worrisome was being conducted in the United States and Canada about forming an Atlantic Common Market with the EEC. The process is described as 'natural' (*shizen seiteki, shizenteki*), which, as seen from the point of view of rhetorics, is an effective way of emphasizing the perceived irresistible force of the movement blooming around the world. The only thing one can do with natural processes is to accommodate oneself to them. The committee points out that Japan is 'tasting loneliness' (*kodoku wo ajiwatte iru*) because of this (Nihon Keizai Chōsa Kyōgikai 1963: 17).

Japan could try to use diplomacy to dissuade the emerging groups from developing into trading blocks and Japan could try to help the process of global economic integration to go on, but its means are seen to be limited. The third possibility is to try to create a regional grouping where Japan could really belong, and end its loneliness. The partners are not to be found in Asia. The committee throws in names like the 'Pacific Common Market' (Taiheiyō kyōdō ichiba), the 'Organization for Pacific Economic Co-operation' (Taiheiyō keizai kyōryoku kikō), and the still more vague 'Pacific Area' (Taiheiyō chi-iki), but adds that unfortunately these are only names without much substance. In practice it is not known what should be placed under the names, and the whole thing 'feels like a dream' (*musō ni suginai*). The most that can be said is that the group would be composed of the United States, Canada, Australia, New Zealand, and Japan, and that these countries should set up a body for comprehensive and diverse economic co-operation (Nihon Keizai Chōsa Kyōgikai 1963: 2).

In spite of the vagueness of the idea, the process involved in forming this group is deemed natural (*shizen no nari iki*). The committee clearly prefers the type of rhetoric where actual Japanese decision-making can be de-emphasized. The world is depicted as a collection of strong currents, among which Japan drifts like a raft, being steered with a very small paddle. This is one way of sticking to the small country theme, and implying that there is not much sense in trying to paddle against the flow. When the Pacific orientation is presented here as a natural current, it probably implies most of all a lack of convincing arguments in favour of the idea. The metaphor allows instead the themes of growth and development to complete the picture of the United States, Canada, Australia and New Zealand forming the most natural grouping to which Japan would belong.

With respect to policy, the committee does not have anything drastic in mind. The most it wants is the establishment of regular government level round-table negotiations among the five countries. Such negotiations should be conducted at least once a year to discuss mutual economic problems. The countries should also exchange information for mutual understanding, in the form of cultural exchanges and spreading knowledge about the economic conditions in the five countries.

The committee does not see it as profitable to include developing countries in the grouping, saying that their problems are so different from those of the industrialized countries that if they were discussed at the same table, the number of possible problems would multiply to such an extent that getting tangible results from discussions would become difficult. Also, free trade between the developed and the developing countries would wreak havoc in the economies of the developed countries. The problem of the developing countries is left for economic developmental assistance, and for the future to resolve itself. The committee expects rapid industrialization in some countries of Southeast Asia, and if they are able to make the transition to become industrialized countries, they could be adopted into the grouping (Nihon Keizai Chōsa Kyōgikai 1963: 3–8).

The central positive argument for the creation of the grouping lies in the development of ocean transport. In terms of time, costs, and the size of shiploads, transportation across the Pacific has become far easier than before. The amount of trade is increasing among the coastal cities of the countries involved. In addition, the economic structure of the United States seems to be changing, the West Coast gaining in importance, so much so that the committee feels confident to say that the economic centre of the United States is shifting from the Northeast to the Pacific Coast. Trade between Japan and the United States had been increasing rapidly in the past; during the seven years between 1954 and 1961 trade had increased five times, and seemed to be increasing further.

The committee presents figures on estimated transportation costs. According to them, it would be most economical in many cases for goods destined for Los Angeles to be imported from Japan. Using the figure of 100 to describe the cost of transport from the East Coast to Los Angeles, Western Europe would require 120, while Japan only 70–90. It would take 4 weeks to make the journey from Europe, 3 weeks from the East Coast, and 2 weeks from Japan. In this sense, not only Japan, but also Australia and New Zealand are comparatively close to the American West Coast. However, the argument becomes much weaker when the committee discloses that these calculations were made by using ships as the only means of transporting goods; if road and railroad transportation were included, as in a real competitive situation, the American economy would again appear as tightly integrated, rather than splitting into two separate parts (Nihon Keizai Chōsa Kyōgikai 1963: 7–8).

As can be inferred from the way the argument is constructed, the main interest of the committee was the United States. The committee had to try to find a way to keep it from turning its back on the Pacific and Japan in the face of the economic temptation emanating from Western Europe. 'It is unnecessary to say' (*iu made mo naku*) that nothing would come out of the grouping if the United States was not interested in it:

> The United States holds the keys to the realization of Pacific integration. Only the United States has the power to make global economic initiatives, and feels conceited about the fact.
> (Nihon Keizai Chōsa Kyōgikai 1963: 12)

Nothing could be achieved without the support of the United States, or rather, the United States should be made to initiate it. That way, its prestige as the initiator of global and regional policies could be honoured, while Japan, which in this connection is nothing more than a small country, could get what she wanted.

The conceit the committee is referring to can be discerned, for instance, in the famous words from the inaugural address of President John F. Kennedy in 1961:

> We shall pay any price, bear any burden, meet any hardship, support any friend, oppose any foe to assure the survival and success of liberty.
> (Quoted from Maga 1990: ix)

David Calleo has remarked that 'if the world were only a theater, the Kennedy Administration would have to be counted as a great success' (1982: 9), on account of the ability of the administration to stir up the imaginations of both national and international audiences with colourful exclamations, slogans, and grand designs. The purpose of the Kennedy Administration was to renew the American position of world leadership, and instill new vigour into the American economy, both of which had slipped at the end of the 1950s. It set out upon this task with bold epideictic rhetoric, differing greatly from the rhetoric the Eisenhower Administration had used. This diminished the perceived Japanese possibilities for initiating international policies, and strengthened the view of the committee that on the international scene Japan would have to work through the United States, and not antagonize it with overly independent initiatives.

The committee points out that the eyes of the United States are focused on the military–political aspects of international activity, and to the Atlantic Ocean and the NATO countries, and less on economics, or the Pacific region (Nihon Keizai Chōsa Kyōgikai 1963: 12–13). Kennedy's package of initiatives included the Trade Expansion Act of 1962, on the basis of which was launched an ambitious world-wide campaign for trade liberalization, named the Kennedy Round of GATT. In principle this looks like what the committee was hoping for, a re-emergence of the globalistic orientation of world integration, but in practice the matter was different. The Trade Expansion Act was specifically directed against the EEC, as a way of ensuring American access to the EEC market, and increase in this way integration between the North American and Western European economic areas. The idea of an Atlantic Community was circulated widely by the Kennedy Administration, and pushing Great Britain into the EEC became an important policy goal. This economic side of the Atlanticist orientation was accompanied by equally strong initiatives to tighten NATO as another Atlantic alliance. The Kennedy Round was a global initiative, but its global aspect was often overshadowed by the special relationship between the United States and Western Europe (Calleo 1982: 14–15). The idea of an Atlantic Community composed of the United States, Canada, the EEC and the EFTA remained as an important theme of public debate throughout the lengthy Kennedy Round negotiations which were concluded in 1967, and continued to be debated even after that (English 1968b). From the Japanese point of view, this was a really worrisome situation. It explains the panicky atmosphere of the committee. The Atlantic orientation of the United States with regard to Japan's case was comparable to the attempted entry of Britain into the EEC in 1961 from the point of view of the countries of the British Commonwealth.

Atlanticism was only a part of the global initiative of the Kennedy Administration. As a matter of fact, it also proposed the creation of a New Pacific Community. However, its meaning differed from the economic grouping about which the committee was thinking. The policy of the Kennedy Administration towards the Pacific and Asia was conducted under the general strategic framework of combating communism. Eastern Asia and Oceania became regarded as one totality under this strategy, without perceiving any special relationship between Japan and the United States, or at least not as strongly as the Japanese felt about it. The idea behind the New Pacific Community initiative was to build a new frontier out of the non-socialist countries of the region, and to shift some of the burden of supporting the economically-weaker Asian countries to the more affluent societies, notably to Japan and Australia. The purpose was to form a strong political and military block in the area, and all economic initiatives were subordinated to the political goal of containing communism (Maga 1990). The creation of the New Pacific Community would have meant an intensification of the Cold War in the region. The Japanese committee did not want to have anything to do with this; rather, their tone in commenting on this was even somewhat sarcastic (Nihon Keizai Chōsa Kyōgikai 1963: 14). Apparently, from their point of view, the United States did not understand the vital priorities. The two countries seemed to be using totally different concepts of the international system.

The situation of the other three countries was different. In 1962 a meeting of the prime ministers of the Commonwealth had taken place in the panicky atmosphere of what to do if Great Britain should leave the Commonwealth. Canada, because of its special relationship with the United States, began to deepen economic ties with it. A discussion had begun about forming an economic unit of the two countries, as well as taking part in European integration. However, interest in Japan had also risen. Canada was a great exporter of wheat, while Japan was a food-importing country. Canada also exported forestry products and minerals to Japan, and other possibilities were conceivable. In January 1963 a ministerial level conference had convened in Tokyo to discuss mutual trade. The idea of a regional Pacific economic grouping does not seem to have been under discussion, but the committee concludes that Canada, at least, would not be against the idea of Pacific integration (Nihon Keizai Chōsa Kyōgikai 1963: 15).

The economy of New Zealand is presented as 'riding on the backs of sheeps and cows', and except for the dairy industry, the country was not very developed industrially. Of all of the three countries, it was the most dependent on the British market, and was thus in the greatest need of searching for new markets. The nearest market was Australia, and a discussion had started about integration of the two countries (Nihon Keizai Chōsa Kyōgikai 1963: 15).

There was a proposal for a New Zealand–Australia Free Trade Area (NAFTA), and because New Zealand was a very small country, the New Zealanders would be content with it. The Australians would not. They needed big markets for their big exports, and in that sense the small market of New Zealand was no solution to Australia's dilemma. Thus, Australia seemed to be reacting most strongly in favour of creating something in the Pacific area. A lively discussion had flared up among academics, business people, and the press about finding export markets nearby. That would also decrease transportation costs considerably compared with freight costs to Europe. Japan, a country importing great quantities of foodstuffs and industrial raw materials, such as the wool, cotton, and iron ore which Australia had to offer, had begun to look interesting in this respect. The governments had been doing nothing thus far, but a convention of business people of both countries was scheduled to take place in Tokyo later in 1963 (Nihon Keizai Chōsa Kyōgikai 1963: 16). The meeting was a success, and in 1964 a similar meeting was held in Canberra (Nagano 1964). Thus, Australia seemed to be the greatest hope for advancing the idea of Pacific integration.

However, the committee also holds great reservations about the practicability of the idea:

> There is a strong doubt about how well our country could melt together with countries professing white Europeanism, and how far these countries would accept Japan in the same grouping with them.

> (Nihon Keizai Chōsa Kyōgikai 1963: 18)

What seems so good and mutually profitable economically, becomes difficult when other aspects of integration are considered. Race and culture may pose a problem. The concept of *Ō-Bei* describes a politico-economic entity. To describe the racial and cultural mixture of this entity, there is another handy concept, *haku-Ō shugi*, meaning 'white Europeanism'. As seen through Japanese eyes, the countries of predominantly European origin seem to form a close grouping among themselves, and an outsider like Japan would stand out as clearly different in their company. This is why the committee proposes only a very careful beginning, namely the round-table discussions, to probe into whether anything at all is possible.

In addition, the committee does not want to propose overly strong policies towards Pacific integration in the beginning, since it might antagonize other Asian countries (Nihon Keizai Chōsa Kyōgikai 1963: 19). It seems that the committee would like to keep the Southeast Asian countries as a reserve. Obviously, the rationale is that if nothing comes out of the Pacific Common Market, or the Organization for Pacific Economic Cooperation, and Japan faces the danger of being isolated outside other regional trading blocks as occurred before the Second World War, Japan could try to turn towards the Asian countries. That had been the solution leading to the war, and although it would be done without military means this time, the historical precedent caused misgivings. Thus the committee comes round to proposing for Japan a course of trying to be in the middle of everything, without taking a definite stand in any direction, yet trying to keep channels open to all directions. At present, the direction of the Pacific countries looks the most promising, and the idea should be developed carefully, but situations might change.

In 1964, Tsukamoto Masao, Abe Masamichi, and Araki Tadao published a book called *Keizai tōgō no kodō, EEC no seika kara OPEC no kōsō made* (The Movement of Economic Integration, From the Outcome of the EEC to the Idea of OPEC), in which they try to clarify the position of Japan with respect to regional integration. At the time, Tsukamoto was the director of the Japan International Co-operation Agency (JICA), a governmental body set up to deal with Japanese development assistance, associated with the Ministry of Foreign Affairs, while Abe and Araki were officials of the same ministry. From a theoretical standpoint, their book is not as sophisticated as the writings of Kojima, but the question they pose about Japan's necessary choice between a Pacific and an Asian orientation is an important one.

The authors start out from the same idea as the committee, namely, that Japan has to look for partners for regional integration. They too present regional integration as the thing to do during the 1960s. However, besides the Pacific direction, they also argue for an Asian direction. Japan has to try to build parallel organizations either in Asia, or in the Pacific. The decision has to be made between these two directions (Tsukamoto *et al* 1964: 164).

The orientation towards Asia crystallizes into the concept of the Organization for Asian Economic Cooperation (OAEC, Ajia keizai kyōryoku kikō), which they associate especially with the name of Okita Saburo. As officials of the Ministry of Foreign Affairs they have access to the report of the three-member group of experts, as well as to the report of the seven-member expert group that had convened in 1963, offering opinions similar to the earlier one. It had also been declared confidential, so they cannot make too specific references to the documents. They do not take into consideration extensive plans for regional integration, like the idea of an Asian Free Trade Area (Ajia jiyū bōeki chi-iki), but rather discard them quickly (*fukanō ni chikai*). The reasons are the already familiar ones: as the levels of development among Asian countries are too widely separated, free trade might harm Japan's traditional industries, while Japan's economic efficiency might harm the development of industries in Asian countries. For the second, Asia is too heterogeneous to act together as a unit, even if the socialist countries are left out. However, trade and economic co-operation can always be increased. In this connection Japan is presented as the sole advanced industrialized country (*yui-itsu no senshin kōgyōkoku*) (Tsukamoto *et al.* 1964: 160–1), and all discussion follows from this high status.

The Asian orientation would have some advantages for Japan. It is not uncommon that romantic undertones appear in the sentences of Japanese writers when they discuss Japan's relationship with Asian countries. One of the authors, obviously Tsukamoto, presents personal reminiscences – which in 1964 was still a strong form of argumentation – of how he has been to Thailand several times before, during, and after the war, and this is what he has seen:

> the standard of living of the Thais is rising rapidly, and one can only look in wonderment at the speed with which roads and bridges are being modernized. During and even after the war there were many Thais who were walking barefoot, but now they are all wearing Japanese-made sandals and sports shoes. Taxis, which earlier had been Samurōs (three-wheeled bicycles) made in Japan, have now changed to Japanese Toyopets, Bluebirds, Princes, and other high quality cars, which run back and forth along beautifully paved streets. All this tells truly how our exports to Thailand are increasing, becoming more diversified, and technologically more advanced at the same pace that the standard of living of the Thais is rising.
>
> (Tsukamoto *et al.* 1964: 161)

The author of this passage can point to a basic continuity in Japan's relationship with Thailand, and by implication, with the Asian developing countries in general. In trade, Japan has continuously been able to have the upper hand in the region, dominating the markets. During the post-war period the situation seems to have become even more favourable for the Japanese, as can be seen in the diversity of the products exported there, from light industrial consumer products like sandals to quality cars. There is a vast and expanding market for Japanese products in the Asian countries, as the living standards of the Asians are rising. The relationship between Asian development and Japan's prosperity is seen to be direct. They support each other, and this lays the groundwork for increasing Japanese co-operation with the region. Even short-term economic profits are painted rosy: 'if one invests wisely $1 million in the region, one can expect before long returns of twice or thrice the amount' (Tsukamoto *et al.* 1964: 162). The authors also argue that the Asian countries are hoping for Japanese help for their economies.

Thus far this has been a kind of restatement of Okita's argument, but Tsukamoto, Abe and Araki go a step further. The OAEC would open a new political vision for Japan:

> If Japan were nationally and internationally allowed to become aware of itself as a great power, as one of the three pillars of the world, Japan should invite all the Asian countries together to build the pyramid of economic co-operation. It is time for Japan to be conscious of its responsibility.
>
> (Tsukamoto *et al.* 1964: 162)

The authors use allegories and vague expressions to discuss a delicate matter. The 'three pillars of the world' was one of Ikeda's slogans, depicting Japan on a par with the United States and the EEC as a supporter of the Western politico-economic system. The 'pyramid of economic co-operation' refers to a centre-periphery structure, though evaluated from the point of view of the flying geese theory. As the sole industrialized and developed country in this context, Japan would naturally occupy the leading position in the pyramid, leading the rest of the Asian countries towards rising prosperity. The Asian orientation would mean travelling the road of a great power, as the leader of one's own region, just like the United States and the EEC led their own peripheries.

It has to be noted that the authors use the conditional case. While the themes of growth and development had elevated Japan's international position, it was still viewed narrowly in terms of Japan's rank on the ladder of technological sophistication, and not as a big power mentality with big power ambitions. The Asian orientation would imply a heavy commitment to support the Asian countries economically, but although aid levels had risen under the Ikeda government, the amount remained modest (Shibusawa 1984: 43). Psychologically, the change in basic policy would also have been difficult, both nationally and internationally. It would have meant leaving economism behind, adopting a political stance, and it is hard to see any reason why the Ikeda government would have changed the platform which brought it to power. The

Japanese left would have opposed the change ardently, as would Japan's neighbours. The vision of Tsukamoto, Abe and Araki in 1964 has to be seen as the opening of a possible new horizon for Japan. They do not say that Japan should embark on the road of a big power, but they say that Japan has come to the point where she has to realize that she can now make that decision.

The other orientation towards regional integration, where Japan would not be a great power, is what the authors call in English the Organization for Pacific Economic Co-operation (OPEC, Taiheiyō keizai kyōryoku kikō). The name is an obvious contrast to the OAEC. This is the grouping of the five industrialized Pacific countries, the United States, Canada, Australia, New Zealand, and Japan. As to the contents of the idea, the authors consider it sufficient to review the report of the Nihon keizai chōsa kyōgikai discussed above, without adding much of their own. The concept of OPEC is as delicate as the concept of OAEC, as it would mean great changes in all participating countries. The authors of this book are as careful as the committee in pointing out the importance of increasing mutual understanding of each other as necessary groundwork before attempting to deepen integration (Tsukamoto *et al.* 1964: 169–73).

As constructed by Tsukamoto, Abe, and Araki, both the Asian and Pacific orientations offer promising possibilities for the Japanese economy, but the psychological situations would be different. Both of them would place Japan at a high rank, but in the first case as the leader of a regional grouping, and in the other as a member in the circle of rich and advanced countries. The first orientation would require a great change in the self-image of Japan as a small country interested only in economic matters, while the second orientation would involve equally grave difficulties in engaging in diverse international communication with the culturally different Pacific countries. The authors refrain from taking sides in favour of either of these orientations, but treat them as mutually exclusive. Naturally, some relations with both groups of countries should be maintained and increased, but Japan's basic orientation has to be chosen between them. In their opinion, Japan cannot refrain from deciding, because regional integration has become the overriding phenomenon of the international system. Japan cannot continue being alone, relying only on global economic integration.

It should be kept in mind that the Asia which is referred to in the book by Tsukamoto, Abe, and Araki means geographically the Asia of ECAFE, with the socialist Asian countries excluded. The situation in 1964 also evoked discussions in the Diet. Kajima Morinosuke, a member of the House of Councillors, was especially worried about the situation. On 6 March, referring to the possibility of Atlantic integration, he demanded Prime Minister Ikeda's opinions about building up something similar in the Pacific area (Kajima 1964: 36–7). In his answer Ikeda outlined the possible areas where regional unity could be strengthened, namely the nations of Asia, nations of the Western Pacific, and nations around the Pacific (Ikeda 1964: 38). His answer is, however, for an unspecified future, and obviously no clear government policy had been formulated on the matter. The discussion tended to centre on the question of China, which would have been a central country in the Asian region mentioned by Ikeda. Kajima emphasized the usual attributes of common racial stock, a common script, and a long common history (Kajima 1964: 24).

The Chinese question had also become acute because France had recently recognized the government of the People's Republic of China. In the immediate situation there seemed, however, to be no possibility for such action on Japan's part. The Chinese government would not recognize the Japan–US Mutual Security Treaty, and remained otherwise hostile, as well. Foreign Minister Ohira Masayoshi also pointed to the attitude of the United States, implying that nothing could be done on the matter (Ohira 1964a: 23). That part of Asia was closed to Japan.

In addition, in 1964, relations with South Korea had not yet been normalized. Although negotiations were going on, the parties had not been able to agree even on questions like the establishment of exclusive fishing grounds (Ohira 1964b: 15). In the immediate East Asian neighbourhood of Japan there were no prospects for building up a regional organization. Also in the more remote Southeast Asian area, although hostility against Japan was lessening, no concrete possibilities were in sight. In the statements of neither Ikeda nor Ohira is there a trace of willingness to initiate an Asian policy where Japan would attempt to become an organizing and politically-leading actor in a Southeast Asian grouping, as Tsukamoto, Abe, and Araki had implied in connection with the Asian orientation.

Japan's tendency to leave Asia went one step further in 1964. In that year Japan was admitted to the OECD, about which Okita Saburo comments: 'Japan has entered the company [*nakama*] of adults, the advanced countries' (1964: 2). The Japanese word *nakama* has several meanings, including a circle of companions, a gang, a group with informal relationships; and it is this kind of circle of 'adult' advanced industrialized nations that Japan had now successfully entered. Although the grouping was loose, Japan was no longer alone. Okita still finds it necessary to qualify Japan's position with respect to the rich Euro–American countries, as its standard of living was not yet on their level, but that notion is again qualified by Japan's rapid economic growth, which Okita now calls 'super high growth' (*chōkōdo seichō*). If Japan's rank was low in terms of the general standard of living, in the dimension of growth it had earned the incontestable rank of umber one (*ichiban*) (Okita 1964: 36). The operation balances the psychological equation, and makes Japan even with the other OECD countries. In addition, in the not-so-distant future, Okita can expect that Japan will really reach their standard of living.

The process of Japan moving away from Asia in terms of its frame of reference was in a sense confirmed by an international event during the following year. The first United Nations Conference on Trade and Development (UNCTAD) convened during the spring of 1965. At the beginning of the conference Japan was in the unique position of being a member of both the Afro–Asian group and the group of developed countries. The arrangement reflected the old idea of Japan being a middle-level country between developing and developed countries. During the early stages of the conference Japan was represented at the meetings of both the Asian countries and the developed Western countries. However, during the middle of the conference an explicit antagonism arose between the developing and the developed nations, and a solid block of the developing countries emerged. Since Japan continued to participate in the meetings of the developed countries, it was thrown out of the meetings of the Asian countries. Consequently Japan, which was already the sixth largest trading nation in the world, was not elected to the working group that drafted trading principles. The Asian group sent only their own members. At the end of the conference when members for the Trade and Development Board – which was to act as a standing follow-up board for the conference – were chosen, Japan was elected. Not from the Asian group as had happened in similar situations before, but from the group of advanced industrialized nations.

Asian antagonism towards Japan seems to have resulted in part from the conflict within the conference, and in part from Japan's voting behaviour. Japan had adopted an attitude conservative even for a developed nation, especially opposing the attempts of the developing countries to remove import barriers on their export products. This was one occasion where Japan was publicly forced to take sides, and Okita Saburo, one of the Japanese delegates to the conference, was clearly shaken by the event (1965: 1–3).

ASIAN DYNAMISM

The discussion in Japan went on, with several authors trying to clarify Japan's position. The new economic dynamism of Asia seemed to be interesting to many authors. One of them was Oki Hiroshi, an official in the Section for Economic Co-operation in the Ministry of Foreign Affairs. In 1965 he published a book entitled *Ajia to Nihon, Ajia keizai hatten ni kyōryoku suru Nihon no yaku-wari* (Asia and Japan, The Role of Japan in Assisting Asian Economic Development). It does not present such clear undertones of Japan as a big power as Tsukamoto, Abe, and Araki expected in this regard, but Oki does argue that Japan has regained its ability to take initiatives internationally. Making the initiative means using foreign policy. Oki distinguishes three different foreign policies of Japan: the foreign policy of peace (*heiwa gaikō*), political foreign policy (*seiji gaikō*), and economic foreign policy (*keizai gaikō*). As used by Oki, they are not analytical concepts, but rather overlapping terms whose borders are not defined. Peaceful foreign policy refers to an orientation towards the world in general, exposing the peaceful and harmless nature of Japan. Oki is careful to qualify his claims about the emerging power of Japan as not meaning any big power policies. It would be carried out mainly through speeches in the United Nations and other similar forums, as well as through helping economic development around the world. Life would be made better for the people, and the world a more peaceful place (Oki 1965: 5–6). Political foreign policy would be practised among the countries of the free world. It would mean supporting some of the global initiatives of the United States, while simultaneously negotiating, e.g., the return of Okinawa to Japanese jurisdiction. Economic foreign policy is by Oki's definition synonymous with economic co-operation (Oki 1965: 67). It also forms a part of the peaceful foreign policy, and is needed around the world, but it is especially aimed towards the Asian developing countries. They are the main interest in Oki's book.

He here links Japan with the Asian countries in a logical framework, obviously inspired by ideas similar to those espoused by Akamatsu. He structures Asia according to the countries' level of development:

1 Countries producing mainly primary products
2 Countries in the process of light industrialization
3 Light industrial countries
4 Countries in the process of heavy industrialization
5 Heavy industrial countries.

(Oki 1965: 181)

Now, in 1965, Oki no longer finds any whole countries on level 1, although large districts in several countries, such as Indonesia, Laos, or Thailand belong here. Taken as a whole, most Asian countries are at stage 2, developing light industries. They are clearly moving upwards from the level on which they had been when they were colonized. They import capital, and their exports still consist mostly of the primary products they have traditionally exported. The products of their light industries are consumed in the home country, but more often than not they are already doing well against imports. However, their industries are still weak, needing protection, and corresponding national policies are usually adopted.

Pakistan, Thailand, and the Philippines have succeeded in climbing to the third stage. Their imports of light industrial goods have greatly diminished, and although primary products still occupy a major part of their exports, industrial goods are also exported. These countries import lots of capital and technology. At stage 4 are countries like Hong Kong, Taiwan, South Korea, India, and China – which Oki has not hesitated to include. The share of their exports dedicated to light industrial goods is fairly high, and except for China, they import even greater amounts of capital and technology for the construction of their heavy industries.

The only advanced industrialized country in Asia naturally occupies stage 5 alone. However, when presented in this way, the distance between Japan and the other Asian countries does not appear to be great. In addition, the same argument with which others could make the perceived distance between Japan and the Euro–American countries become insignificant, namely rapid development, is now applied by Oki to the Asian countries. They grow fast, and they climb rapidly upwards. If development continues, some of them will be approaching the level of the advanced countries in the foreseeable future. There are instances where Oki places Japan and some other Asian countries into a structurally similar position. For example, in terms of their trading structures, Japan and Hong Kong are said to be very much alike, importing raw materials and exporting processed goods. Other countries, like Taiwan, are also approaching this stage (Oki 1965: 92). Oki introduces a new concept, 'relatively advanced countries' (*sōtaiteki senshinkoku*), which allows him to group together Japan, Hong Kong, India, China, and 'others' (Oki 1965: 184), obviously referring to Taiwan, South Korea, and Singapore.

As can be expected, Oki does not use the term integration when referring to Japan's relationship with these countries, but speaks of economic co-operation. Trade in raw materials and industrial products should be expanded between the countries, and Japanese investments and developmental assistance in the region should be increased (Oki 1965: 81–135). The argument is the familiar one under the theme of development, that for a long time to come the region would offer a vast and expanding market for Japanese products. Oki can thus be seen as favouring the Asian orientation, although he does not talk about Japan assuming any role of political leadership in the region, but stays in the economic sphere.

It is important to emphasize the theme of economism here. Only because he closes out the political sector can Oki make up this kind of constructive scheme where Japan appears closely connected with the Asian countries. Where the discussants transgress the borderline of economism, as Tsukamoto, Abe, and Araki did by depicting Japan as a regional political leader, or when the amorphous political situation in Asia is discussed, something inhibiting regionalism in Asia always appears. With this it does not mean that there is something unrealistic in what Oki is doing, but rather that parts of reality have to be shut out in difficult situations for constructive thinking to be able to proceed (Korhonen 1990: 33–6).

In Oki's case there had also been a change in the political situation, which made it easier to place less emphasis on the political sector. In June 1965 a breakthrough was finally made in the Japanese–Korean negotiations on normalising relations. Japan agreed to pay South Korea US $200 million as war reparations, and US $300 million as aid. In addition, the flow of private funds was expected to rise rapidly. As it turned out, the lessening of tension took time; even though diplomatic relations were established, it took two years until the first Japanese investment in South Korea was authorized, and the level of investment remained low until the early 1970s (Shibusawa 1984: 44). However, that is not important here. In 1965 Oki could expect that a transfer of capital and technology would aid the development of South Korea, political tension between the countries would diminish, and the relationship shift towards an economic one. The same could be expected to happen eventually also with China, the whole of East Asia moving towards an economic orientation.

The Japan Economic Research Center (JERC) was established in 1964. It was a private organization, situated in the Nikkei Building in Otemachi, the economic centre of Tokyo. Its purpose was to further research into the problem areas and future of Japan's economy. To this end it organized various studies, study groups and conferences, bringing academics together with government and business circles, also sponsoring international participation and personnel exchange. Okita Saburo became its first director, and JERC soon moved to the centre of discussion on regional integration in Japan. In September 1965 it organized a conference among Japanese economists to discuss ways of increasing trade with the developing countries. In light of the recent UNCTAD meeting it was deemed necessary to start discussion of Japan's situation in the Asian–Pacific area in earnest.

Of the discussants, Fujii Shigeru, especially, argues about the importance of perceiving the strength of the Asian economies. Like Oki, he also places great emphasis on the 'magical' attribute of the high speed of growth, which during the 1960s began to appear in many Asian countries. Fujii especially praises Hong Kong and Taiwan, while noting that India seems to be slipping somewhat. Other countries praised are Burma, Ceylon, Indonesia, South Korea, Malaysia, Pakistan, the Philippines, and Thailand; presented in alphabetical order, without an attempt to differentiate Asia into different regions. The list of products that Fujii presents as displaying especially good rates of development is impressive: cotton textiles, paper, cement, iron and steel, phosphorous fertilizers, potassium fertilizers, sulphuric acid, caustic soda, and soda ash; in other words, not only light industrial products, but also cruder heavy and chemical industrial products (Fujii 1965: 1–5).

This new Asia, as presented by Fujii, is an economic threat to Japan. He does not point out the beneficial effects of Asian development on Japan's export trade, but rather concentrates on its harmful effects. Japanese exports to the area are shown to be declining as a result of local production, trade among the Asian countries, and governmental measures against Japanese trade. Fujii remarks, though, that many countries have tended to run continuous deficits in their trade with Japan. In addition, many Asian countries are already competing with the Japanese in third markets, often successfully, in product categories like cotton goods, various other light manufactures, plywood and cement (Fujii 1965: 5–11).

Fujii notes that thus far the countries have not been able to compete very successfully in the Japanese market, except in one apparently threatening case. It became famous among Japanese economists, acquiring the status of a fixed expression: 'the Hong Kong flowers'. In 1965 the plastic flowers made in Hong Kong, used in decorating homes and public places, had been able to conquer the Japanese market, driving the Japanese flower makers into near oblivion. Earlier, Japan had been the principal producer. The production of plastic flowers had increased rapidly in Japan during the 1950s, reaching their peak in 1960. Exports to the United States and other international markets had risen accordingly. However, from 1961 onwards the Japanese began to lose international markets in favour of the Hong Kong flower makers, and also imports to Japan began to rise considerably. Production in Japan fell rapidly, so that in 1964 it was already below the 1956 level, and was continuing to fall (Fujii 1965: 16).

There were also other sundries, the production of which required cheap manual labour, and which were beginning to be imported to Japan. Most of them were wooden, bamboo, and straw products, such as furniture and various other consumer goods. Also, more zippers were being imported. The place of origin was usually Hong Kong or Taiwan. Japanese producers were being pushed out of the international markets, too (Fujii 1965: 17–18). The resemblance to the history of Japanese development was obvious: new competitors entering markets with incredibly cheap, miscellaneous consumer products which looked harmless, but with which the countries could conquer important niches. Later the products would diversify, and their quality rise. An especially shattering event in this sense seems to have been the easy conquering of the Japanese market by the Hong Kong flowers.

The importance of this kind of exercise is in creating a new frame of reference for Japan with respect to Asia. The rank of Asia is rising in the economic dimension, and there is no longer a need to depict Japan as being alone in Asia as the only developed country. The attribute of economic dynamism is, in the middle of the 1960s, spreading outward from Japan to include the Asian countries as well. It changes the generally backward image of Asia towards a more positive one. Following the theme of development, Kojima and Okita had expected this to happen, and now it was happening. In Oki's case, the new image of Asia is positive enough to act as a counterpart to interest in the Pacific countries, but still not strong enough to elicit enthusiasm towards deep economic integration with them. In Fujii's case a more threatening image is created. However, in both cases the dynamism of Asia becomes an additional reason for taking the Asian countries into consideration in all visions of Japan's future.

THE PAFTA PROPOSAL

At the same conference on trade expansion by the developing countries Kojima Kiyoshi and Kurimoto Hiroshi, an official of the Japan ECAFE Association, presented a paper which subsequently came to dominate discussion on Japan's prospects for regional integration. The name of the September version was *Taiheiyō kyōdō ichiba to Tōnan Ajia* (A Pacific Common Market and Southeast Asia) (Kojima and Kurimoto 1965). In November an international conference was held on the same subject, and the Japanese participants presented revised versions of their papers. The name of the November version was 'A Pacific Community and Asian Developing Countries' (Kojima and Kurimoto 1966a).

Although both Kojima and Kurimoto were given as authors of the paper, they wrote separately, Kurimoto's contribution appearing as an appendix to the text by Kojima, and they will therefore be separately analysed. The main text and the principal ideas were contributed by Kojima. There is also a rewritten version of the paper in Japanese (Kojima and Kurimoto 1966b), but analysis here will be concentrated on the first two versions. They constitute the original proposal of PAFTA. Argumentation in these versions is fresher, being still in the formative stages, and thus more open to analysis. The part written by Kojima was also published, again with some rewriting, in his book *Japan and a Pacific Free Trade Area* (1971: 71–104).

Because of different languages, different audiences, and the development of the argument over time, there are some differences in the versions. The basic one is that the first version is more marked by doubts as to the pros and cons of regional integration, to be discussed with the home audience. The latter version is more sophisticated, easier to read, and argued more persuasively as a proposition to be accepted by an international audience. The audience at the international conference was composed of economists from various Asian countries and one from the United States; later the English version was distributed widely in the Pacific countries. It must be emphasized, however, that the differences between the versions are not great, but rather a matter of emphasis.

Both versions begin by emphasizing that what follows is 'a highly hypothetical enquiry' (Kojima and Kurimoto 1965: 1; 1966a: 93), meaning that although the idea makes some sense economically, its practical feasibility is still felt to be questionable. The idea of Pacific integration is presented as a research problem:

> what would be the scale, character, and mutual economic benefits for members of a Pacific Free Trade Area if one were to be established among the United States of America, Canada, Japan, Australia and New Zealand in the forseeable future.
>
> (Kojima and Kurimoto 1966a: 93; 1965: 1)

The theoretical basis for Kojima's proposal goes back to his study on the concept of integration in 1962 and on his policy proposal for arranging trilateral trade between the United States, Japan, and the Asian countries. At that time he had been sceptical about treating the Pacific countries as an economic region with which Japan could integrate, but now he has changed his mind. It is interesting to note that while in previous discussion Japan had been placed as the last member in lists of the five countries, Kojima now places her in the middle. It was with this kind of tiny changes of emphasis that Japanese thinking on Pacific integration proceeded. Although Kojima calls his study hypothetical, he also uses the expression 'foreseeable future'; time is still unspecified, but at least it is seen as a concrete possibility, no longer as a dream. The idea of the five countries forming an economic grouping was by 1965 common knowledge in Japan, but thus far discussion had proceeded in vague terms, based more on feelings than actual knowledge of the situation between the countries. With this study Kojima moves discussion on to the firmer ground of a scientific study on the economic strengths and weaknesses of the countries in question. The strength of Kojima's argument is that he lays bare, from an economic point of view, the basic relationship between the Pacific countries. This laid a firm foundation on which subsequent discussion could be based.

However, in 1965 neither of the versions was yet ready. There were inconsistencies in the argument. A clear indication of the preliminary state of the idea is the number of different names that Kojima uses in describing the idea. The titles of the texts, as presented above, clearly indicate that the European Economic Community has been used as their model. The goal of integration is given as the formation of an 'economically integrated free trade area such as already exists with the European Economic Community' (Kojima and Kurimoto 1966a: 94). However, these names are used interchangeably with 'Taiheiyō jiyū bōeki chi-iki' (Kojima and Kurimoto 1965: 1), i.e., 'Pacific Free Trade Area' (Kojima and Kurimoto 1966a: 93). It would point to a more EFTA-like approach. Basically, Kojima's approach is only that of free trade, consistent with his earlier opinions. He does not present any ideas regarding a customs union, and still less of political unity, or creation of supranational organizations to stand over the member countries. That would explain the use of the latter names, while references to 'Community' might at least partly result from the fact that the EEC was without doubt both more well known and the more prestigious of the two Western European organizations. Using a name modelled after it would mean giving Pacific integration equally prestigious overtones to those of the EEC.

In the earlier text the name 'Taiheiyō senshinkoku jiyū bōeki chi-iki' (Kojima and Kurimoto 1965: 12), or 'A Pacific Advanced Countries Free Trade Area' is also used. In the same version Kojima also uses the abbreviation PAFTA, the whole name being given in English as 'Pacific and Asian Free Trade Area' (ibid.: 2), which conflicts with the previous name. This probably indicates that Kojima is still vacillating somewhat between the Asian and the Pacific orientations. The later version uses PFTA throughout, where Asia has been dropped. In later discussion, both by Kojima and others, the name returned to the more easily pronounced PAFTA, where the first 'A' comes from the second letter in the word 'Pacific' (Kojima 1971: 71). For the sake of consistency, the abbreviation PAFTA will be used throughout the following in the latter sense.

Interestingly enough, in the later version Kojima also calls PAFTA sarcastically a 'rich men's club' (Kojima and Kurimoto 1966a: 103), as the PAFTA might lead to a still more drastic break with the Asian countries. A solution might be to include the Asian countries into the grouping through an associated membership in the way many African countries were associated with the EEC. In a footnote he also remarks about the possibility of including the Latin American countries as associate members, and in another mentions that the entry of the United Kingdom would also be welcome (Kojima and Kurimoto 1965: 2; 1966a: 96).

The vagueness of the question of membership indicates that Kojima does not want closed integration, and in both versions he still insists that the best course for Japan would be free trade on a global basis. However, his views about the threatening aspects of European integration seem to have become even stronger than before. The earlier version especially argues from the basis of a threat emanating from Europe. Kojima seems to have become worried even about the prospect of the EFTA joining the EEC, which might not result in a more open EEC, but in an even more closed Western European integration. Against this economic threat he strongly advocates that Japan has to start studying measures to set up a counterforce (*taikō seiryoku*) (Kojima and Kurimoto 1965: 2), the PAFTA being his solution. In the later version the argument is directed more towards the United States, Kojima pointing out that, in view of the possibility of the appearance of an 'inward looking Europe', the United States might well find closer integration in the Pacific desirable' (Kojima and Kurimoto 1966a: 93–4).

There is also a brief mention of the tendency of the United States to look 'towards the possibility of ultimately going in with Europe' (ibid.: 93). It is only a small one. The general structure of his argument is that he declines to make the liaison between North America and Western Europe present to his audience, but instead constantly argues for a liaison between North America, Japan, Australia and New Zealand. The prospects for an Atlantic Community had also diminished at the time. Following President Charles de Gaulle's veto of Britain's entry into the EEC in 1963 the GATT negotiations between the United States and the EEC had made a turn for the worse, and at the time of Kojima's proposal there was still no relaxation in the tension (Kojima 1980: 3). France in particular had adopted an antagonistic stance towards trade liberalization with the United States, especially on the question of agricultural products, and maintained a restrictionist attitude towards United States's investments. There was also a corresponding tension between France and the United States in NATO, although in 1965 French troops still remained under the unified command. These tensions caused a shift in rhetoric in Washington. The image of an Atlantic Community dropped lower in Washington's hierarchy of values, and in its place the concept Atlantic partnership, a more distant relationship, began to be talked about (English 1968b: 28–30). The United States still tended to be more interested in Atlantic affairs than Pacific ones, and Kojima's proposal has to be seen partly as an attempt to increase a Pacific orientation in the global policies of the United States, but the main idea in 1965 seems to have been the setting up of a counterforce to the EEC. This idea of a counterforce explains the extremely wide membership Kojima contemplates. If Western Europe was to create an economic block with Africa, and the socialist world would be another block, Japan would still thrive quite well in a grouping composed of North, Central, and

South America, Oceania, Asia, Great Britain, and the British Commonwealth.

In addition to this defensive or negative argument, Kojima also uses positive arguments. One of them is that if PAFTA was formed, and the attention of all of the five rich countries directed towards the Pacific and Asia, it would be a 'miracle drug' (Kojima and Kurimoto 1965: 2) to the developing Asian economies. It would mean increased trade, investments, and development aid to the region. The general idea is that a group of rich countries could do this far better than one poor Japan. In light of the recent conflict in the UNCTAD Conference with the developing countries, Japan being criticized for not opening her import restrictions against them, the enlargement of the export markets of the Asian countries would obviously make the situation easier for Japan.

Another positive argument concerns the economic viability of PAFTA as a statistical entity. The statistical figures Kojima uses as the basis for his calculations are presented in Table 3.1.

Table 3.1 Statistical characteristics of the Pacific Free Trade Area, 1963

	GNP (US $ million)	Population (thousands)	Per capita income (US $)
USA	583,918	186,591	3,083
Canada	39,781	18,600	1,591
Japan	59,672	94,930	512
Australia	17,320	10,705	1,283
New Zealand	4,436	2,485	1,499
Total	705,127	313,311	
Average			1,837
United Kingdom	84,000	53,441	1,248
EEC	247,491	175,432	1,088

Source: Kojima & Kurimoto 1965: 39

It is always necessary to keep in mind that at that time the United States was still in an economic class of her own. In terms of GNP the United States was more than twice as big as the whole EEC. Its importance for Japan was also at least twice as great, and probably more because it was nearer – and this was without taking non-economic factors into consideration. Of the remaining PAFTA countries, Japan was the strongest in terms of GNP, but not very much stronger than Canada. Japan was also second in terms of population, but on the lowest position in terms of national income per capita. Like Okita before, Kojima also points out that Japan's

situation resembles in many ways that of Italy in European integration (Kojima and Kurimoto 1965: 4), as Italy was also relatively
poor compared with France, the Federal Republic of Germany, and
the Benelux countries.

It may be useful to speculate here about some matters that Kojima
only hints at. For instance, in the earlier version, he mentions in
passing that the United States might be too big for PAFTA (ibid.:
4). If we left the United States out of the calculation, we could get
a grouping with a total GNP of US $121,000 million, and with a
population of 127 million. According to the purely economic criteria
of Kojima, this would show that even without the United States the
four countries could create an economically feasible grouping among
themselves. Its size would be about half of the EEC in terms of
GNP, and two-thirds in terms of population. Japan would, however,
be a dominant member in this grouping, especially if the industrial
structures of the countries were taken into consideration. This idea
is not discussed by Kojima at all. Perhaps it would not make sense
even as a logical possibility. As in the discussion of the concept of
OPEC above, Kojima does not show a willingness to use any overtones of a big power in connection with the idea of PAFTA but
treats Japan constantly as a small country. In addition, Japan could
not possibly be seen as integrating 'glue' in any institutional scheme.
Japan would be alien to the three countries, with hardly any historical ties with them. Clearly in PAFTA it would be the United States
towards which all of the other countries would orient themselves.
Japan can study, take part in, and even propose the formation of a
grouping like PAFTA but, as formulated already by the Nihon keizai
chōsa kyōgikai in 1963, she cannot create a grouping like this based
on her own power. Japan has to get the United States to do it.

On the other hand, Kojima also included the figures for the United
Kingdom in his table of statistics without explaining the reason. If
we were to speculate further, and substitute the United Kingdom
for the United States, we would get an organization roughly equiva-
lent to the EEC. Its population would be almost the same, 180
million, and its GNP only a little lower, US $205,000 million. Here,
Japan would be getting together with the British Commonwealth,
including the three Pacific countries, as well as a number of Asian
and African countries. Naturally, this kind of speculation sounds
ridiculous. The Commonwealth countries have long historical ties
among themselves, and economically Japan and Great Britain would
just be competitors. In addition, Great Britain was relatively stag-
nant economically, and would no longer have been strong enough

to accommodate Japan as a junior partner – and it is exactly a junior partnership in a larger grouping that seems to be in Kojima's mind for Japan.

Kojima's third positive argument concerns the industrial structures of the participating countries, and the effects on them of tariff elimination. Kojima uses the concept of the intensity of trade, meaning the amount of trade that is conducted between any two countries over and above the amount that would be expected in a purely abstract situation of global free trade. He found that the trade intensity is above normal among the five PAFTA countries. They especially tended to export quite a lot to the other countries in the area, but tended to import from outside the area. The United States and Canada on the one hand, and Australia and New Zealand on the other, form especially close trading relationships. In 1965 the latter two countries had already signed an agreement to create a free trade area between themselves, coming into effect on 1 January 1966.

Japan traded quite extensively with the United States and Australia. It generally consisted of complementary trade, exchanging primary products for manufactured ones (Kojima and Kurimoto 1965: 5–6; 1966a: 97). Japanese exports went to the United States (27 per cent), all five countries (33 per cent), and Southeast Asia (32 per cent). The rest (35 per cent) went to other places around the world. The general situation was thus such that the trade of Japan could be divided into three parts of roughly equal size, which makes Kojima warn that Japan should not be too preoccupied with Pacific integration at the cost of forgetting Asia. Especially in the earlier version he emphasizes that, in terms of trade, Japan stands between Asia and the Pacific (Kojima and Kurimoto 1965: 5–6). However, with respect to the overall international market, the Asian Pacific region, which absorbed 65 per cent of Japan's exports, was extremely important. (Actually Kojima calls it the *Taiheiyō-Ajia chiiki*, meaning 'Pacific–Asia area', placing the word 'Pacific' first, as it had not yet become a fixed expression, being one of the names still evolving). If the tendency to form economic blocks continued, Japan would have had to place the guaranteeing of good relations with this area above everything else.

However, the process of the relative diminishing of trade with the Asian countries, which had started during the 1950s, was still continuing. Since the partial liberalization of Japan's trade after 1960, which meant mainly the liberalization of imports of some primary products, Japan's trade with the five Pacific countries had been further intensified in contrast to its trade with Asian countries. For instance, Japan imported large quantities of soy beans, rice, maize, sorghum, raw cotton, iron ore, and coking coal from the United States; sugar, iron ore, copper, and coking coal from Australia; and iron ore, copper, and coking coal from Canada. Except for cotton, imports were increasing. This leads to the following comment:

> the import of primary goods is being made in increasingly large quantities from the Pacific advanced countries, whose supplies are better in quality, cheaper in price, better in quality control and more punctual in delivery. The liberalization of trade is causing Japan to turn its back to Asia.
>
> (Kojima and Kurimoto 1966a: 104).

The process is not wished for by Kojima, but the phenomenon is still a factor favouring the Pacific orientation.

When we look at the industrial structures of countries, and divide products into four groups, namely heavy and chemical industries (K), light manufactures (L), natural resource intensive products (N), and agricultural products (A), the global situation was that the countries which had a comparative advantage in K-products were the United States, Japan, and Western Europe – which actually had the highest ratio. The strongest comparative advantage Japan had was in L-products, where it had the highest relative share. It was in a competitive relationship with Western Europe and the Asian developing countries in these products, but complementary with the four Pacific countries. In A-products, Canada, Australia, New Zealand, Asian developing countries, and to a large extent also the United States, were competitive with each other, and complementary only with Japan and Western Europe. In N-products, only Canada had a large share, and Australia and the United States a moderate one, lower than Southeast Asia. Japan's share was extremely low, and thus it was in an extremely complementary situation with all of the countries within the Asian Pacific area (Kojima and Kurimoto 1965: 10; 1966a: 99).

Several things follow from this: The four other PAFTA countries are competitive with the Asian developing countries in exporting A- and N-products. If trade liberalization were to take place among the five countries, Japan's trade might shift even more strongly towards them, if special measures were not adopted to help the Asian countries in their export trade. They would need assistance to develop their production to increase their competitiveness, and the four PAFTA countries would need to make structural adjustments in their economy. A similar problem is also seen to exist in the expansion of the trade in manufactured goods if trade liberalization were to take place only among the five. Because of its comparative advantages in both K- and L-products, Japan might hamper the possibilities of the Asian developing countries to export to the other PAFTA countries if special measures were not taken to help them (Kojima and Kurimoto 1966a: 103–7).

It also seems clear that Japan would benefit more than any of the other five countries if trade were liberalized among them. According to the first version, if tariffs were eliminated, Japan's exports to the four other countries would increase by 55 per cent, but her imports by only 12 per cent (Kojima and Kurimoto 1965: 14). The reason is that Japanese exports tend to be products which generally have higher duties than the kinds of products it imports. If Japan were to engage in similar integration with Western Europe (EEC + EFTA), its exports would grow by only 27 per cent, but imports by 40 per cent. Therefore Kojima comments that it would be wise not to integrate with Western Europe, but with the Pacific countries. That idea he praises enthusiastically (*hijōni nozomashii yūrina kōka da . . .*) (ibid.: 1965: 15). These arguments are obviously meant for national consumption, to increase Japanese interest in the idea. Although Kojima in principle valued global integration above regional integration, the latter now began to look like a viable and highly recommendable second-best solution.

In the later version, recalculations are made and the expected benefits toned down. Kojima does not mention whether it is because of more correct methods of calculation, or because of a different audience. The figure for the increase of Japan's exports is 21 per cent, not much above the figure at which they were already in reality rising, and the figure for the increase of imports, 6 per cent. After this, Kojima mentions that 'Japan would be able to improve her balance of trade with the area which was deficit by $1,000 million in 1963' (Kojima and Kurimoto 1966a: 101). In this way it is made to appear as right and proper that Japan would be able to improve its trading situation with the other countries. Naturally, it may be that Kojima did not have fresher figures at hand, but it may also be that Kojima used the most convenient year to back up his proposal for the international audience. Japan's balance of trade was already getting better in 1964, and in 1965 it was already back in the black (Nakamura 1987: 51). The United States would increase its trade somewhat, keeping quite well in balance. The situation for all of the three remaining countries would deteriorate, suggesting 'the need of industrialization' for them (Kojima and Kurimoto 1966a: 102).

Thus, according to Kojima's calculations, Japan would fare quite well whether the world trading situation remained the same as it had been, based on GATT, or whether it would take part in Pacific integration. The United States would gain somewhat with Pacific integration, or at least it would not seem to lose anything by it. The argument to turn the attention of the United States away from Atlantic integration rests on this basis. The other three countries would be the losers. They were built up as supporting economies for Great Britain, but now they were clearly in need of finding new markets, and changing their economic structures. From Kojima's point of view, they should rapidly start to advance along the course of the flying geese, decreasing the share of A- and N-products in their exports, adding more industrial products. In this way they would fit better into Pacific integration, and not stand in the way of the Asian countries in their exports of A- and N-products. The high levels of income and education in Canada, Australia, and New Zealand would point to a direct orientation towards K-products in their industrialization so that, in the case of L-products also, they would make way for the Asian developing countries.

Kojima also points out that recently Japan had approached full employment, so that the problem of employing its huge population was disappearing. Because full employment would lead to a rise in wages, Japan would rapidly lose competitiveness in several L-industries (Kojima and Kurimoto 1965: 22), placing them clearly in the category of sunset industries. Thus, Japan would also start paving the way for the import of L-products from the Asian developing countries. It would even be easy from the point of view of the export expansion resulting from PAFTA. The trade expansion of the Asian countries would be managed carefully, which is the basic sense of the idea of associated membership. With the greater market of PAFTA, their exports would increase, and as they would need to import all they could to continue their development, export trade from PAFTA to the Asian countries would also increase. Japan would be well situated in this regard. The PAFTA proposal of Kojima was, thus, in face of the possible threat emanating from European integration, a way of securing Japan's trading position in an optimal way, while allowing it to retain its trading relationship with the Asian countries, the market second in importance. Kojima's proposition amounts to adopting a general Pacific orientation in

Japan's economic foreign policy without, however, turning her back on Asia.

The part written by Kurimoto stands as a curious appendix to the text of Kojima. The main problem as he sees it is the balance of payment deficits suffered by the Asian developing countries. To correct it, he advocates that as a first stage the advanced Pacific countries should gradually stop importing agricultural products from each other, and transfer supply sources to the Asian developing countries. In the second stage these countries should refrain from exporting agricultural products to third parties like Europe, and curtail their own production to the level of minimum self-sufficiency, leaving the international agricultural markets completely to the developing countries (Kojima and Kurimoto 1965: 22–6; 1966a: 107–11).

The idea has a superficial similarity to Kojima's proposition, but nothing more. It would cut the strength from Kojima's argument for PAFTA with respect to Canada, Australia and New Zealand. The United States would also be affected. The only function Kurimoto's piece would appear to have is as a political offensive towards the Asian developing countries. As it is situated at the end of the paper, it might leave a good taste in the mouth of Asian readers who might be alarmed by the formation of a 'rich men's club', which would give the Asian countries the status of a mere associated member. In that sense, Kurimoto's proposition would be purely persuasive, albeit clumsy, politics aimed at the Asian countries. On the other hand, even that function is limited. Kurimoto does not try to make room for the industrialization of Asian countries, but rather argues in favour of developing them as agricultural economies. There is a discrepancy between Kojima and Kurimoto, which perhaps most of all shows the immaturity of the paper, as if it had been hastily put together for the conference.

Too much should not be read into the PAFTA proposal about its orientation towards developed countries (comp. Chung 1981: 14–17). PAFTA included more than an idea of keeping Asia as a reserve in case Pacific integration did not proceed smoothly. The proposal reflects the rise in Japan's international status and level of development, and in that sense Japan had left Asia, but only in that sense. The Asian countries are kept constantly in the picture. The PAFTA proposal should be viewed under the theme of Asia, as an attempt to define optimally, in an economic sense, the relationship between Japan and Asian countries. It can be seen as an attempt to assist the latter according to the flying geese pattern of development.

In the rewritten Japanese version of 1966, which was published in February, a special concluding chapter is added, where the benefits for Asia are emphasized (Kojima and Kurimoto 1966b: 94–5).

In his *Sekai keizai nyūmon* (Introduction to World Economics), published in December 1966, Kojima conducts most of his discussion of the PAFTA concept from the point of view of Asian countries. Although he hopes for the success of the Kennedy Round, he also criticizes it because it had begun to look as if the trade liberalization it would bring would mostly benefit the industrialized countries. It left countries producing agricultural products and light manufactures without much change in their international trading situation. PAFTA is presented here as a corrective measure to the Kennedy Round (Kojima 1966: 103–4).

He calculates that at least Hong Kong, Taiwan, Singapore and India were on a level of development where they would be strong enough to benefit greatly from free access to the markets of the five Pacific countries. The other Asian countries would still need assistance from the industrialized countries for their light industries. They could, however, export raw materials and agricultural products. He calculates also that the brunt of the exports from Asian countries would be borne by the United States. Exports there would expand by US $330,000,000, to Canada by US $20,000,000, to Japan by US $40,000,000, to Australia by US $30,000,000, and to New Zealand by US $14,000,000. Asian exports would rise 15 per cent, and light industrial products would occupy the greatest share of the rise of Asian exports, giving a great boost to Asian development (Kojima 1966: 114–16). As a market, and as a source of capital and technology, PAFTA is presented as the parent organization (*botai*) to Asian development.

It is probably because of a different audience that Kojima emphasizes PAFTA's Asian and Pacific aspects differently in different settings. It seems that in the actual proposal, intended to initiate political action among an international audience, he concentrates on the relationships between the five industrialized countries. In this text written for home consumption, in the middle of general economic discussion, the Asian aspect can come into the foreground.

Bela Balassa's typology of the degrees of regional economic integration, which had been widely used in the study of integration during the 1960s (Nye 1971: 28–9), and which Kojima had also known in 1962, although he did not then take special interest in it (Kojima 1962a: 56, 61), can be used in setting Kojima's proposal into perspective. Balassa distinguishes between five different categories of economic integration, from the loosest type to tighter forms, starting from (1) a free trade area, where tariffs and quantitative restrictions between countries are abolished, but each country retains its own tariff policy towards non-members; (2) in a customs union the whole group adopts common tariffs against non-members; (3) in a common market not only trade restrictions, but also restrictions on factor movements are abolished among members; (4) in an economic union national economic policies are harmonized to remove discrimination due to them; and (5) in total economic integration also monetary, fiscal, social, and countercyclical policies are harmonized, and a supranational authority whose decisions are binding for member states is set up (Balassa 1962: 2).

In view of these possible degrees of economic integration, Kojima's PAFTA proposal appears as the loosest form. He proposes only the formation of a free trade area, not even a customs union, much less any of the more extensive forms of integration. In one sense Kojima goes beyond the simple free trade area approach, as he advocates a common trade and aid policy towards the Asian countries. Also, the proposal as an application of the theory of the flying geese pattern of development could in a sense be seen as a harmonization of economic policies, but the sense is different from Balassa's stage 4. The purpose of PAFTA was general expansion of trade in the widest possible area outside Europe and the socialist countries, but it should be seen as a very loose form of regional integration. PAFTA was modelled to be harmonious with GATT and the ideal of global economic integration.

JAPAN, THE BRIDGE

In 1967 Miki Takeo became the foreign minister of Japan, and adopted Kojima's proposition as the economic basis for his foreign political visions. Kojima's scientifically-backed construction made the idea of Pacific integration look practical, and usable in politics. Although Kojima himself does not claim so, on the basis of timing and political actions it is possible to argue that on this foundation first Miki, and after him other politicians including Miyazawa Kiichi and Ohira Masayoshi (Kojima 1980: 21–5) were able to build more political constructions.

Miki Takeo was the first politician to help make the idea of Pacific integration known in wider circles both in Japan and abroad. In 1967 the slogan *Miki kōsō*, i.e., 'Miki Plan', or 'Miki Conception' emerged. In its economic substance it followed Kojima's proposition, but it was argued by means of using more political rhetoric. Kojima's argumentation was meant for professional economists, but Miki constructs his arguments so that the idea can be sold to wider audiences. He turns the idea of economic integration into a political ideology.

In his public speeches Miki further extends the definition of Japan with respect to other countries:

> Japan has now arrived to take a place after the United States and the Soviet Union, on the same level with Great Britain and the EEC.
>
> (Miki 1984a: 292)

By 1967 Japan had become the third largest national economy in the world after the United States and the Soviet Union, surpassing each of the Western European countries. It had become number three in this dimension, and consequently Japan could now be presented as standing at the same rank as Great Britain and the EEC countries. The rank was so distinct that there was no longer any need to qualify the statement with the complex reference to standards of living and rapid growth; the statement could now simply stand on its own.

At the same time, Miki carefully presents Japan also as a member of the Asian countries (*Ajia no ichi in*). This is still qualified by emphasizing that Japan remains the only advanced industrialized country in Asia, balanced by the notion that the situation may not necessarily remain so in the future. He uses the expression 'the new breeze of Asia' (*Ajia no shinfū*) to describe the new economic dynamism of the Asian countries. Miki talks also about their diminishing interest in war and ideological tensions, presenting them as following the economistic example of Japan. The Vietnam War is spoiling the picture, but Miki has hopes that it will end soon. China is in the middle of the Cultural Revolution, but Miki is confident that before long – 'perhaps after ten years, perhaps after fifty years' – China, too, will be moved by the new breeze of Asia, especially if ideological tensions are allowed to disappear, and economic cooperation increases (Miki 1984c: 308). The Japanese themes of economism, growth and development are thus thickly spread over the Asian countries with the slogan of the new breeze of Asia.

Miki strongly emphasizes that Japan is a member of two groups, the advanced industrialized countries, especially the Pacific advanced countries, and the Asian countries. For these two groups to be combined into a meaningful whole from the point of view of Japan, a special geographical reference is needed. This is the expression

'Asian–Pacific area' (*Ajia-Taiheiyō chi iki*), which Miki constantly uses in his speeches. He is treating the whole area as one entity which develops together and increases the mutual security and prosperity of all of the participating countries. It is a geographical term, and as such it is outside the sector of politics. That makes it useful for the political end of discussing increased economic co-operation, not only among the non-socialistic countries, but also with China, and even the Soviet Union. All countries whose shores are washed by the Pacific Ocean can be included in the concept, while ideological differences can be de-emphasized. This is important from the point of view of Japan's security, and Japan would benefit also from increased trade.

At the same time, the concept is also a means of moving towards a more meaningful geographical definition of Asia from Japan's point of view. Miki is still vague on this point; he can very well name the Pacific countries as the United States, Canada, Australia and New Zealand – but he hardly mentions the Asian countries. In fact, he hardly refers to Asian matters west of Indo-China, and at least in this sense the concept of Asia relevant to Japan is in a process of being defined through the term 'Pacific'. It begins to mean what is today known as East Asia, Indo-China, and the countries of the Association of the Southeast Asian Nations (ASEAN). It is a small enough place in which to concentrate Japan's still limited projects of developmental aid and other economic co-operation. It also diminishes the enormous heterogeneity of countries and cultures contained in the European concept of Asia. It is perhaps most accurate to say that Miki's conception does not exclude the rest of Asia, and in all situations he argues against closed groupings, but the Pacific parts of Asia are emphasized more than the rest. The Latin American countries are also usually missing from Miki's frame of reference, but we can at least say that they are potentially contained in the concept of an Asian–Pacific area. Miki is creating a new geographical concept to structure the surface of the globe in a way that is meaningful to the Japanese.

Miki also uses the category of time to argue for the newness of the situation. One of his ways is to divide the twentieth century into three parts. The first third is characterized by the First World War, the second by the Second World War, but the last third of the century, beginning in 1967, was supposed to be a period of peace (Miki 1984a: 286). The argument is based on the idea that the spread of nuclear arms is awakening the world to the same revelation Japan awoke to at the end of the war, that militarism and ideological politics do not pay; economism does (Miki 1984b). By means of economism and peaceful politics Japan had risen from extreme poverty to prosperity, and the same road of economic construction is open to all other countries. With the new breeze of economic development blowing in Asia, more and more countries seem to be adopting that road. The future prospects of Asia are emphasized, and if the remaining third of the twentieth century were to be spent on peaceful construction, the twenty-first century (*nijū isseiki*) (Miki 1984a: 286) would present a peaceful and prosperous Asian Pacific region. Both the geographical category of the Asian Pacific region, and the temporal category of the next thirty years and beyond, are essential ingredients of the Miki Conception.

'The Twenty-first Century' had become a catchword by 1967, following a boom of future studies in Japan. It was a continuation of the theme of growth, and resulted in a multitude of various visions. The model of Japanese visions was research that had been conducted in Western Europe and the United States during the 1960s (Okita 1967: 9), but in Japan future studies acquired a special meaning. They were extremely economistic, most discussants being economists, and there was a tendency among them to equate future research with economics (*miraigaku wa keizaigaku to onaji koto da*) (Sakamoto J. 1967b: 264).

The time was appropriate for that kind of national exercise. In 1965, 20 years had passed since the end of the war. In 1967, it had been 100 years since Emperor Meiji had ascended the throne. The crowning event in 1967 was Japan's economy becoming the second largest among the Western trading nations. These factors were duly noted by the discussants (Koyama 1967: 30). Various government agencies built up visions of Japan's future (Okita and Murobuse 1967: 258–71). Okita Saburo remarked that especially long-term visions were in full bloom (Okita 1967: 9). The Japan Economic Research Center organized seminars and international conferences where both the historical record of Japan's growth and its economic development were studied, and various visions were formed (Shinohara and Fujino 1967).

The euphoric rhetoric of these studies is easily comparable with the rhetoric of the Ikeda Plan, and confidence in the future is based on confidence in the continuation of economic growth. In a JERC survey of the opinions of Japanese economic experts, it was found that 40 per cent of them expected Japan's present high rate of growth (9–11 per cent) to continue up to 1975, although the majority (54.4 per cent of them) expected growth to slow to a yearly rate of

6–8 per cent. That is also the rate at which the majority of 61.5 per cent of them expected the Japanese economy to grow between 1975 and 1985 (Okita and Murobuse 1967: 250). As the economists well knew, the growth rate of 6–8 per cent meant doubling the size of the economy during a 10-year period, and they were thus conservatively following the Ikeda Plan (Koyama 1967: 30–1; Matsumoto 1967: 121). That high growth must end was not seriously questioned, and this gave the basic undertone to all visions of the time.

The idea of 100 years since the ascension of Meiji easily translated to the idea of 100 years from 1967, which brought in the concept of the twenty-first century (Koyama 1967: 27; Nakayama 1967: 1; Sakamoto J. 1967a: 5; Okita *et al.* 1967: 51). In practice, studies tended to be restricted to the following 20 or 30 years, and the next century was left unmapped. However, that rather tended to heighten the emotional load of the idea of *nijū isseiki*. As its contents were not defined, the idea assumed the general dynamism of the theme of growth, a shining bright future towards which Japan was moving.

For instance, the future Tokyo of 1985 is compared with London and New York as the central point of Asia, just as London is presented as the central point of Europe, and New York that of the Americas. The text does not go any further than the year 1985, but it gives grounds for the reader's imagination to continue the trend, as it is full of exclamations about the enormous developmental energy (*kyodaina hatten no enerugii*) of Tokyo. The other component of the image is that there are no more examples for Tokyo to follow, either in Japan or in other countries. Tokyo has come to stand in the vanguard (*sentan*) of the development of world history (Okita and Sakamoto J. 1966: 7–8). Other similar images afloat at the time included the idea of Japan as a special state (*tokuchō kokka*), and as a grand experimental state on the cutting edge of world history (Sakamoto J. 1967a: 24; Koyama 1967: 26–7). Thus far Japan had been presented as a follower, but here the image of global leadership in terms of the flying geese theory is presented.

This image of the twenty-first century is, however, strictly econo-mistic. Military or political images are not floated alongside it. There is expected to be a convergence of the capitalist and socialist systems, and development is expected to take off in the developing world. This sets the stage for the ending of political tensions, and for real world-wide economic integration (Okita *et al.* 1967). Japan is given the attributes of a peaceful cultural country (*heiwakokka-bunkakokka Nihon*) (Okita and Sakamoto J. 1966: 8), a country which does not use military power (*buryoku wo tsukawanai kokka*), and a country which is big, but not strong in the military-political sense (*ōkii ga kyōkoku de wa nai kokka*) (Sakamoto J. 1967a: 24). In spite of the grand economistic attributes given her, Japan is still seen as a small country in the global political system. However, here we are approaching the end of that theme.

This is also the sense in which Foreign Minister Miki Takeo's references to the twenty-first century in the Asian Pacific region have to be understood. His idea meant that in the twenty-first century the Asian Pacific region will become a great, prosperous, and important place, but exclusively concentrated on economic development. All of the three Miki slogans, *Ajia no shinfū, Ajia-Taiheiyō chi iki,* and *nijū isseiki* belong together, forming one package.

In his rhetoric, Miki deliberately reinterprets the meanings of such value-laden geographical terms as east, west, north, and south. The problem of Asian Pacific development is depicted as being at the point of intersection of East–West and North–South problems (Miki 1984c: 305–6). East and West do not, however, have the meaning they have when seen from the Western European perspective, from which both communism and Asia would be situated in the East, while Democracy and the Euro–American area would be situated in the West. In the rhetoric of the *Ō-Bei* countries the West tends to be a concept valued positively, while the East tends to have a negative value. The more Japan approaches the *Ō-Bei* countries the more this usage of words is bound to disturb the Japanese, and Miki's reinterpretation of the terms can be seen as a reflection of this. In Miki's rhetoric, the West represents Asia, which is situated on the western side of the Pacific Ocean. It is the word of the yellow people and Asian culture. The East represents the eastern side of the Ocean, the white people with their culture of European origin. The construction is not purely geographical, however, because Miki also places Australia and New Zealand into the East together with the United States and Canada.

The construction has several useful meanings. First, it is a way of elevating the status of Asia by linking it with the positively laden word, West. Second, it is a way of excluding the political East–West dimension from the discussion, making it appear irrelevant in the Asian Pacific setting. Third, it is a way of placing Japan into a doubly Western situation, initially as a member of the group of Western advanced industrialized countries, then as a member of the Western Pacific countries.

North and South are equally value-laden terms. They appeared during the 1960s, and were used extensively, for instance, in the first UNCTAD Conference in 1964; North representing the developed countries, South the developing countries. Usually Miki uses the terms in this sense in the Asian Pacific setting, but he also plays with the idea of using geography as the determinant, i.e., making Australia and New Zealand represent South, while Japan, South Korea, and Taiwan would represent North (Miki 1984e: 313–14). Here too, Japan would appear in a doubly positive position of being a Northern country in two settings.

Although the ranking dimensions are thus occasionally mixed, Miki also at times emphasizes the differences between the two parts of the Asian Pacific area:

> White Pacific and yellow Asia, leading Pacific and following Asia, Pacific of the western culture and Asia of the eastern culture: the two are different in all fields. There is only one common human interest that binds them together, namely the psychological and material wish towards a more prosperous way of living.
>
> (Miki 1984d: 311)

In Miki's sense, prosperity includes both economic prosperity, which would be created by increased trade and development of the whole region, and the prosperity of security, which would also be created by economic development, and by letting the ideological and political tensions fade away. The diminishing of conflicts in Asia would directly increase the security and well-being of the Pacific countries, too. Miki obviously has in mind things like American soldiers not needing to fight in Korea or Vietnam, nuclear proliferation in Asia being stopped, and both Australia and New Zealand not being drawn deeply into the structure of the Cold War.

Like the economists, Miki also argues that to help Asia develop, the assistance of all of the Pacific countries would be needed. He presents, for instance, statistics, according to which Asia is the most neglected of all developing regions in terms of developmental assistance: Africa receives US $6 per head yearly, Latin America US $4.20, and Asia US $3.30. If the massive aid given to Vietnam is excluded, Asia receives only US $1.60 per head yearly (Miki 1984c: 307). Miki in no way defines Asia, but the accuracy of the argument itself is not important; what is important is the mathematical formula used to back it up. The argument is based on the idea of balance, making it appear as rightful that aid to Asia should be increased. Japan is depicted here as too small to be able to do much by itself, so that the main point is to draw the United States to commit itself heavily to the economic development of Asia. In spite of the self-satisfied exclamations of the economic success of Japan, Miki also returns to the idea of the smallness of Japan in this kind of practical context.

Besides the new geographical definition of the Asian–Pacific area, the temporal dimension of mutual future prosperity, and the argument of common humanity, there is also an additional 'glue' which ties the region together. That is Japan. Japan can act in the role of creating a bridge across the Pacific (Miki 1984c: 306). Japan is not only geographically located between the two coasts of the Pacific, but it is also both an Eastern and a Western country. It is among the industrialized Pacific countries, and geographically an Asian country. It combines both Western and Eastern cultures. Japan would thus be in the centre of two worlds. It would serve in a mediating role between them when seen on the regional level, and benefit enormously from the central role when seen on the level of Japan's national interest.

It is important to note here, when analysing the very powerful images Miki creates, that he does not talk about an 'Asian–American area'. It would in a sense be much more logical as a geographical term, depicting the two continents where people live and engage in their activities, connected by the salty water between them. One reason may be that Australia and New Zealand have to be included – but neither is the expression 'Austral–Asian–American area', nor other such combination used. Handy political slogans, such as 'Double-A Area', 'Triple-A Area', or even 'A-Class Area' could be created out of such geographical terms. However, they would place Japan only in the Asian group, and it is just this exclusive image from which the Japanese try to escape. Such expressions would not adequately convey the new identity the Japanese are creating for themselves as a *Pacific* country.

Miki's final probe into the ideology of the Asian–Pacific area relates to the future. The world – as a politico-economic-cultural entity – formerly revolved with Europe as its centre. At that time the part of Asia that Japan is situated in came to be referred to as the Far East, (*Kyokutō*), beyond 'Central East' (*Chūkintō*) and 'Near East' (*Kintō*). Miki finds this degrading. Reality has questioned the central position of Europe, but, so to speak, vocabulary and the general way of using language retain the former world system. Europe should be dropped from its central place also on the conceptual level. Miki's answer is the Asian–Pacific area. A new world situation is developing, and with a view to the twenty-first century, Miki envisages the emergence of a new era, the 'Asian–Pacific era' (*Ajia-Taiheiyō jidai*), when the Asian–Pacific area will replace Europe as the centre of the world (Miki 1984d: 310).

The Miki Conception plays on all of the important themes of the discussion of post-war Japanese economists. Over these themes he weaves the exclamations of the boom of future studies during 1966–7, and the geographic image of the Asian–Pacific region developed in the discussion on integration. Miki's rhetoric uses extremely strong images of a common destiny for the Asian Pacific countries. The destiny leads them as a group towards material prosperity, global importance, and splendid historical grandeur. This common destiny creates conceptual unity in the grouping. Another unifying element, Europe as a common enemy – although this image is far from strong – is also used. Finally Japan, as the Bridge over the Pacific, as the essential member in connecting the Asian and the Pacific countries with each other, is presented as the centre of the centre of the future world.

EXPOSURE TO INTERNATIONAL DISCUSSION

In June 1966 the Asian and Pacific Council (ASPAC) was created, primarily instigated by South Korea. It was promoted as an association for regional co-operation, and the first meeting was attended by ministers from Australia, the Republic of China, Japan, the Republic of Korea, Malaysia, New Zealand, the Republic of the Philippines, Thailand, and the Republic of Vietnam. The Kingdom of Laos sent an observer. From the point of view of the discussion being conducted in Japan the name of the association was, so to speak, right, but membership was too limited, and the objectives were considered with misgivings. ASPAC had among its expressed objectives the increase of cultural and economic co-operation with the other member countries, but its main objective was political and ideological, i.e., the creation of a regional association to assist the front-line countries of South Vietnam, South Korea, and Taiwan in the containment of communism. ASPAC never became an influential organization, and after 1972 it no longer had meetings at the council level (Shibusawa 1984: 45, 87).

An association like this can naturally be developed in various directions. While attending the second meeting of ASPAC in July 1967 in Bangkok, Miki strongly argues that ASPAC should not be developed as an anti-communist association (Miki 1984e). Instead he argues for developing ASPAC as an economic organization with open membership, which should be enlarged, although he does not elaborate on this point in his speech.

However, clearly ASPAC was not what the Japanese integration-ists were looking for, and instead Miki gave his support to the PAFTA proposal of Kojima Kiyoshi. In March and April of 1967 he dispatched Kojima on a mission to the four Pacific countries and England to sound out possibilities for an international academic conference to discuss the establishment of a Pacific Free Trade Area. Kojima's mission was successful and he was able to recruit suitable participants for the conference (Kojima 1980: 2; letter 1992). The conference was held in January of 1968 in the Japan Economic Research Center, which as a private organization was an ideal place for a low profile probe of the international reception of Kojima's proposal. The title of the conference was *Pacific Trade and Develop-ment*. Kojima Kiyoshi and Okita Saburo together took care of organ-izing the meeting. In contrast to ASPAC, the members of the conference were carefully chosen so that they were all economists, rather than politicians. It was a way of ensuring that discussion remained within the professional economic sphere, and did not leak unnecessarily into the political sector. In their preface the organizers emphasize that 'our study should be academic and free from various pressures except truth' (Kojima and Okita 1968: i). 'Academic' in their sense, however, means just trying to remain outside the sector of politics, understood as ideological, military, or power-political topics of discussion. The conference certainly constituted a politi-cal act, as a move towards restructuring the Asian–Pacific inter-national economic system. Kojima and Okita clearly emphasize that they are policy-oriented, claiming that their studies 'should certainly stimulate, within 3 or 5 years, moves by nations around the Pacific Basin towards closer economic co-operation'.

However much the organizers tried to shun the political sector, it inevitably crept into the conference with the participants. The coun-tries were in different situations with respect to Pacific integration, and as they considered themselves as representatives of their coun-tries, the different national interests of the countries were reflected in their presentations. What kept the conference together was Koji-ma's PAFTA proposal, to which all participants reacted in their various ways. An indication of the value of the PAFTA proposal as a well-thought-out idea was the way it had been able to captivate the interest of other Pacific economists, whether they were for or against it.

The basic point in the PAFTA idea, especially as coloured by

Miki, was that the whole Asian–Pacific area constituted a clear region, and the five Pacific countries formed a still closer unit. A basic issue dividing the participants was whether they accepted this proposition, or whether they conceptualized differently the geographical situation.

All Japanese participants had adopted the idea. Kojima himself in his presentation talks about the Pacific as 'one of the two major centres of world trade and ranks alongside Western Europe'. The Pacific here means PAFTA, and its counterpart is the EEC. Kojima compares the ranks of PAFTA and the EEC, showing that intra-area trade in the EEC was in 1958 smaller than intra-PAFTA trade, comprising respectively 5.98 per cent and 7.99 per cent of world trade. However, since then EEC trade had grown faster, so that in 1965 intra-EEC trade already comprised 12.00 per cent, but intra-PAFTA trade only 10.38 per cent of world trade. A similar comparison is made between 'European trade', meaning trade among all Western European countries, and 'extended Pacific trade' among PAFTA, Asia excluding the socialist countries, and Latin America. Between 1958 and 1965, the former had increased its share of world trade from 19.38 per cent to 29.45 per cent, while the latter had risen from 20.36, when it had been higher, to only 21.71 per cent. In economic dynamism Western Europe thus ranks higher, and the situation elicits the following comment from Kojima:

> Extended Pacific area trade is another centre of world trade, but it has not grown so fast as has European trade, mainly due to the stagnation in exports of primary produce from developing countries in Asia and Latin America. The extended Pacific area could be the largest centre of world trade if there were closer co-operation in expanding trade and development within the area, since it has greater potential in the endowment of its population, natural resources, and capital awaiting development than already-well-developed Europe.

(Kojima 1968a: 155)

The construction of the situation in these terms makes sense only from the point of view of treating Pacific integration as a political ideology as Miki had done. The Asian–Pacific area is treated as existing in the real world, and a history is given to it. The year 1958 is logical as the beginning of the EEC, but at the same time it makes it possible to rank the two entities in a way that gives the Asian–Pacific region a glorious past. At that time it had been at a higher rank than Europe, but the situation had turned to a dismal present. At the end of the quotation Kojima clearly treats Pacific integration as a political programme which should be advanced, and the number one position in the world should be 'taken back'.

According to Kojima's argument, Latin America belongs to the idea of Pacific integration. It would be necessary from the point of view of making the United States interested in the proposal. It is interesting that here Kojima can construct an entity called Asia and Latin America (ALA) (Kojima 1968a: 156), but only in the connection that Japan is at the same time placed inside the group of the five Pacific countries. Like Miki, Kojima and the other Japanese representatives at the conference never use the expression Asia–America. Japan has to be identified principally as a Pacific country.

The importance of a PAFTA-type of regional integration has also risen in Kojima's eyes because the Kennedy Round of GATT negotiations for tariff reduction had ended in 1967. They had dragged on for years, and especially from Kojima's point of view, the results were not encouraging. The level of tariff reductions was not high, and important commodities, like agricultural products, remained protected by many countries. In addition, the difficulty of the Kennedy Round negotiations, and the negative trade balance of the United States, suggested that another major round of global tariff reductions would not be feasible during the next 10, or even 20, years. That seemed to be another step in the slow process leading away from the era of global economic integration. This has turned him in favour of regional economic integration among the PAFTA countries, in the sense of a complete free trade area (Kojima 1968a: 163, 168). He no longer has any doubts on the matter. PAFTA would ensure that Japan would not be shut out of the markets of these English-speaking countries, and left alone with the poor Asian countries, as happened during the process leading to the Second World War. In addition to the preferred Japanese ways of identifying themselves, this material factor also necessitates the Japanese placing so much emphasis on the Pacific group of five countries.

On the other hand, PAFTA was only an argument. It was a reconstruction of reality on the rhetorical level, but not a material reality. PAFTA should not develop towards a closed trading block, the development potentiality of the Asian and Latin American countries should be allowed to come to fruition, and the possible harmful effects of free trade among the PAFTA countries should be taken care of. For the practical realization of the PAFTA proposal, with all these objectives in mind, Kojima emphasizes the importance of proceeding through functional, rather than institutional, integration

(Kojima 1968a: 176). PAFTA should not be set up with a declaration as an institutional entity, but rather the groundwork should be done first through functional co-operation. To this end Kojima proposes the adoption of three moral codes of international behaviour:

1 A code of good conduct in the field of trade policy, which means moving towards dismantling trade barriers among the five, particularly those that inhibit imports of agricultural products and light manufactures.
2 A code of overseas investment not only among the five advanced countries but also towards the developing countries. It would minimize fears of American capital domination, and maximize protection of United States balance of payments.
3 A code of aid and trade policies towards associated Asian and Latin American developing countries, to encourage their development and help their trade expand.

As a practical expression of these codes Kojima proposes the setting up of two organizations, a Pacific Bank for Investment and Settlement, and an Organization for Pacific Aid and Development (OPTAD). The features of the latter should be similar to those of the OECD, including committees on trade, investment, and aid. With these new proposals PAFTA is removed somewhat more to the future, as the final institutional goal of co-operation, while the functional OPTAD becomes the immediate goal.

Other Japanese presentations tend to echo similar views, and together they present a fairly unified front. In discussing agricultural trade over the Pacific ocean, Hemmi Kenzo starts with a similar comparison between the EEC and the Pacific area, arguing that the latter is 'the second biggest trading area of agricultural commodities in the world' (Hemmi 1968: 251). If the potential of the region for growth and development – this qualification has by now become a fixed expression – was taken into view, it should be seen as the most important trading area for those commodities.

Ashiya Einosuke starts directly from Kojima's ideas, concentrating on devising a plan for a bank, to be called Pacific Bank for Investment and Settlement. It would be necessary on two counts. First, as Kojima's calculations had shown, Japan would be the country to benefit most from free trade among the five countries, while Canada, Australia and New Zealand would be the losers, at least in the initial stages. The Bank would assist them in their probable balance of payment difficulties, and in building their industries towards a more competitive direction. Second, the Bank would be an instru-

ment for directing capital to the Asian and Latin American developing countries, to help them in making the extraction of their raw
materials and agricultural products more efficient, as well as in
advancing development of their light industries. Ashiya does not
clearly face the problem of from where the capital for the Bank
would come (Ashiya 1968).

Okita Saburo and Ohnishi Akira presented a paper dealing with
Japan's role in Asian economic development. Japan, as the economic
leader of the Asian countries, is presented as having a moral obligation to continue its 'high growth tempo', so that she can develop
herself as a market for the products of the Asian developing countries. Japan could also provide for imports of technologically-sophis-
ticated products needed by the developing countries, as well as give
aid in general. The Asian developing countries would also need
larger markets than Japan, markets that could be provided by the
advanced Pacific countries combined. At the same time, even though
Japan could quite well provide for a large part of the imports needed
by them, it would not be able to provide for the capital they would
need:

> the GNP of North America is 15 times the aggregate GNP of
> all the countries in Latin America, and the GNP of Western
> Europe as a whole is 10 times that of Africa. However, Japan's
> GNP only equals to the aggregate GNP of the nations in South
> and Southeast Asia. Thus aid to the developing countries in Asia
> is too gigantic a problem for Japan alone. It naturally follows
> that the joint and coordinated aid efforts by the five developed
> countries in the Pacific area are highly desirable in the light of
> the proportion of the aggregate economic output of the developed
> nations to that of the developing nations in the Asian–Pacific
> region.
>
> (Okita and Ohnishi 1968: 371)

Although Japan has attained the economic rank of the Western
European countries like Britain, West Germany and France, as
Okita and Ohnishi also emphasize (Okita and Ohnishi 1968: 359),
it is still too small a country for the task of directing massive capital
flows to the Asian developing countries. The formulation of the
argument is a clever construction, a contemporary development of
Okita's arguments during the 1950s. It allows Okita and Ohnishi to
place Japan on the same proud rank with Western European and
North American countries but, arguing from an economic perspective, succeeds in avoiding the politically-sensitive issues of a political,

great power status. At the same time Japan, as a national economy, is contrasted with the economic regions of North America and Western Europe, so that Japan's problem really can be made to appear as gigantic. The implications of the numerical values given, 15, 10, and 1 are very easy to grasp. Okita and Ohnishi can thus argue both from the perspective of a high rank and the position of a small country at the same time. The key word in the quotation is the inconspicuous 'naturally', which implies that another unnamed partner in the Asian–Pacific region has the moral obligation to foot the bill.

The position in greatest contrast with the Japanese is that of the economists from the United States. They also present a fairly unified front. They are conscious that their country would be the one that would pay, and are reluctant to advance discussion on any but their own terms. They refuse to accept the Japanese geographical concepts, but instead argue with the globalistic concepts of a hegemonic superpower. They like to concentrate on discussing the Kennedy Round and its effects. When they discuss regional integration, they either stay on the non-committed abstract level of economic theory, treating regionalism as the second-best solution when 'superior courses of action', namely global integration, are closed off (Cooper 1968: 306). Another way is always to speak of efforts at regional integration in the plural, e.g., customs unions, free trade areas, or free trade arrangements, always trying to keep more than one such existing or hypothetical arrangement under discussion (Johnson 1968: passim). Nor do they ever use the concept Asian–Pacific area, but always keep these two words separate, in quite different contexts.

The other striking difference from the Japanese rhetoric is that economic goals are subsumed under political goals. For instance, Ranis, who treats foreign assistance as 'one of the most important tools of foreign policy', discusses the whole issue of aiding Asian developing countries as a way of helping the free world countries to compete with the communist block (Ranis 1968: 334–5). He does not separate conceptually military and economic assistance, but discusses them together.

It is interesting that even the word 'contain', which was used extensively in the military-political rhetoric of the United States as 'containing communism', is also used in a similar way in the economic sphere. The American economists talk about 'containing' the discriminatory effects of the EEC (Johnson 1968: 234). In view of the recent conclusion of the Kennedy Round, and the balance-of-payment problems, the United States is not expected to be willing to contemplate any additional moves towards free trade. Johnson considers the possibility of increasing economic co-operation with Canada, but on other types of regional co-operation he comments:

> At the present time, the constellation of circumstances that would most probably evoke a new U.S. initiative would be the opportunity to strike back at the countries of the European Economic Community, from which the external pressure for the new restraint policies has come, through the formation of a free trade area with E.F.T.A. and Canada that would discriminate strongly against E.E.C. exports of manufactures. But the development of the war in Vietnam might lead the United States to contemplate a Pacific Free Trade Area as a means of strengthening its political position in Asia vis-a-vis Communist China.
>
> (Johnson 1968: 239–40)

Johnson represents simultaneously both the London School of Economics and the University of Chicago, which may explain part of his special geographical emphasis on North America and Western Europe, but he is only the most vocal representative in this matter, there being no essential difference between him and the other American economists. The argument is based on the situation of a superpower, which is conscious of its capability to strike left and right with trade wars or military wars against countries that have angered it. This is the only position from which regional integration is contemplated. Between the proposed North Atlantic Free Trade Area (NAFTA) and PAFTA, the first is clearly preferred, while 'Pacific free trade would be a sequel and extension or adjunct of Atlantic free trade'. Johnson recommends, however, a narrower Pacific free trade arrangement among Australia, New Zealand and Japan, suitable for these 'relatively small, not yet fully mature industrial economies'. He also accuses these countries, as well as Canada, of trying to 'enjoy a free ride' during the Kennedy Round negotiations, trying to benefit from tariff reductions between the United States, Britain, and the EEC, while not offering any of their own (Johnson 1968: 244–50).

Alone among the countries concerned, the United States retains the highest rank according to Johnson's rhetoric, while the others are shown in their proper place as immature and small economies. They are treated conceptually just like the Japanese are treating the Asian countries. They are advised to create a free trade area among themselves, and offered only an associative relationship within the grouping of more mature economies (comp. Kojima 1968a: 154).

The Canadian position is less unified. One of the Canadian economists, Bruce Wilkinson, makes a Kojima-type of statistical study of the PAFTA countries from the point of view of Canada, thus accepting the Japanese way of conceptualizing that part of the world (Wilkinson 1968). The other Canadian, H. Edward English, does not accept Kojima's vocabulary at all, but likes to talk about a Pacific free trade group, or a free trade association. He also refuses to accept the Japanese concept of the Asian–Pacific area, as well as their way of treating PAFTA as a unit:

> the Pacific area is not really a region; it is a hemisphere or a little more . . . there are three regions involved, one large – North America, one medium sized – Japan, and the other small – Australia and New Zealand.
>
> (English 1968a: 23–4)

Both Canadians like to argue in a way which places them in a high rank. In their case that means emphasizing North America as a region, and the close relationship Canada has with the United States. English, especially, emphasizes Canada's Atlantic identity, her long history as part of the British Empire, and her trading relations with European countries – up to the point of calling Japan a 'non-Atlantic' country (English 1968a: 18).

However, the Canadians use economic rhetoric, without showing enthusiasm for supporting the political objectives of the United States. They also both give serious consideration to the idea of Pacific integration, although they tend to leave the Asian countries out of the discussion. They are most concerned about the economic structure of their country. Canada is competitive in exporting agricultural products and raw materials. Canada also has a wide industrial base, but built up behind protective walls, so that it is not very competitive internationally. The productivity of the Canadian economy at that time was on the average one-third lower than that of the American economy. The problem with PAFTA is that it would place Canada in a competitive relationship with both Australia and New Zealand in the export of primary products, while the low wages of Japan would make it difficult to compete with Japan in industrial products. Problems would be smaller in a North American free trade arrangement; the lower Canadian wages would close at least some of the gap in productivity between the two countries. However, both Canadians are after all fairly confident that before long free trade conditions would improve the state of their economy, even make it prosper, assuming an appropriate adjustment period. At present various political groups favouring the continuance of protection seem to be strong in Canada, but still it would be useful to further study the idea of economic integration involving the Pacific (English 1968a: 22; Wilkinson 1968: 49).

What is curious after one has become familiar with the Japanese position – which tends to regard the other four countries as a culturally unified block of English-speaking countries – is that Australia and New Zealand do not figure extensively in the discussion of the Canadians. The countries had never had an especially extensive trading relationship, and even that was declining. It is the United States which looms large on the Canadian horizon as a market, Japan holding the second place, but Australia and New Zealand do not feature highly in their arguments.

The small New Zealand presents a special case. Especially as constructed by Leslie V. Castle, of all the countries, New Zealand had held the closest relationship with Britain:

> Most immigrants were of British stock and retained close family and business ties with the 'Old Country' or 'Home'. There was a common language, a common sense of destiny and purpose. New Zealand regarded itself as an outpost of England and of Empire.
>
> (Castle 1968: 100)

New Zealand developed much like a county of England, only situated on the other side of the globe. Even as an agricultural country it was highly specialized in serving the British market. The three key products were butter, lamb, and cheese. Over a period of several decades New Zealanders grew used to relying on the British to absorb a steady increase of about 3 per cent per annum of New Zealand's exports with slowly increasing prices. Thus they were used to a secure source of income, which was on a fairly high level. No other markets were needed, nor sought for. New Zealanders were used to a peaceful existence, a tranquil pastoral life, with stable rather than rising incomes. Even the climate was good. These were the nostalgic good old days.

Things began to take a turn for the worse during the 1950s, when the production of meat and milk in Britain rose rapidly. European and North American producers began to export their surpluses to world markets, while continuing to protect their own. GATT does not feature much in the vocabulary of the New Zealanders, except as a source of disillusionment. The final blow came when Britain applied to the EEC in 1961 without making a blanket reservation for agricultural products. The move was greeted with 'a mixture of rage and incredulity', as many had not believed that Britain could even contemplate imposing tariffs on New Zealand products while allowing imports from the EEC to enter duty free. De Gaulle's veto in 1963 came as a temporary relief. The New Zealanders concentrated on securing a bargaining position for themselves. It meant in practice that 'the generally agreed official line appears to be that the best outcome can be achieved if New Zealand does not reduce her degree of dependence on the United Kingdom market' (Castle 1968: 90).

However, new markets also began to be sought. The easiest solution appeared in the neighbourhood. The New Zealand–Australia Free Trade Agreement (NAFTA, not to be confused with the idea of a North Atlantic Free Trade Area, also abbreviated as NAFTA) was signed in 1965. However, it did not mean much. Its coverage was narrow, confined to products which were already being traded, and only a few items of manufactured products were included. It reflected bitter opposition of the New Zealand Manufacturer's Federation and New Zealand's commitment to guaranteeing employment. The Minister of Industries and Commerce declared that no industry should be damaged by the Agreement (Castle 1968: 96).

New Zealand had developed various industries, like meat preserving and freezing, dairy products, pulp, paper, and other forestry products, fertilizer plants, vehicles, and farm machinery. The entire production catered, however, almost completely for the home market behind very high protective walls. Very little was exported except foodstuffs. An example is the New Zealand electronics industry: 'The entire market is not quite large enough to cater for one optimum-size plant producing radios, yet in 1965 there were some 26 firms engaged in the production of radio sets or components' (McDougall 1968: 123).

New Zealand would not be able to adjust its industries quickly enough to be able to compete internationally, and the markets for agricultural products were contracting in the traditional market. In this situation only Japan appeared as a 'really bright spot' (Castle 1968: 92). Although the government, and the nationalistic pro-British farmers were slower to act, economists were beginning to eye Japan with interest. Japan was protectionist with respect to local production, just like the United States, but with a big population on a small land area, and with the economy growing fast, Japan would clearly be in need of importing lots of foodstuffs. Especially if a free trade arrangement could be created, New Zealand could very well compete in the Japanese market. Only Japan looked like a possible alternative to the British market. The problem would be the concessions the New Zealanders would have to make to increase imports from Japan, but the creation of more competitive industries really seemed necessary. To guarantee even the stability of incomes, exports should be diversified, and a larger share of them should be composed of industrial products. The long tradition of protection and easy life would, however, make any opening of the economy a long and arduous process, as the feeble attempt of NAFTA had demonstrated.

To Castle, PAFTA seems like an interesting proposition. However, he really discusses Australia and Japan, as well as wider Asian markets which might also start to absorb more dairy products if living standards were to rise there. Of Canada and the United States he remarks that they 'need not be left out of account' (Castle 1968: 107). Disillusionment about their past trading practices no doubt explains much of this.

The Australian case was similar to that of New Zealand, except that its economy was larger, and consequently it had never been able to be as dependent on a single market as the neighbouring country. Ian A. McDougall, formerly of Australia, at the time at Massey University in New Zealand, is even more critical of countries engaging in agricultural protection than Castle. He only discusses his own idea of a Japanese–Australian–New Zealand Free Trade Area (JANFTA). The high growth of Japan is the centre of his argument. Growth would improve Japan's prospects for future absorption of increasing quantities of not only agricultural products, but also minerals. Japan had already displaced Britain as the most important export market for Australia in this sense. However, just as in Canada and New Zealand, the industrial sector of Australia was varied, but well protected. An example corresponding to the radios of New Zealand was car production in Australia, where 14 firms were engaged in the manufacture or assembly of motor vehicles, and a wide range of cars, station-wagons and other vehicles were produced (McDougall 1968: 130–1). An indication of the state of the economy was that the largest foreign market for the manufactured products of Australia was New Zealand. However, McDougall also recognizes the necessity of creating competitive export industries and, like the Canadians, he is optimistic of the chances of Australia, providing that a period of careful adjustment be allowed. While discussing his JANFTA, McDougall also thinks that 'at a later date' other countries, too, such as Canada, the United States, and some of the less-developed economies of the Pacific Basin, could be included (McDougall 1968: 133), but he wants to start very carefully.

Peter Drysdale is, among all of the non-Japanese attendants at the Conference, the one most interested in Kojima's original proposal. He uses throughout his paper the concept of PAFTA. He has in a sense taken a large part of Kojima's argument and applied it to the Australian case. Although he is also very critical of the protectionism of the United States, which places heavy duties, not only on Australia's dairy exports, but also on her exports of wool and minerals, Drysdale points out that, at least as an origin of imports, the United States had in the previous years displaced Britain from first place (Drysdale 1968: 194). Looking thus at the pattern of overall trade, the Pacific as a whole constitutes a major part of Australia's world.

Drysdale is also the most optimistic of the non-Japanese economists in his general outlook, using more than others arguments derived from classical free trade theory. He shows a high degree of reliance on the prospects of the Australian manufacturing industry. It is interesting that he also constructs such a view of the world that he can argue optimistically from the position of a high rank, claiming that 'Australians, proudly, are the Norwegians of the Pacific' (Drysdale 1968: 208) – whatever he means by that.

The greatest similarity between Drysdale and the Japanese economists is that he also discusses extensively the Asian countries, both from the moral point of view regarding raising their living standards, and from the point of view of export markets (Drysdale 1968: 212–13). As he constructs it, the Australian position in relation to them is similar to Japan's. He regards Australia and Japan as occupying a similar kind of mentor role, derived in particular from the case of the Territory of Papua-New Guinea, which was under Australian guardianship at the time.

Looking at the whole discussion in the Conference, there is a striking difference between the rhetoric of the Japanese and the other participants. The Japanese appear to have a different mentality. They are always talking about growth and development. These words and similar expressions appearing continuously in their texts relate to a movement upwards, towards a positively evaluated future. The other economists are talking more about stability, ways of guaranteeing the present level of well-being, or modest improvements on it. They do not build nebulous visions about the future.

Even Drysdale, the most optimistic of them, does not build visions of the Pacific as the centre of the world in the next century.

The reception of Kojima's PAFTA proposal by the economists of the Pacific countries was thus mixed. If we look at the central concept, only the Canadian Wilkinson and the Australian Drysdale adopted it as the basis for their papers. No one used the concept of the Asian–Pacific area, although Drysdale came close.

There also appeared a clear division among the countries, which did not run between Japan and the rest, but between North America and Oceania. The latter countries were the warmest towards regional economic integration including Japan, while the former were the coolest. Probably the greatest disappointment was the position of the United States. It was interested more in the Atlantic area, while the Pacific area received attention only of a secondary degree, and even that tended to be coloured with ideas of military and political strategy. The Americans perceived no urgency. They tended to think that nothing special needed to be done immediately, while all of the others were thinking in terms of the immediate necessity of some first steps. However, even the American participants were not hostile to the idea, but mildly interested, leaving the door open for future discussion. In his analysis in 1990 of the reasons why the Pacific Free Trade Area could not eventually be set up, Kojima gives substantially the same reasons, which had already come out in this first conference (Kojima 1990: 3–7).

The final communiqué put together at the end of the conference calls for step-by-step moves towards closer co-operation in trade policies among Pacific economies, and for more co-ordination in their aid policies. It also stressed the need for continued public discussion of these problems in all of the countries, as well as for their consideration by their respective governments. The participants also agreed that a new conference should be held soon, in about a year's time, and the place was set to be the East–West Center in Hawaii (Pacific Trade and Development Conference 1968: iii-iv). The place was obviously well chosen symbolically. The conference thus ended by acting as a small but not uninfluential lobby in the direction of their national publics and governments. It also took the first steps towards transforming itself into a permanent body for international discussion.

4 Conclusion

This study has analysed Japanese discussions of the 1950s and 1960s on international economic integration. The selection of Japan as the only country to be studied has had its drawbacks. Only brief references have been made to discussion in other Asian countries, in connection with the Economic Commission for Asia and the Far East (ECAFE), although related discussions have also been held in other similar international meetings (Kojima 1980: 2). Discussion processes in Australia, New Zealand, Canada and the United States have not been studied beyond those at the first Pacific Trade and Development Conference. Using the perspective of Japan has been one-sided, but then, discussion in the other countries does not seem to have been very widespread, being confined mainly to newspapers and some business circles (Drysdale 1981; Pacific Basin Economic Co-operation Committee 1967).

The Japanese discussion process seems to have been the most fruitful. ECAFE plans were not proceeding very well; the Asians were not in a position to engage in far-reaching regional integration; even the Association of Southeast Asian Nations (ASEAN) which was formed in 1967 by Thailand, the Philippines, Malaysia, Singapore, and Indonesia was barely working during the 1960s, and only after the end of the Vietnam War in 1975 did it begin to play a more important regional role. In spite of the early stirrings of discussion, the vision of the four other Pacific countries tended to be directed towards Europe. With the Kennedy Round of the General Agreement on Tariffs and Trade (GATT) negotiations going on, and Britain's entry into the European Economic Community (EEC) blocked for the time being, during the 1960s these countries had no immediately pressing reason to start a wide discussion about a Pacific orientation, although the situation of the Oceanian countries was somewhat different from that of the United States and Canada.

During the 1960s Japan was in the unique position of being situated in the middle of the Asian–Pacific area in more than one sense: in terms of her geography, culture, international rank, industrial structure, economic capabilities, and trading relations. The Pacific War and the Cold War together had ruptured Japan's traditional relationship with her nearest Asian neighbours, and when the possible threat from European integration hit the region in the early 1960s, Japan was already in the process of trying to find a meaningful place for herself in the region. Here was a suitably critical situation, providing a reason to do something, and during the 1960s the self-confidence for grand visions emerged. Probably these factors explain why discussion on regional integration in Japan started so early and so earnestly among intellectuals, and why they found a ready response among politicians. As seen in the Pacific Trade and Development Conference in 1968, Japanese discussion on Pacific integration by that time had become more advanced than in the other countries. In spite of the internationalism of the Japanese discussants and their connections with foreign ideas, the Japanese discussion developed on Japanese terms, in a Japanese setting, and formed a distinct body of texts.

The following general conclusions can perhaps be made. Japanese discussion on regional integration was spurred on by external influences. There were the cautious discussions conducted in United Nations circles during the 1950s, but the most important ones were the formation of the EEC and the spread of the idea of regional economic integration around the globe. Also, demands made at the turn of the decade under the auspices of GATT for opening the Japanese economy to freer trade contributed to an intensification of discussion on Japan's external economic relations.

In Japan the question of integration came to be discussed at a time of rising self-esteem in connection with rapid economic growth and development. This brought out the problem of Japan's identity, an indication of which was the importance of the category of geography in the discussion. The transformation of Japan's identity took place in the form of small changes in the definitions given for Japan and qualifications of those definitions.

The first stage of these changes begins at the end of the Second World War, when Japan was interpreted pessimistically as an impoverished, small, weak, and backward Asian country. She was dependent on the United States in terms of military security and economic survival. She was placed inside the hegemonic world structure of the United States, and consequently her foreign political orientation was determined by this dominant power. Japan was defined as an Asian country, and the term 'Asia' at that time was given very low prestige. This definition was balanced by one positive qualifier, the fact that Japan was an industrialized country, and in this sense a little ahead of the other Asian countries. The difference was not seen to be great, however, as Japan was often compared with countries like India and China. China was even seen to be eclipsing Japan as the new regional power in East Asia.

In spite of perceiving herself as an Asian country Japan had difficulties in linking herself with the other Asian countries. There were varying degrees of hostility and distrust towards Japan, an attitude most pronounced among her geographically, historically and culturally closest Asian neighbours. Moreover, the two Koreas and the two Chinas were front-line countries in the Cold War, while Japan tried to stay far away from actual involvement there. Japan moved towards an economistic orientation, while the other East Asian countries remained preoccupied with a militaristic and ideological orientation. Trade with China had fallen to a low level. Although trade with Southeast Asian countries was growing, its relative importance was diminishing, the general post-war expansion of trade taking place between industrialized countries. During the first 15 years after the war Japan remained basically alone in Asia, making only discreet attempts towards economic co-operation and image healing through war reparations payments.

The year 1960 opens the second stage. The Ikeda Plan was crucial here: with its deliberate optimism and pride, it brought a definite change to the picture. The attribute of rapid economic growth became attached to the definition of Japan, and that raised her rank at a stroke. Rapid growth was an area where Japan could be better than any other country in the world. The idea was heightened by various additional factors. It offered an opportunity to brush off some of the indulgence in self-pity engaged in during the early post-war years. It was also a ranking dimension favoured by Japanese economism. As Japan had succeeded in the field most important for her on her own terms, it tended to intensify the Japanese economistic orientation. The goal of economic growth surfaced in the rest of the world at the same time, with plans for growth in the Organization for Economic Co-operation and Development (OECD) countries, and the declaration of the United Nations Development Decade. Accompanied by a period of thaw in the Cold War, this change made it possible for the Japanese to view themselves, not as a backward nation, but a nation in the vanguard of modernism: peaceful in her foreign policies and economically very successful. This laid the basis for the opening of a completely new foreign political horizon.

The Japanese international frame of reference began to change, the *Ō-Bei* countries replacing the Asian countries as the principal referents. However, at first a complex of qualifiers had to be employed. When the claim of being on the same level with the Euro–American countries was made, it had to be qualified by bringing the category of future into the picture. The structure of the claim was that at present Japan was still behind the Euro–American countries in terms of her living standards and the backwardness of some of her industries, this qualification then being negated by the idea of rapid growth, which in the future would make the previous qualifier unnecessary. The relative ease of the shift into this definition was made possible by Japan's history when, as a colonial Great Power, she had once been of the same rank as the Euro–American countries. The mental structure was already in existence in the Japanese social consciousness, and it only needed to be activated. The ranking dimensions were different from the earlier ones, economic growth and development replacing colonialism and military might, but the structure was similar. It was this factor that brought forth the demand that Japan *must* continue growing fast to be able to again attain the level of the Euro–American countries.

The third stage is reached with the discussion of regional integration during the years 1962–5. The potential economic threat emanating from Europe, and the perceived shift from global to regional integration, forced the Japanese to look for a specific region to which they could belong. In practice there were two directions, the Southeast Asian developing countries, and the four advanced Pacific countries. There were two other hypothetical directions, namely, the historical grouping of countries within the Sinic cultural sphere, and the geographical grouping of the socialist countries, but both of these directions were closed because of the political situation, and hardly appeared in discussion. Especially conspicuous in the discussion of integration was the total silence about the nearest geographical neighbour, the Soviet Union.

Both of the open directions had their advantages. Regarding the Asian orientation there had also existed a ready, historical mental image, dating especially from the 1930s and early 1940s, when the Japanese had pictured their country as the leader of Asia. This image had drawbacks, as it also contained the images of colonialism and militarism, a re-emergence of which was opposed by the

Japanese, and by the Asian countries. Neither would the new military strength of the Asian countries, nor the hegemonic position of the United States, have allowed Japan to appear on the Asian scene as a military and political leader at the time.

However, the theory of the flying geese pattern of development provided a way to circumvent psychological predilection. As an economic theory, using the image of development as a procession of leaders and followers along a one-dimensional road, it made possible the depiction of Japan in the position of a leader in Asia. The idea was confined strictly to the economic sector, had a component of prestige for Japan, and displayed a sense of responsibility towards helping Asian economic development. The future-oriented theory provided a way of identifying Japan with the Asian countries without historical burdens. There was a developmental time-lag, but otherwise Japan and the Asian countries were in a similar situation of rising towards higher levels of prosperity. Although Japan was distancing herself from Asia both mentally and in terms of her trading relationships, Asia was a place to reckon with in regard to the future. There was not one discussant in the literature analysed who advocated a policy of turning Japan's back on Asia; on the contrary, all of them to varying degrees advocated deepening her relationship with the Asian countries.

On the other hand, an Asian orientation also had its drawbacks. The concept of Asia used by the Japanese was not practical. Although they usually limited it by excluding the countries west of Pakistan, and the socialist Asian countries, the area was still too big regarding Japanese capabilities of economic assistance. The nearly total absence of China and the Koreas from the picture was a serious handicap to this orientation. In addition, Japan had neither the capabilities nor the motivation, nor any reason to start challenging the position of the United States. The creation of a regional grouping – if it would have been possible considering the misgivings of the Asian countries – without the participation of the United States might have led in that direction. There was little wish to be a great power in that sense.

Regarding Japan's psychological identity and her national interests, understood here in terms of general security and economic profit, the Pacific orientation seemed to be the ideal solution. The four advanced Pacific countries appeared as the most natural group to belong to with respect to Japan's new self-understanding as an advanced industrialized nation. The event during the first United Nations Conference on Trade and Development (UNCTAD) in

1965, when Japan was thrown out of the group of Asian nations, pointed in the same direction. Among the Pacific Free Trade Area (PAFTA) countries Japan would appear as a fairly advanced industrialized nation; admittedly poorer in gross national product (GNP) per capita and standard of living than Australia, Canada, and New Zealand, but more advanced than those countries in terms of her industrial structure. In terms of trading relations, a PAFTA would have guaranteed Japan reasonably large markets, even if Western Europe had followed the example of the socialist countries and turned into a closed economic block. Related to this was the fact that, in view of the discussion of a North Atlantic Free Trade Area, Japan faced a situation resembling the 1930s, when it was pushed out of the markets of the Euro–American countries and left alone with the poor Asian countries. That period led to the policy of Japan militarily conquering her own regional block. This was unthinkable and undiscussable during the 1960s. Although the Pacific orientation represented regionalism, it was open regionalism in as wide a way as possible. It was a logical extension of the security arrangement with the United States, although the economists did not explicitly refer to that fact, that aspect coming into the discussion through the small country theme. This orientation would have allowed Japan to remain a small country with respect to the enormous economic and military size of the United States, and to continue her rapid economic development without the danger of being pushed towards a political and military orientation.

As a member of the exclusively economic Pacific grouping, Japan could have increased co-operation with the Asian countries without political big power connotations. In the light of Asian distrust of Japan, that approach would also have been the most viable. The economic development of the Asian countries could have been assisted, but the financial burden of assistance and the burden of being their market would have been borne by the PAFTA countries as a group. Japan would have benefited economically both from trade expansion among the PAFTA countries, as well as from the expanding importing capabilities of the Asian countries, and thus the difficulties of opening Japan more to international trade would have been largely circumvented. At the same time that kind of development would have increased the overall security of Japan. As the whole Asian–Pacific structure would have been defined in economic terms, the entire ideological, political, and military confrontation in Asia would have been limited. An economistically oriented Asia would have presented the new Japan without military ambitions a far more secure environment than before. This is the way Kojima Kiyoshi's original PAFTA proposal has to be understood, as the crowning of the third stage. It was an accurate mapping of the new Pacific horizon.

The fourth stage of the process begins with the adoption of Kojima's proposal as the basis for further discussion. The Pacific industrially advanced countries came to represent a new regional identity for Japan. This was also the time when Japan had become larger than any of the Western European countries in terms of her GNP, and thus the second largest national economy in the Western trading system. This was the ultimate point to which Japan could advance as a small country. As other components of the structure remained the same, however, there was still no reason to drop that attribute. During this stage it was possible to define Japan principally as a Pacific country, and it was in connection with the Asian countries that specific qualifiers, such as the geographical situation, had to be used. The Pacific identity was the ground on which Miki Takeo's bridge over the ocean could be built, always carefully phrasing his reference to this geographical entity as the Asian–Pacific area. The category of the future, referring to growth, development, and economic dynamism, was further strengthened, and the place it was attributed to shifted once again with Miki's ideological expansion of Kojima's rather down-to-earth Pacific horizon. The concept shifted to point in the direction of building from the Asian–Pacific area a new centre of the world for the twenty-first century, Japan being in the centre of that centre.

These Japanese ideas appeared too nebulous for others at first, as exemplified by the discussions in the first international conference on Pacific economic co-operation, but they provided the basis for an intensification of discussion on Pacific integration during subsequent years. The Japanese began the process by conceptualizing the geographic terms, as well as the economic and ideological rationale, for future discussion.

After that, nothing very spectacular happened for ten years. The Pacific Free Trade and Development conferences became a yearly gathering of economists, known as the PAFTAD conferences. Already in 1969 Asian participation was included, with participants from South Korea, Taiwan, Hong Kong, the Philippines and Indonesia, and during the 1970s the conferences widened still, with even occasional participation of economists from the Soviet Union. Another professional regional grouping was also born during the 1960s. In Tokyo in 1967, a preliminary meeting was organized for setting up a Pacific Basin Economic Co-operation Committee (Pacific Basin . . . 1967), and in 1968 in Sydney, Australia the Pacific Basin Economic Council (PBEC) held its first general meeting. It was a gathering of business executives from Australia, Japan, New Zealand, the United States and Canada. Also, as in the case of PAFTAD, the membership of the PBEC expanded to include Asian business people.

These two organizations kept the idea of Pacific integration alive. The number of individuals participating was not very great, but they tended to develop a similar frame of mind, and their numbers grew gradually. Establishing new personal connections, recruiting new participants for meetings, teaching and lecturing, publishing in various forums, and giving out press releases, the two organizations built up a respectable tradition of discussion. The idea attained a certain permanence.

Meanwhile, on the material level important changes were taking place. The Second World War receded another decade into the past. The Vietnam War ended in 1975, and ASEAN developed into a respectable regional organization. The Oil Crisis in 1973 ended Japan's rapid growth, but in her place South Korea, Taiwan, Hong Kong and Singapore, as well as the Southeast Asian countries, continued to grow rapidly, following the Japanese example. At the end of the 1970s the economic focal point of Asia was no longer dominated by Japan; these other countries were also becoming important. The countries of the Indian Ocean were separated from the concept of Southeast Asia, and came to be referred to as South Asian countries. They were separated from the new East and Southeast Asian economic dynamism, and receded into the periphery of the Pacific horizon. Also, mutual economic ties among the Asian Pacific countries developed rapidly through trade and investment. In 1977 Deng Xiaoping returned to power in China, moved Chinese national and foreign politics towards an economistic orientation, and began to open the country. Already in 1978 a Treaty of Peace and Friendship was concluded with Japan, and on New Year's Day in 1979 diplomatic relations were established with the United States.

The Oil Crisis had sent Western Europe into relative stagnation, and because the Western Pacific continued to grow rapidly, trade over the Pacific became greater than trade over the Atlantic at the end of the decade. This was something that had been expected to happen in the twenty-first century, but the phenomenon had taken only a decade. In this sense, the Asian and Pacific countries became more important to the United States than Western Europe. The same also happened in the cases of Canada, Australia and New Zealand, while the latter two countries especially became more and more conscious of themselves as Pacific countries, Europe having only historical relevance. The American trade balance continued to deteriorate, which led to trade frictions, not only with Japan, but also with the new East Asian 'tigers'. An idea emerged that some kind of multilateral forum might be needed to handle these issues. Demographic changes in the United States continued; the Atlantic Northeast lost importance, while the Sun Belt and West Coast gained. A few years after the defeat in Vietnam, after the first shock had been overcome, a need for a new policy towards Asia began to be felt. Due to all these factors the situation became ripe for a new general introduction to the idea of Pacific integration.

The person who made the introduction was Ohira Masayoshi, who became prime minister in December 1978. Ohira had graduated from Hitotsubashi University and spent his early career as an economist in the Ministry of Finance. When Ikeda Hayato entered politics he took Ohira with him from the ministry as his personal secretary in 1949, and later in the 1960s Ohira inherited Ikeda's faction in the Liberal-Democratic Party. Ohira had also been acquainted with Okita Saburo since 1939, when both had been young officials working together for a time in China. Ohira needed a grand design for his premiership, and Pacific integration looked suitable. In March 1979 he established a study group to aid him in formulating policy. It was composed of respected economists and bureaucrats. Okita became its chairman until his resignation in November, when he was appointed Minister of Foreign Affairs in Ohira's Cabinet (Okita 1983: 99; Ohira Masayoshi kaisōroku kankōkai 1983). Kojima Kiyoshi was not a member, but he acted as a consultant to the study group.

The group produced an interim report in November 1979, and a final report in the following year entitled *Kan Taiheiyō rentai no kōsō* (The Concept of Pacific Rim Solidarity) (Kan Taiheiyō rentai kenkyū grūpu 1980). The title of the translated English version is given as 'Report on the Pacific Basin Cooperation Concept'. There is some variation in the names, which has been apparent also in subsequent discussion. The Pacific rim (*kan Taiheiyō*) refers to the principal trading nations around the Pacific, as they are the ones that provide the carrying force for co-operation. The principal problem with this metaphor is that it depicts a thing that is hollow at the centre, and that implies a certain weakness. The concept also leaves the small Pacific island nations out of the picture. The other metaphor, basin, does not have that defect, but it may be too geographic, and it evokes an image of a place where you wash your hands (Wolff 1979). Perhaps these problems have had something to do with the fact that neither of the concepts has become dominant in discussion. Actually, the most-widely-used concept at the beginning of the 1980s turned out to be that of the Pacific Community, which is also used in the report of the Japanese study group. The word 'community' evokes images of a common feeling of belonging together, of shared values, and of shared destiny. It goes well with the concepts of solidarity and co-operation. At the end of the 1970s these were not yet concepts describing a real situation, but rather beautiful, harmonious goals toward which action should be directed.

The other conceptual framework of the report is very similar to the one Miki Takeo had used a decade earlier. It is built around a successful past of rapid economic growth, the present spread of economism around the countries of the region, and the common destiny of the prosperous twenty-first century, which did not seem to be very far away any more. The political strength of the report was that it remained patient, committed to the long-range view, even emphasizing that haste should be avoided at all costs.

For instance, it did not take up questions of formal institutions or membership, because such questions might have caused trouble. The principal idea was to build up mutual co-operation in economic and cultural fields, solidarity, and a feeling of community as groundwork for the twenty-first century. Difficult questions might be taken up later, when a sufficiently strong functional community would have been built up from below. However, from the examples used in the report it can be seen that the five advanced Pacific nations would naturally be included, but also the ASEAN countries – Thailand, the Philippines, Malaysia, Singapore and Indonesia – were seen as necessary building blocks of the community, without which nothing could proceed. These ten countries formed the new nucleus of the Pacific integration concept. The newly industrialized-economies (NIEs) of South Korea, Taiwan, and Hong Kong were also seen to be important, but so was China. Because these countries brought with them political problems, they were placed on a second tier of importance – but as long as the membership question was not taken up formally, co-operation could be advanced with all of them. A third tier was formed by the Latin American countries, the Pacific island countries, the Soviet Union, and other socialist countries in East and Southeast Asia. Economic co-operation could be extended to all of them if they were willing, but it would not have been a serious loss if some of them had preferred to stay out.

As trade, aid and private investment were already increasing rapidly, it was not important to emphasize them as forms of co-operation. Instead, emphasis was on increasing mutual knowledge and feelings of community: more research, more studying abroad, more working abroad, more cultural exchange, more tourism, more communication through submarine cables, relay satellites and computer networks, and above all, more discussions. Discussions should be increased at all levels, but co-ordinated top level discussions should also be organized. The PAFTAD and the PBEC conferences had provided unspectacular but very successful examples of community building among like-minded individuals from different countries, and that kind of activity should be expanded. From now on private level participation should only be mixed gradually with government level participation. A new international conference series should be started, mainly on the private level at first, with a small committee to be established as a steering body for management purposes. The idea is to avoid bureaucracy and the hardening of co-operation patterns; only gradually, after many successful conferences have been held, would the committee slowly be expanded and attain a degree of permanence. Simultaneously, work groups of specialists would be created to conduct studies and promote joint projects in special fields. After a long time, the possibility of establishing a real inter-governmental organization could be considered.

The subsequent practice of Pacific integration has followed the recommendations of the Japanese study group almost to the letter. Prime Minister Ohira and Foreign Minister Okita toured the Pacific countries, visiting China in December 1979; Australia, New Zealand and New Guinea in January, 1980; and the United States, Mexico and Canada in May of the same year. Most important in this connection was the visit to Australia, where Ohira and Australian Prime Minister Malcolm Frazer agreed to support a non-governmental international seminar to explore the Pacific Community idea. The prime motivators of the seminar were, however, Okita and Sir John Crawford. Ohira himself died of a heart attack in June, but the process he helped to initiate continued as planned. The seminar was held at the Australian National University in Canberra in September (Crawford and Seow 1981), and with it the Pacific Economic Co-operation Conference (PECC) was born.

The original participants in the Canberra seminar were the United States, Canada, Japan, Australia, New Zealand, the five ASEAN countries, South Korea, Papua New Guinea, Fiji and Tonga. Each country's delegation typically involved one senior government official, one business leader, and one academic. In subsequent conferences a similar combination was continued, so that PECC combines a variety of government officials, academics and business executives under one organizational framework. In terms of countries, membership has gradually widened: such Latin American countries as Mexico, Peru and Chile have started to participate. Hong Kong, China and Taiwan are all members; the feat was accomplished when Taiwan agreed to use the name Chinese Taipei. The possibility of the Soviet Union joining was debated in the latter half of the 1980s. Observers from other international organizations, such as the Asian Development Bank, the United Nations Economic and Social Commission for Asia and the Pacific (ESCAP; formerly ECAFE), and the OECD have been present in conferences. The second PECC was held in Bangkok in 1982 and the basic organizational form was established there. PECC consists of yearly general conferences, a standing committee which organizes the conferences and activities during interconference periods, national PECC committees in each country, and special task forces. There is a separate task force for trade in manufactures, trade in agricultural products, trade in minerals, and investment and technology transfer. The task forces report to the general conference. The whole process involves a variety of international meetings, consultations, and review committees. PECC has produced a number of personal contacts, a pile of publications, and fairly wide publicity in the region.

Also the number of other publications, written both within and without the region, expanded rapidly throughout the decade. Good representative examples are the Committee on Foreign Affairs's *The Pacific Community Idea* (1979), the Joint Economic Committee's *Pacific Region Interdependencies* (1981), Masuda Ato's *Taiheiyō kyōdōtai ron* (1980), Japan Center for International Exchange's *The Pacific Community Concept* (1980), Han Sung-joo's *Community-Building in the Pacific Region* (1981), Whitlam's *A Pacific Century* (1981), Institut du Pacifique's *Le Pacifique, 'Nouveau Centre du Monde'* (1983), Linder's *The Pacific Century* (1986), Leviste's *The Pacific Lake* (1986), Seki Hiroharu's *The Asia-Pacific in the Global Transformation* (1987), Bey's *Ajia Taiheiyō no jidai* (1987), and Okita Saburo's *Approaching the 21st Century* (1990). Kojima Kiyoshi's two volumes *Taiheiyō keizaiken no seisei* (1980; 1990) provide a good analysis of the expansion of discussion, especially concerning the PAFTAD and PECC processes.

The move towards a still more governmental level organization started in 1989, when the Asia–Pacific Economic Co-operation (APEC) was established, primarily by Australian instigation, at a meeting of foreign and economic ministers in Canberra. The development of APEC has followed a rationale similar to the other organizations for Pacific integration: it has centred on sustaining economic growth, development and trade liberalization in the area, excluding the difficult political sector, and has proceeded in a low-profile, piecemeal fashion. During subsequent meetings in Singapore (1990), Seoul (1991) and Bangkok (1992) it was always emphasized that the meetings were informal. However, an important decision was made during the Bangkok meeting when the ministers decided to establish a standing Secretariat in Singapore, starting in January 1993 (APEC Secretariat 1993a). With this move APEC was transformed from an informal discussion group to a formal institution. Even at present it is not a decision-making body. According to the first Executive Director of APEC, William Bodde, Jr., there have been discussions about moving gradually to the stage of concluding economic agreements and making common policy decisions among member governments, eventually resulting in a free trade area, but that stage does not seem to be approaching yet (Bodde 1993).

Most of the activity of APEC takes place in its work groups, of which there are 12. They are mostly engaged in creating data bases and publications on trade and investment issues, tariffs and non-tariff barriers, resources, communications, tourism, technology transfer, etc. They also engage in various kinds of planning, seminars, study tours and other activities. Although the original project began at the end of the 1960s, the process of increasing mutual knowledge and understanding is still continuing. In 1993 a special Eminent Persons Group was established to create forecasts for regional trade up to the year 2000. Okita Saburo was nominated as the Japanese representative to the group, but he passed away at the age of 78 soon after his nomination, after devoting a lifetime of work to regional development in Asia and the Pacific (APEC Secretariat 1993b).

The membership of APEC is somewhat different from PECC. It was started in 1989 by the original five countries of Kojima's PAFTA proposal, the six ASEAN countries (with Brunei added to them in 1984), and South Korea. This was the politically-easy nucleus from which to start. Since then APEC has been enlarged once at the end of 1991, when Hong Kong, China, and Taiwan – again under the name of Chinese Taipei – entered the organization. APEC is thus at present an organization for the established industrialized countries and the high growth areas of the Western Pacific. The small Pacific island countries, Latin American countries, and Russia are missing. It may be that membership will be enlarged in the future, so that APEC will come to resemble PECC on a more governmental level, but that may not necessarily happen.

At the end of the 1980s the world was entering a new movement towards regional integration, starting with the Single European Act adopted by the Commission of the European Community in 1985. The remaining European Free Trade Association (EFTA) countries began to approach the European Community (EC), either through the European Economic Area concept, or by trying to join the EC itself. After the changes in the former socialist Eastern European countries in 1989, and the collapse of the Soviet Union in 1991, the idea of greater European integration began to be circulated, with the widest geographical images depicting a unified Europe from Scotland to Sakhalin, or even from Vancouver to Vladivostok. American regional integration has also moved apace. The United States signed a free trade agreement with Canada in 1988, and negotiations for creating a North American Free Trade Agreement (NAFTA, not to be confused with the two NAFTA conceptions of the 1960s) between the United States, Canada and Mexico are under way, with the US ratifying the agreement in 1993. Also, ideas of some sort of economic integration between all American nations have been circulating.

In the Western Pacific, similar regional schemes have been presented. In 1990 Chinese economist He Xin proposed that China and Japan, along with other East Asian countries, form an economic grouping among themselves (He 1990). His proposal was not an official one, but it appeared in the *Beijing Review*, and can be seen as a probe. There have been other similar probes, the most famous one from Malaysia in 1991, proposing the formation of an East Asia Economic Group (EAEG) among ASEAN, Japan, and other unnamed Western Pacific countries. The EAEG was seen as a response to European and American regional integration processes, but even the Malaysian proposal emphasizes that the EAEG has to be compatible both with GATT and APEC (Consulate General of Malaysia 1991). Later it was renamed the East Asia Economic Caucus (EAEC) to avoid too strong connotations of a block. Japanese response to these kinds of probes has thus far been vague. Since Miki Takeo and Ohira Masayoshi no other leading Japanese politician has been equally enthusiastic about promoting integration in the area, and exclusively Western Pacific integration might jeopardize the special relationship with the United States.

The probes underline, however, how Japan has become an acceptable partner in regional integration from an Asian point of view. That is a great change compared with the situation in the 1960s and 1970s. A distinct sense of belonging together, a sense of community has been emerging, at least in the Western Pacific. Although the idea is highly debatable, it is possible that in the present state of flux in the international system there might emerge a division of the world into a European, an American, and a Western Pacific block. As He emphasized in his proposal, that would not mean the emergence of a new Greater East Asian Co-prosperity Sphere with Japanese domination, because the other Western Pacific countries would be stronger now, able to hold Japan in check.

On the other hand, the situation is still in many ways similar to the one during the 1960s. There does not seem to be a wish for the formation of actual blocks, but rather the setting up of loose regional groupings with better bargaining power, under the ideology of global free trade. The Asian–Pacific region is a large and loose area, and its importance in a period of threatening integration in other regions is the same as in Kojima's original proposal in 1965, a place big enough for dynamic countries to thrive.

Drastic changes in the global politico-economic system can happen very fast, and it is difficult to predict when such changes will occur. If nothing drastic happens, a rational anticipation of future development in the Asian–Pacific region might lead one to expect a gradual strengthening of APEC. As a loose and economistic organization, APEC – assisted by PECC, PAFTAD and PBEC – might be able to override deepening co-operation among Eastern Pacific countries as separate from Western Pacific countries, and act as a government level link across the ocean. Since foreign ministers also participate in meetings, political and security issues could also be finally put on to the agenda. Such a change is needed now that the Cold War no longer structures interaction in the area, while the global importance of the area continues to rise. Or, if economism remains its basic unifying factor, APEC could develop towards a real Pacific Free Trade Area. However, in view of the slow pace of community building in such a diverse region, such developments probably will have to wait until the fabled twenty-first century.

Bibliography

PUBLISHED MATERIAL

Primary research material

Akamatsu Kaname (1932) 'Waga kuni keizai hatten no shuku gōben shōhō', in *Shōgyō keizai ron*, dai 15 kan jōsatsu, Nagoya: publisher unknown, 179–210.

—— (1945) 'Shinkōkoku sangyō hatten no gankō keitai', in *Keizai shinchitsujo no Keisei genri*, kōhen dai 3 sho, Tokyo, 299–314.

—— (1959) 'Wagakuni sangyō hatten no gankō keitai – kikai kigu kōgyō ni tsuite', *Hitotsubashi rongyō* 11, 514–26.

—— (1975a) [1927] 'Wie ist das vernünftige Sollen und die Wissenschaft des Sollens bei Hegel möglich? Zur Kritik der Rickert'schen Abhandlung "Über idealistische Politik als Wissenschaft" ', in Monkasei (ed.), *Gakumon henro. Akamatsu Kaname sensei tsuitō ronshū*, Tokyo: Sekai keizai kenkyū kyōkai, 46–62.

—— (1975b) [1961] 'A theory of unbalanced growth in the world economy', in Monkasei (ed.), *Gakumon henro. Akamatsu Kaname sensei tsuitō ronshū*, Tokyo: Sekai keizai kenkyū kyōkai, 24–45.

—— (1975c) [1962] 'A historical pattern of economic growth in developing countries', in Monkasei (ed.), *Gakumon henro. Akamatsu Kaname sensei tsuitō ronshū*, Tokyo: Sekai keizai kenkyū kyōkai, 1–23.

—— (1975d) [1967–8]. 'Gakumon henro', in Monkasei (ed.), *Gakumon henro. Akamatsu Kaname sensei tsuitō ronshū*, Tokyo: Sekai keizai kenkyū kyōkai, 9–68.

Arisawa Hiromi, Okita Saburo and Wakimura Gitaro (1951) 'Tōnan Ajia to Nihon keizai – zadankai', *Sekai* 12, 56–9.

Asahi shimbunsha yoron chōsashitsu (1976) *Asahi shimbun yoron chōsa 30 nen shi, Showa 21 nen 3 gatsu – 51 nen 3 gatsu*, jō, ka, Tokyo: Asahi shimbun.

Ashiya Einosuke (1968) 'A Pacific bank for investment and settlement – its conception', in Kojima Kiyoshi (ed.), *Pacific Trade and Development, Papers and Proceedings of a Conference held by the Japan Economic Research Center in January 1968*, Tokyo: The Japan Economic Research Center, Paper no. 9, 307–24.

Asia–Pacific Economic Cooperation Secretariat (APEC) (1993a) *Asia–Pacific Economic Cooperation (APEC)*, Information sheet, Singapore.

Asia–Pacific Economic Cooperation Secretariat (APEC) (1993b) *APEC Secretariat Established in Singapore*, press release, 12 February 1993, Singapore.

Bey, Arifin (1987) *Ajia-Taiheiyō no jidai*, Tokyo: Chuo Koronsha.

Bodde, William, Jr. (1993) 'An interview on regional economic issues', *The Asian Wall Street Journal*, 20 May 1993.

Castle, L. V. (1968) 'New Zealand trade and aid policies in relation to the Pacific and Asian region', in Kojima Kiyoshi (ed.) *Pacific Trade and Development, Papers and Proceedings of a Conference held by the Japan Economic Research Center in January 1968*, Tokyo: The Japan Economic Research Center, Paper no. 9, 79–108.

Committee on Foreign Affairs (1979) *The Pacific Community Idea. Hearings before the Subcommittee on Asian and Pacific Affairs of the Committee on Foreign Affairs, House of Representatives, Ninety-Sixth Congress, First Session*, Washington DC: US Government Printing Office.

Consulate General of Malaysia (1991) *East Asia Economic Group (EAEG)*, mimeo.

Cooper, Richard N. (1968) 'Financial aspects of economic cooperation around the Pacific', in Kojima Kiyoshi (ed.) *Pacific Trade and Development, Papers and Proceedings of a Conference held by the Japan Economic Research Center in January 1968*, Tokyo: The Japan Economic Research Center, Paper no. 9, 283–306.

Crawford, Sir John and Seow, Greg (eds) (1981) *Pacific Economic Cooperation: Suggestions for Action*, Singapore: Heinemann Asia.

Drysdale, Peter (1968) 'Pacific economic integration, an Australian view', in Kojima Kiyoshi (ed.) *Pacific Trade and Development, Papers and Proceedings of a Conference held by the Japan Economic Research Center in January 1968*, Tokyo: The Japan Economic Research Center, Paper no. 9, 194–223.

Ebihara Takekuni (1962) 'Tōnan Ajia bōeki no shōrai', in Kojima Kiyoshi (ed.) *Tōnan Ajia keizai no shōrai kōzō*, Tokyo: Ajia keizai kenkyūjo, Ajia keizai kenkyū shiriizu, dai 37 shū, 153–85.

English, H. Edward (1968a) 'Canada and Pacific trade policy', in Kojima Kiyoshi (ed.) *Pacific Trade and Development, Papers and Proceedings of a Conference held by the Japan Economic Research Center in January 1968*, Tokyo: The Japan Economic Research Center, Paper no. 9, 3–29.

Fujii Shigeru (1965) *Ajia shokoku no seihin, hanseihin yushutsu to senshinkoku no sangyō chōsei*, Tokyo: Nihon keizai kenkyū sentā, Nanpoku mondai konfarensu, kenkyū hōkoku 3 (sono 2).

Gaimushō tokubetsu chōsa iinkai (1990) [1946] 'Nihon keizai saiken no kihon mondai', in Arisawa Hiromi and Nakamura Takafusa (eds) *Shiryō. Sengo Nihon no keizai seisaku kōsō, dai ikkan, Nihon keizai saiken no kihon mondai*, Tokyo: Tokyo daigaku shuppankai, 143–263.
English version: (1977) *Basic Problems for Postwar Reconstruction of Japanese Economy. Translation of A Report of Ministry of Foreign Affairs' Special Survey Committee, September 1946*, Tokyo: The Japan Economic Research Center.

Han Sung-joo (ed.) (1981) *Community-Building in the Pacific Region: Issues and Opportunities*, Seoul: Asiatic Research Center, Korea University.

Hemmi Kenzo (1968) 'The agricultural gap in the Pacific', in Kojima Kiyoshi (ed.) *Pacific Trade and Development, Papers and Proceedings of a Conference held by the Japan Economic Research Center in January 1968*, Tokyo: The Japan Economic Research Center, Paper no. 9, 251–74.

He Xin (1990) 'The development of China's economy – Chinese scholar He Xin's talk with Japanese Professor Yabuki Susumu (III), *Beijing Review*, 3–9 December 1990, 7–14.

Ikeda Hayato (1964) 'Reply', in Kajima Morinosuke, *Current Problems of Japan's Foreign Policy. A record of the interpolations on Japan's foreign policy by Morinosuke Kajima in the Budget Committee of the House of Councillors, and other related documents*, Tokyo: Kajima Institute Publishing Company, 37–8.

Itagaki Yoichi (1949) 'Ajia jinkō mondai to keizai hatten', *Chuo Koron* 5, 18–23.

Japan Center for International Exchange (1980) *The Pacific Community Concept. Views from Eight Nations. Proceedings of the Asian Dialogue at Oiso*, The JCIE Papers, Tokyo.

Johnson, Harry G. (1968) 'A New World trade policy in the post-Kennedy Round era. A survey of alternatives, with special reference to the position of the Pacific and Asian regions', in Kojima Kiyoshi (ed.) *Pacific Trade and Development, Papers and Proceedings of a Conference held by the Japan Economic Research Center in January 1968*, Tokyo: The Japan Economic Research Center, Paper no. 9, 234–50.

Joint Economic Committee (1981) *Pacific Region Interdependencies. A Compendium of Papers submitted to the Joint Economic Committee, Congress of the United States*, Washington DC: US Government Printing Office.

Kajima Morinosuke (1964) *Current Problems of Japan's Foreign Policy. A record of the interpolations on Japan's foreign policy by Morinosuke Kajima in the Budget Committee of the House of Councillors, and other related documents*, Tokyo: Kajima Institute Publishing Company.

Kan Taiheiyō rentai kenkyū grūpu (1980) *Kan Taiheiyō rentai no kōsō*, Ohira sōri no seisaku kenkyūkai hōkokusho 4, Tokyo: Ōkurashō insatsu kyoku.

English version: 'Report on the Pacific Basin co-operation concept' (1981), in Joint Economic Committee, *Pacific Region Interdependencies. A Compendium of Papers submitted to the Joint Economic Committee, Congress of the United States*, Washington DC: US Government Printing Office, 17–63.

Karashima Kanesaburo (1948) 'Ajia wa naze kawatta ka', *Sekai* 10, 13–22.

Keizai kigakuchō (1955–9) *Keizai hakusho*, Tokyo.

Keizai shingikai (1960) *Kokumin shotoku baizō keikaku*, Tokyo.

Kobayashi Yoshimasa (1951) 'Senryō wa Nihon ni nani wo motarashitaka', *Chuo Koron* 1, 58–61.

Kojima Kiyoshi (1956) *Kōeki jōken*, (The Terms of Trade) Tokyo: Keisō shobō.

—— (1958) *Nihon bōeki to keizai hatten* (Japan's Trade and Economic Development), Tokyo: Kunimoto shobō.

—— (1960) (ed.) *Ronsō. Keizai seichō to Nihon bōeki* (Economic Growth and Japan's Trade), Tokyo: Kōbundō.

—— (1961a) 'Sekai keizai no kōzō hendō to dai ichi ji shōhin bōeki', in *Ajia dai ichi ji shōhin no kihon mondai*, chōsa kenkyū hōkoku sōsho, dai 9 shū, Tokyo: Ajia keizai kenkyūjo, 11–44.

—— (1961b) 'Dai ichi ji shōhin kakaku hendō no mekanizumu', in *Ajia dai ichi ji shōhin no kihon mondai*, chōsa kenkyū hōkoku sōsho, dai 9 shū, Tokyo: Ajia keizai kenkyūjo, 45–108.

—— (1961c) 'Kanshū ni atatte', in Arubāto O. Hāshuman, *Keizai hatten no senryaku*, Tokyo: Ganshodō, 7–9.

—— (1962a) *EEC no keizaigaku*, Tokyo: Nihon hyōronsha.

—— (1962b) 'Dai ichi ji shōhin bōeki to kyōdō ichiba', in *Ajia no dai ichi ji shōhin bōeki*, Ajia keizai kenkyū shiriizu, dai 27 shū, Tokyo: Ajia keizai kenkyūjo, 57–116.

—— (1962c) 'Tōnan Ajia keizai kyōryoku no kōzu', in Kojima Kiyoshi (ed.) *Tōnan Ajia keizai no shōrai kōzō*, Ajia keizai kenkyū shiriizu, dai 37 shū, Tokyo: Ajia keizai kenkyūjo, 187–229.

—— (1962d) 'Amerika, Nihon, Tōnan Ajia sankaku bōeki no kihon rosen', in Kojima Kiyoshi (ed.), *Tōnan Ajia keizai no shōrai kōzō*, Ajia keizai kenkyū shiriizu, dai 37 shū, Tokyo: Ajia keizai kenkyūjo, 13–61.

—— (1962e) (ed.) *Tōnan Ajia keizai no shōrai kōzō*, Ajia keizai kenkyū shiriizu, dai 37 shū, Tokyo: Ajia keizai kenkyūjo.

—— (1962f) *Sekai keizai to Nihon bōeki*, Tokyo: Keisō shobō.

—— (1966) *Sekai keizai nyūmon. Nihon bōeki no kankyō*, Tokyo: Nihon keizai shimbunsha.

—— (1968a) 'Japan's interest in the Pacific trade expansion', in Kojima Kiyoshi (ed.) *Pacific Trade and Development, Papers and Proceedings of a Conference held by the Japan Economic Research Center in January 1968*, Tokyo: The Japan Economic Research Center, Paper no. 9, 153–93.

—— (1968b) (ed.) *Pacific Trade and Development, Papers and Proceedings of a Conference held by the Japan Economic Research Center in January 1968*, Tokyo: The Japan Economic Research Center, Paper no. 9.

—— (1971) *Japan and a Pacific Free Trade Area*, Berkeley and Los Angeles: University of California Press.

—— (1975) 'Gankō keitai ron to purodakuto saikuru ron – Akamatsu Kaname keizaigaku no ittenkai', in Monkasei (ed.) *Gakumon henro. Akamatsu Kaname sensei tsuitō ronshū*, Tokyo: Sekai keizai kenkyū kyōkai, 227–45.

—— (1977) *Japan and a New World Economic Order*, Tokyo: Tuttle.

—— (1978) *Japanese Direct Foreign Investment. A Model of Multinational Business Operations*, Tokyo: Tuttle.

—— (1980) *Taiheiyō keizaiken no seisei*, Tokyo: Sekai keizai kenkyū kyōkai.

—— (1990) *Zoku, Taiheiyō keizaiken no seisei*, Tokyo: Bunshindō.

Kojima Kiyoshi and Kurimoto Hiroshi (1965) *Taiheiyō kyōdō ichiba to Tōnan Ajia*, Tokyo: Nihon keizai kenkyū sentā, Nampoku mondai konfarensu, kenkyū hōkoku 3 (sono 3).

—— (1966a) 'A Pacific economic community and Asian developing countries', in *Report of a JERC International Conference, Measures for Trade Expansion of Developing Countries*, Tokyo: Japan Economic Research Center, 93–133.

—— (1966b) 'Taiheiyō kyōdō ichiba to Tōnan Ajia', in Okita Saburo (ed.) *Teikaihatsukoku no bōeki to kaihatsu*, Tokyo: Nihon keizai kenkyū sentā, sōsho 3, 67–95.

Kojima Kiyoshi and Okita Saburo (1968) 'Preface', in Kojima Kiyoshi (ed.) *Pacific Trade and Development, Papers and Proceedings of a Conference held by the Japan Economic Research Center in January 1968*, Tokyo: The Japan Economic Research Center, Paper no. 9, i-ii.

Koyama Kenichi (1967) 'Nihon no shakai henka no mitōshi', in Nakayama Ichiro (ed.) *Nijū isseiki no sekai*, Nihon keizai kenkyū sentā sōsho 11, Tokyo: Nihon keizai shimbunsha, 26–50.

Kuno Osamu (1950) 'Amerika no atarashii Ajia seisaku – Owen Rachimoa hakase no shinteian', *Sekai* 5, 67–72.

Leviste, Jose P., Jr. (ed.) (1986) *The Pacific Lake, Philippine Perspectives on a Pacific Community*, Manila: The Philippine Council for Foreign Relations in co-operation with SGV Foundation, Manila.

McDougall, I. A. (1968) 'The prospects of the economic integration of Japan, Australia and New Zealand', in Kojima Kiyoshi (ed.) *Pacific Trade and Development, Papers and Proceedings of a Conference held by the Japan Economic Research Center in January 1968*, Tokyo: The Japan Economic Research Center, Paper no. 9, 109–41.

Matsumoto Kunio (1967) 'Shōhi kōzō', in Okita Saburo and Murobuse Fumiro (ed.) *1985 nen no nihon keizai*, Nihon keizai kenkyū sentā sōsho 10, Tokyo: Nihon keizai shimbunsha, 121–35.

Miki Takeo (1984a) [1967] 'Nichi-Bei ampo ga gaikō no kichō', in *Gikai seiji to tomoni enzetsu hatsugen shū*, jōken, Tokyo: Miki Takeo shuppan kinenkai, 286–94.

—— (1984b) [1967] 'Kaku kakusan bōshi jōyaku seiritsu e doryoku', in *Gikai seiji to tomoni enzetsu hatsugen shū*, jōken, Tokyo: Miki Takeo shuppan kinenkai, 295–304.

—— (1984c) [1967] 'Taiheiyō wo tōzai no kakehashi ni', in *Gikai seiji to tomoni enzetsu hatsugen shū*, jōken, Tokyo: Miki Takeo shuppan kinenkai, 305–9.

—— (1984d) [1967] 'Watakushi no Ajia Taiheiyō kōsō', in *Gikai seiji to tomoni enzetsu hatsugen shū*, jōken, Tokyo: Miki Takeo shuppan kinenkai, 310–12.

—— (1984e) [1967] 'ASPAC, hankyō kaigi ni shinai', in *Gikai seiji to tomoni enzetsu hatsugen shū*, jōken, Tokyo: Miki Takeo shuppan kinenkai, 313–15.

—— (1984f) *Gikai seiji to tomoni enzetsu hatsugen shū*, jōken, Tokyo: Miki Takeo shuppan kinenkai.

Minobe Ryokichi (1949) 'Keizai kyū genzoku no yōsei to genjitsu', *Chuo Koron* 3, 16–22.

Monkasei (1975) (ed.) *Gakumon henro. Akamatsu Kaname sensei tsuitō ronshū*, Tokyo: Sekai keizai kenkyū kyōkai.

Nagano Shigeo (1964) *Dai ni kai Nichi-Gō keizai gōdō iinkai ni shusseki shite*, Nihon keizai chōsa kyōgikai, no. 17.

Nagata Kiyoshi (1948) 'Jiremma ni tatsu Nihon keizai – tenkai no michi wa Herakureitosu no mukashi ni tsūjite iru', *Chuo Koron* 1, 12–17.

Nakayama Ichiro (1967) (ed.) *Nijū isseiki no sekai*, Nihon keizai kenkyū sentā sōsho 11, Tokyo: Nihon keizai shimbunsha.

Nihon keizai chōsa kyōgikai (The Japan Economic Investigating Committee) (1963) *Taiheiyō keizai kyōryoku no hōkō ni tsuite*, Chōsa hōkoku 63-1, Tokyo.

'Nipponkoku kempō' [1946] in Hoshino Eiichi, Matsuo Hiroya and Shiono Hiroshi (henshū daihyō) *Shoroppō*, Tokyo: Yūhikaku, Showa 63 nen. English version: *The Constitution of Japan*. Ministry of Foreign Affairs, Public Information and Cultural Affairs Bureau, Facts about Japan, 1981.

Ohira Masayoshi (1964a) 'Reply', in Kajima Morinosuke, *Current Problems of Japan's Foreign Policy. A record of the interpolations on Japan's foreign policy by Morinosuke Kajima in the Budget Committee of the House of Councillors, and other related documents*, Tokyo: Kajima Institute Publishing Company, 23.

—— (1964b) 'Reply', in Kajima Morinosuke, *Current Problems of Japan's Foreign Policy. A record of the interpolations on Japan's foreign policy by Morinosuke Kajima in the Budget Committee of the House of Councillors, and other related documents*, Tokyo: Kajima Institute Publishing Company, 14–16.

Ohira Masayoshi kaisōroku kankōkai (ed.) (1983) *Ohira Masayoshi kaisōroku*, Tokyo: Kagoshima shuppankai.

Oki Hiroshi (1965) *Ajia to Nihon, Ajia keizai hatten ni kyōryoku suru Nihon no yakuwari*, Tokyo: Nihon kokusai mondai kenkyūkai, kokusai mondai shiriizu 47.

Okita Saburo (1947) 'Bōeki to gaishi e no kōsatsu. Shukushō saiseisan kokufuku no hōto', *Chuo Koron* 7, 13–18.

—— (1950) 'Ajia keizai to Nihon keizai', *Sekai* 4, 44–9.

—— (1956a) *Toonan Ajia no hatten riron* (The Development Theory of Southeast Asia), Tokyo: Nihon gaisei gakkai, gaisei kōza shiriizu, Tōnan Ajia II.

—— (1956b) *The Rehabilitation of Japan's Economy and Asia*, Tokyo: Ministry of Foreign Affairs.

—— (1958) 'Nihon wa ikani kiyo subeki ka', *Chuo Koron* 1, 98–104.

—— (1960) *Nihon keizai no shōrai* (The Future of Japan's Economy), Tokyo: Yūki shobō.

—— (1962) 'Ajia keizai kyōryoku no shomondai' ('The problems of Asian economic co-operation'), *Chuo Koron* 2, 72–80.

—— (1964) *Myōnichi no Nihon keizai. Mazushii keizai kara yutakana keizai e*, Tokyo: Jitsugyō no Nihonsha.

—— (1965) 'Japan and the developing nations', *Contemporary Japan* 28, 2: 1–14.

—— (1966) (ed.) *Teikaihatsukoku no bōeki to kaihatsu*, Tokyo: Nihon keizai kenkyū sentā, sōsho 3.

—— (1967) 'Hajimeni', in Okita Saburo and Murobuse Fumiro (eds) *1985 nen no Nihon keizai*, Nihon keizai kenkyū sentā, sōsho 10, Tokyo: Nihon keizai shimbunsha, 9–13.

—— (1975) 'Akamatsu sensei wo tsuioku suru', in Monkasei (ed.) *Gakumon henro. Akamatsu Kaname sensei tsuitō ronshū*, Tokyo: Sekai keizai kenkyū kyōkai, 145–6.

—— (1983) *Japan's Challenging Years. Reflections of my lifetime*, Canberra: Australia–Japan Research Centre, Australian National University.

—— (1985) 'Prospect of the Pacific economies', in *Pacific Economic Cooper-*

ation, Issues and Opportunities. Report of the Fourth Pacific Economic Cooperation Conference, Seoul, April 29 – May 1, 1985, Seoul: Korea Development Institute, 18–29.

—— (1990) *Approaching the 21st Century. Japan's Role*, Tokyo: The Japan Times.

Okita Saburo and Murobuse Fumiro (1967) (eds) *1985 nen no Nihon keizai*, Nihon keizai kenkyū sentā sōsho 10, Tokyo: Nihon keizai shimbunsha.

Okita Saburo and Ohnishi Akira (1968) 'Japan's Role in Asian Economic Development', in Kojima Kiyoshi (ed.) *Pacific Trade and Development, Papers and Proceedings of a Conference held by the Japan Economic Research Center in January 1968*, Tokyo: The Japan Economic Research Center, Paper no. 9, 359–84.

Okita Saburo and Sakamoto Jiro (1966) (eds) *20 nen go no Tokyo*, Nihon keizai kenkyū sentā sōsho 6, Tokyo: Nihon keizai shimbunsha.

Okita Saburo, Eto Shinkichi and Ohnishi Akira (1967) 'Sekai to Ajia no shōrai', in Nakayama Ichiro (ed.) *Nijū isseiki no sekai*, Nihon keizai kenkyū sentā sōsho 11, Tokyo: Nihon keizai shimbunsha, 51–75.

Pacific Basin Economic Cooperation Committee (1967) *Record of the meeting for setting up a Pacific Basin Economic Cooperation Committee, April 26–27, 1967*, Tokyo.

Pacific Trade and Development Conference (1968) 'Communique', in Kojima Kiyoshi (ed.) *Pacific Trade and Development, Papers and Proceedings of a Conference held by the Japan Economic Research Center in January 1968*, Tokyo: The Japan Economic Research Center, Paper no. 9, iii-iv.

Ranis, Gustav (1968) 'U.S. aid policies in Asia', in Kojima Kiyoshi (ed.) *Pacific Trade and Development, Papers and Proceedings of a Conference held by the Japan Economic Research Center in January 1968*, Tokyo: The Japan Economic Research Center, Paper no. 9, 334–58.

Royama Masamichi (1948) 'Nihon no jissō to seitō no keizai seisaku', *Chuo Koron* 2, 4–12.

—— (1951) 'Futatsu no sekai to Ajia no kadai', *Chuo Koron* 1, 241–9.

Ryu Shintaro (1951) 'Kuenai Nihon – Nihon keizai no yume', *Chuo Koron* 1, 17–21.

Sakamoto Jiro (1967a) '21 seiki no Nihon keizai', in Nakayama Ichiro (ed.) *Nijū isseiki no sekai*, Nihon keizai kenkyū sentā sōsho 11, Tokyo: Nihon keizai shimbunsha, 5–25.

—— (1967b). 'Miraigaku kaigi wo furikaette', zadankai, in Nakayama Ichiro (ed.) *Nijū isseiki no sekai*, Nihon keizai kenkyū sentā sōsho 11, Tokyo: Nihon keizai shimbunsha, 262–78.

Sekiguchi Keitaro (1950) 'Kokusai shōhin ichiba no dōkō', *Chuo Koron* 10, 49–55.

Serita Hitoshi, Ogata Shoji, Sashima Yoshinari, Suzuki Eiichi and Matsumoto Shigeharu (1951), 'Dai san ji sekai taisen ni tsuite – zadankai', *Chuo Koron* 1, 63–86.

Shimizu Ikutaro (1951) 'Nihonjin', *Chuo Koron* 1, 4–16.

Shinohara Miyohei and Fujino Shozaburo (1967) (eds) *Nihon no keizai seichō. Seichō konfarensu no hōkoku to tōron*, Nihon keizai kenkyū sentā sōsho 8, Tokyo: Nihon keizai shimbunsha.

Sugi Takashi (1950) 'Tōnan Ajia ni uchikomareta sambon no kusabi', *Chuo Koron* 6, 31–7.

Tsuchiya Kiyoshi (1951) 'Nichi-Bei keizai kyōryoku no hōkō to kibo to naiyō', *Chuo Koron* 6, 23–9.

Tsukamoto Masao, Abe Masamichi and Araki Tadao (1964) *Keizai tōgō no kodō. EEC no seika kara OPEC no kōsō made*, Tokyo: Nihon kokusai mondai kenkyū jo, kokusai mondai shiriizu 42.

Whitlam, E. Gough (1981) *A Pacific Century*, Cambridge and London: Australian Studies Endowment and Council on East Asian Studies, Harvard University.

Wilkinson, Bruce (1968) 'Canadian trade, the Kennedy Round and a Pacific Free Trade Area', in Kojima Kiyoshi (ed.) *Pacific Trade and Development, Papers and Proceedings of a Conference held by the Japan Economic Research Center in January 1968*, Tokyo: The Japan Economic Research Center, Paper no. 9, 30–71.

Wolff, Lester L. (1979) 'Discussion of the Pacific community idea', in *Hearings before the Subcommittee on Asian and Pacific Affairs of the Committee on Foreign Affairs, House of Representatives, Ninety-Sixth Congress, First Session*, Washington DC: US Government Printing Office, 83.

Yamaguchi Shogo (1946) 'Nihon keizai to sekai keizai. Nihon keizai saiken no tame no jakkan no mondai', *Chuo Koron* 9, 23–31.

Yokota Kisaburo (1946) 'Sekai kokka ron', *Sekai* 9, 17–29.

Other literature

Allen, G. C. (1962) *A Short Economic History of Modern Japan 1867–1937, with a Supplementary Chapter on Economic Recovery and Expansion 1945–1960*, London: Unwin.

—— (1965) *Japan's Economic Expansion*, Herts: Royal Institute of International Affairs and Oxford University Press.

—— (1975) 'Professor Kaname Akamatsu', in Monkasei (ed.) *Gakumon henro. Akamatsu Kaname sensei tsuitō ronshū*, Tokyo: Sekai keizai kenkyū kyōkai, 328–31.

Amaya Naohiro (1975) *Hyōryū suru Nihon keizai. Shin sangyō seisaku no bijon*, Tokyo: Mainichi shimbunsha.

Appelbaum, Richard P. and Henderson, Jeffrey (eds) (1992) *States and Development in the Asian Pacific Rim*, London and New Delhi: Sage.

Aristotle (1959) [about 330 BC] *The 'Art' of Rhetoric*, London: Harvard University Press and William Heinemann.

Axelbank, Albert (1977) *Black Star Over Japan. Rising Forces of Militarism*, Tokyo: Tuttle.

Baerwald, Hans H. (1959) *The Purge of Japanese Leaders under the Occupation*, Berkeley and Los Angeles: University of California Press.

Balassa, Bela (1962) *The Theory of Economic Integration*, Watford: Allen and Unwin.

Bamba Nobuya and Howes, John F. (1980) (eds) *Pacifism in Japan. The Christian and Socialist Traditions*, Kyoto: Minerva Press.

Barthes, Roland (1990) 'Die alte Rhetorik. Ein Abriß', in Josef Kopperschmidt, (ed.) *Rhetorik. Band I. Rhetorik als Texttheorie*, Darmstadt: Wissenschaftliche Buchgesellschaft, 35–90.

Beasley, W. G. (1985) *The Modern History of Japan*, Tokyo: Tuttle.

Boltho, Andrea (1975) *Japan, An Economic Survey 1953–1973*, Bungay: Oxford University Press.

Calleo, David P. (1982) *The Imperious Economy*, Cambridge: Harvard University Press.

Calvert, Peter (1986) *The Foreign Policy of New States*, Kent: Wheatsheaf.

Chung Hoon-mok (1981) 'Economic integration in the Pacific basin: a historical review', in Han Sung-joo (ed.) *Community-Building in the Pacific Region: Issues and Opportunities*, Seoul: Asiatic Research Center, Korea University, 3–29.

Clyde, Paul H. and Beers, Burton F. (1971) *The Far East. A History of Western Impact and the Eastern Response, 1830–1970*, Englewood Cliffs: Prentice Hall.

Correspondents of *The Economist* (1963) *Consider Japan*, London: Duckworth.

Cusumano, Michael A. (1985) *The Japanese Automobile Industry. Technology and Management at Nissan and Toyota*, Cambridge and London: Harvard University Press.

Destler, I. M., Fukui Haruhiro and Sato Hideo (1979) *The Textile Wrangle, Conflict in Japanese–American Relations, 1969–1971*, Ithaca and London: Cornell University Press.

Drysdale, Peter (1981) 'Australia and Japan in the Pacific and world economy', in Peter Drysdale and Kitaoji Hironobu (eds) *Japan and Australia. Two societies and their interaction*, Hong Kong: Australian National University Press, 419–38.

—— (1983) 'Foreword', in Okita Saburo, *Japan's Challenging Years. Reflections of my lifetime*, Canberra: Australia–Japan Research Centre, Australian National University, vi–x.

Dubro, Alec and Kaplan, David E. (1987) *Yakuza. The Explosive Account of Japan's Criminal Underworld*, Aylesbury: Futura.

Edström, Bert (1988) *Japan's Quest for a Role in the World. Roles Ascribed to Japan Nationally and Internationally 1969–1982*, Dissertation, Stockholm: Institute of Oriental Languages, University of Stockholm.

Elsbree, Willard H. (1953) *Japan's Role in Southeast Asian Nationalist Movements 1940 to 1945*, Cambridge: Harvard University Press.

Emmerson, John K. (1976) *Arms, Yen and Power. The Japanese Dilemma*, Tokyo: Tuttle.

English, H. Edward (1968b) *Transatlantic Economic Community: Canadian Perspectives*, Toronto: Private Planning Association of Canada/University of Toronto Press.

Frank, Andre Gunder (1967) *Capitalism and Underdevelopment in Latin America*, London: Monthly Review Press.

Galtung, Johan (1971) 'A structural theory of imperialism', *Journal of Peace Research* 8, 2: 81–117.

—— (1976) *Self-reliance: Concept, Practice and Rationale*, Oslo: Chair in Conflict and Peace Research, University of Oslo.

—— (1980) *The True Worlds. A Transnational Perspective*, New York: The Free Press.

—— (1989) *Solving Conflicts. A Peace Research Perspective*, Honolulu: University of Hawaii Institute for Peace.
Galtung, Johan, O'Brien, Peter and Preiswerk, Roy (1980) (eds) *Self-reliance. A New Development Strategy?* London: Bougle-l'Ouverture.
General Agreement on Tariffs and Trade (GATT) (1971) *Japan's Economic Expansion and Foreign Trade 1955 to 1970*, GATT Studies in International Trade, no. 2, Geneva.
Gilpin, Robert (1984) *War and Change in World Politics*, Cambridge: Cambridge University Press.
Haas, Ernst B. (1958) *The Uniting of Europe. Political, Social and Economic Forces 1950–1957*, London: The London Institute of World Affairs and Stevens and Sons.
—— (1964) *Beyond the Nation-State. Functionalism and International Organization*, Stanford: Stanford University Press.
Halliday, Jon and McCormack, Gavin (1973) *Japanese Imperialism Today. 'Co-prosperity in Greater East Asia'*, New York: Monthly Review Press.
Haushofer, Karl (1923) *Japan und die Japaner. Eine Landeskunde*, Leipzig und Berlin: B. G. Teubner.
Hegel, G. W. Fr. (1970) [1837] 'Aus Hegels Vorlesungen über die Philosophie der Weltgeschichte', in *Recht, Staat, Geschichte, eine Auswahl aus seinen Werken*, Feuchtwangen: Alfred Kroner, 351–432.
—— (1980) [1840] *Vorlesungen über die Philosophie der Geschichte*, Stuttgart: Reclam.
Hidaka Rokuro (1987) *Sengo shisō wo kangaeru*, Tokyo: Iwanami shinsho.
Higgins, Benjamin (1968) *Economic Development. Principles, Problems and Policies*, London: Constable.
Hindmarsh, Albert E. (1936) *The Basis of Japanese Foreign Policy*, Cambridge: Harvard University Press.
Hirschman, Albert O. (1960) *The Strategy of Economic Development*, Forge Village: Yale University Press.
Hoyt, Edwin P. (1986) *Japan's War. The Great Pacific Conflict 1853–1952*, New York: Da Capo.
Ienaga Saburo (1978) *The Pacific War. World War II and the Japanese, 1931–1945*, New York: Pantheon Books.
Inoguchi Takashi (1986) 'Japan's images and options: not a challenger but a supporter', *Journal of Japanese Studies* 12, 1: 95–119.
Institut du Pacifique (1983) *Le Pacifique. 'Nouveau Centre du Monde'*, Paris: Berger-Levrault/Boréal Express.
Iriye Akira (1972) *Pacific Estrangement. Japanese and American Expansion 1897–1911*, Cambridge: Harvard University Press.
Iwasaki Ikuo (1983) (comp.) *Japan and Southeast Asia. A Bibliography of Historical, Economic and Political Relations*, Singapore and Tokyo: Institute of Southeast Asian Studies and Library, Institute of Developing Economies.
Japan Center for International Exchange (1982) *The Pacific Community Concept. A Selected Annotated Bibliography*, The JCIE Papers, Tokyo.
Johnson, Chalmers (1986) *MITI and the Japanese Miracle. The Growth of Industrial Policy 1925–1975*, Tokyo: Tuttle.
Jones, F. C. (1954) *Japan's New Order in East Asia. Its Rise and Fall 1937–45*, London: Oxford University Press.

Kahn, Herman (1970) *The Emerging Japanese Superstate: Challenge and Response*, Englewood Cliffs: Prentice Hall.

Kato Norihiro (1985) *Amerika no kage*, Tokyo: Kashutsu shobō shinsha.

Kennedy, Paul (1989) *The Rise and Fall of the Great Powers. Economic Change and Military Conflict from 1500 to 2000*, New York: Vintage.

Keohane, Robert O. and Nye, Joseph S. (1977) *Power and Interdependence. World Politics in Transition*, Boston and Toronto: Little, Brown and Co.

Khamchoo, Chaiwat (1986) *Japan's Southeast Asian Policy In the Post-Vietnam Era (1975–1985)*, Dissertation, Department of Political Science, University of Washington.

Kierkegaard, Søren (1980) [1845] *Staadier paa Livets Vei*, Haslev: Gyldendal.

—— (1982) [1844] *Begrebet Angest. En simpel psychologisk-paapegende Overveielse i Retning af det dogmatiske Problem om Arvesynden af Vigilius Haufniensis*, Haslev: Gyldendal.

Kjellén, Rudolf (1918) *Die Großmächte der Gegenwart*, Leipzig and Berlin: B. G. Teubner.

Kjellén, Rudolf and Haushofer, Karl (1935) *Die Grossmächte vor und nach dem Weltkriege*, Leipzig and Berlin: B. G. Teubner.

Korhonen, Pekka (1990) *The Geometry of Power. Johan Galtung's Conception of Power*, Tampere: Tampere Peace Research Institute, Research Reports no. 38.

—— (1992) *The Origin of the Idea of the Pacific Free Trade Area. A Study of Japanese Rhetorical Categories and Discussion on International Integration 1945–1968*, Dissertation, Jyväskylä: University of Jyväskylä.

—— (1994) 'On the theory of the flying geese pattern of development', *Journal of Peace Research* 31, 1 or 2 (forthcoming).

Kosai Yutaka (1986) *Kōdo seichō no jidai. Gendai Nihon keizaishi nō to*, Tokyo: Nihon hyōronsha.

Krause, Lawrence B. and Sekiguchi Sueo (1976) 'Japan and the world economy', in Hugh Patrick and Henry Rosovsky (eds) *Asia's New Giant. How the Japanese Economy Works*, Washington DC: The Brookings Institution, 383–458.

Lake, David A. (1983) 'International Economic Structure and American Foreign Economic Policy 1887–1934', *World Politics* 35, 4: 517–43.

Lebra, Joyce C. (ed.) (1975) *Japan's Greater East Asia Co-Prosperity Sphere in World War II. Selected Readings and Documents*, Kuala Lumpur: Oxford University Press.

Lincoln, Edward J. (1988) *Japan. Facing Economic Maturity*, Washington DC: The Brookings Institution.

Linder, Staffan Burenstam (1986) *The Pacific Century. Economic and Political Consequences of Asian-Pacific Dynamism*, Stanford: Stanford University Press.

Maddison, Angus (1982) *Phases of Capitalist Development*, Hong Kong: Oxford University Press.

Maga, Timothy P. (1990) *John F. Kennedy and the New Pacific Community 1961–63*, Bristol and Maesteg: Macmillan.

Masamura Kimihiro (1987) *Sengoshi*, jō, ka, Tokyo: Chikuma shobō.

Masuda Ato (1980) *Taiheiyō kyōdōtai ron*, Tokyo: Kasankai.

Mills, C. Wright (1970) *The Sociological Imagination*, Bungay: Penguin.

Minami Ryoshin (1986) *The Economic Development of Japan. A Quantitative Study*, New York: St. Martin's Press.

Mitrany, David (1943) *A Working Peace System*, London: The Royal Institute of International Affairs.

—— (1975) *The Functional Theory of Politics*, Bristol: London School of Economics.

Mommsen, Wolfgang J. and Osterhammel, Jurgen (eds) (1986) *Imperialism and After. Continuities and Discontinuities*, Chatham: The German Historical Institute and Allen and Unwin.

Momoi Makato (1977) 'Basic trends in Japanese security policy', in Robert A. Scalapino (ed.) *The Foreign Policy of Modern Japan*, Berkeley and Los Angeles: University of California Press, 341–64.

Momose Hiroshi (1990) (ed.) *Yōroppa shokoku no kokusai seiji*, Tokyo: Tokyo daigaku shuppankai.

Morgenthau, Hans (1929) *Die internationale Rechtspflege. Ihr Wesen und ihre Grenzen*, Frankfurter Abhandlungen zum Kriegsverhütungsrecht, Part 12, Leipzig: Robert Noske.

Myers, Ramon H. and Peattie, Mark R. (eds) (1984) *The Japanese Colonial Empire 1895–1945*, Princeton: Princeton University Press.

Myrdal Gunnar (1961) *Beyond the Welfare State. Economic Planning in the Welfare States and Its International Implications. The Storr Lectures, Yale University, 1958*, Bristol: Duckworth.

—— (1964) [1956] *An International Economy. Problems and Prospects*, Tokyo: Harper and Row and John Weatherhill.

—— (1965) [1957] *Economic Theory and Underdeveloped Regions*, London: Methuen.

Nakamura Takafusa (1986) *Shōwa keizaishi*, Tokyo: Iwanami.

—— (1987) *The Postwar Japanese Economy. Its Development and Structure*, Tokyo: University of Tokyo Press.

Nakane Chie (1985) *Japanese Society*, Tokyo: Tuttle.

Newby, Laura (1988) *Sino–Japanese Relations. China's Perspective*, Worcester: The Royal Institute of International Affairs and Routledge.

Nish, Ian (1975) 'Economic bases of Japan's foreign relations', *Rivista Internazionale di Scienze Economiche e Commerciali* 4, 353–66.

Nurkse, Ragnar (1959) *Patterns of Trade and Development. Wicksell Lectures, 1959*, Uppsala: The Wicksell Lecture Society with the Social Science Institute, Stockholm University, the Stockholm School of Economics and the Swedish Economic Society.

Nye, Joseph S. (1971) *Peace in Parts. Integration and Conflict in Regional Organization*, Boston: Little, Brown and Co.

—— (1990) *Bound to Lead. The Changing Nature of American Power*, New York: Basic Books.

Otake Hideo (1987) 'The Zaikai under the Occupation: the formation and transformation of managerial councils', in Robert E. Ward, and Sakamoto Yoshikazu (eds) *Democratizing Japan. The Allied Occupation*, Honolulu: University of Hawaii Press, 366–91.

Palonen, Kari (1983) 'Politics as a dramatic action situation', in Ilkka Heiskanen and Sakari Hänninen, (eds) *Exploring the Basis of Politics. Five Essays on the Politics of Experience, Language, Knowledge and History*, Ilmajoki: The Finnish Political Science Association, 11–31.

—— (1985) *Politik als Handlungsbegriff. Horizontwandel des Politikbegriffs in Deutschland 1890–1933*, Commentationes Scientiarum Socialium 28, Helsinki: The Finnish Society of Sciences and Letters.

—— (1987) *Tekstistä politiikkaan. Johdatus tulkintataitoon*, Jyväskylä: Department of Political Science, University of Jyväskylä, Publications 54.

Papinot, E. (1976) [1910] *Historical and Geographical Dictionary of Japan*, Tokyo: Tuttle.

Patrick, Hugh and Rosovsky, Henry (1976) 'Japan's economic performance: an overview', in Hugh Patrick and Henry Rosovsky (eds) *Asia's New Giant. How the Japanese Economy Works*, Washington DC: The Brookings Institution, 1–61.

Peattie, Mark R. (1984) 'Japanese attitudes towards colonialism', in Ramon H. Myers and Mark H. Peattie (eds) *The Japanese Colonial Empire 1895–1945*, Princeton: Princeton University Press, 80–127.

Penrose, E. F. (1975) 'My Nagoya era and Professor Akamatsu', in Monkasei (ed.) *Gakumon henro. Akamatsu Kaname sensei tsuitō ronshū*, Tokyo: Sekai keizai kenkyū kyōkai, 323–6.

Perelman, Chaim (1982) *The Realm of Rhetoric*, Notre Dame: University of Notre Dame Press.

Pluvier, Jan (1974) *South-East Asia from Colonialism to Independence*, Kuala Lumpur: Oxford University Press.

Rapp, William V. (1975) 'Gankō keitai bunseki no kakuchō – sangyō nai gankō keitai teki hatten to Nihon no sangyō seisaku', in Monkasei (ed.) *Gakumon henro. Akamatsu Kaname sensei tsuitō ronshū*, Tokyo: Sekai keizai kenkyū kyōkai, 249–61.

Reischauer, Edwin O. (1984) *The Japanese*, Tokyo: Tuttle.

Ricardo, David (1987) [1817] 'Principles of political economy and taxation', in *Authorized facimile of The Works of David Ricardo with a notice on the life and writings of the author, John Murray, London 1888*, Ann Arbor: UMI Out-of-Print Books on Demand, 1–260.

Röpke, Wilhelm (1959) *International Order and Economic Integration*, Dordrecht: Reidel.

Rostow, W. W. (1961) *The Stages of Economic Growth: A Non-Communist Manifesto*, Cambridge: Cambridge University Press.

Rowland, Robert C. (1987) 'On defining argument', *Philosophy and Rhetoric* 20, 3: 140–59.

Sakamoto Yoshikazu (1978) 'Japan as an international being', *Peace Research in Japan 1977–78*, 1–12.

—— (1985) *Gunshuku no seijigaku*, Tokyo: Iwanami.

—— (1987a) 'Nihon senryō no kokusai kankyō', in Sakamoto Yoshikazu and R. E. Vōdo (eds) *Nihon senryō no kenkyū*, Tokyo: Tokyo daigaku shuppankai, 3–45.

—— (1987b) 'The international context of the Occupation of Japan', in Robert E. Ward and Sakamoto Yoshikazu (eds) *Democratizing Japan. The Allied Occupation*, Honolulu: University of Hawaii Press, 42–75.

Sasaki Ryuji (1989) *Sekaishi no naka no Ajia to Nihon*, Tokyo: Ochanomizu shobō.

Seki Hiroharu (1987) *The Asia–Pacific in the Global Transformation – Bringing 'The Nation-State Japan' Back In*, Tokyo: Institute of Oriental Culture, University of Tokyo.

Senghaas, Dieter (1985) *The European Experience. A Historical Critique of Development Theory*, Leamington Spa/Dover: Berg.

Shibusawa Masahide (1984) *Japan and the Asian Pacific Region. Profile of Change*, London and Sydney: The Royal Institute of International Affairs and Croom Helm.

Shinohara Miyohei (1982) *Industrial Growth, Trade, and Dynamic Patterns in the Japanese Economy*, Tokyo: University of Tokyo Press.

Shiraishi Takashi (1989) *Japan's Trade Policies 1945 to the Present Day*, Worcester: Athlone Press.

Singh, Lalita Prasad (1966) *The Politics of Economic Cooperation in Asia. A Study of Asian International Organizations*, Columbia: University of Missouri Press.

Steven, Rob (1990) *Japan's New Imperialism*, Hong Kong: Macmillan.

Storry, Richard (1968) *A History of Modern Japan*, Harmondsworth: Penguin.

Summa, Hilkka (1989) *Hyvinvointipolitiikka ja suunnitteluretoriikka. Tapaus asuntopolitiikka*, Espoo: Yhdyskuntasuunnittelun täydennyskoulutuskeksen julkaisuja A 17.

Thayer, Nathaniel B. (1969) *How the Conservatives Rule Japan*, Princeton: Princeton University Press.

Tinbergen, Jan (1958) *The Design of Development*, Baltimore: The Economic Development Institute and John Hopkins Press.

Toulmin, Stephen (1983) [1958] *The Uses of Argument*, Westford: Cambridge University Press.

Tsuneishi, Warren M. (1966) *Japanese Political Style. An Introduction to the Government and Politics of Modern Japan*, New York and London: Harper and Row.

Turner, Barry and Nordquist, Gunilla (1982) *The Other European Community. Integration and Cooperation in Nordic Europe*, London: Weidenfeld and Nicolson.

Uchida Kenzo (1987) 'Japan's post-war conservative parties', in Robert E. Ward and Sakamoto Yoshikazu (eds) *Democratizing Japan. The Allied Occupation*, Honolulu: University of Hawaii Press, 306–38.

United Nations (UN) (1959) *The Latin American Common Market*, Department of Economic and Social Affairs.

—— (1964) *World Economic Survey 1963. I Trade and Development: Trends, Needs and Policies*, New York.

Väyrynen, Raimo (1988) *Pienet valtiot kansainvälisissä suhteissa*, Helsinki: Valtion painatuskeskus.

Vernon, Raymond (1966) 'International investment and international trade in the product cycle', *Quarterly Journal of Economics* LXXX, 2: 190–207.

Ward, Robert E. and Sakamoto Yoshikazu (eds) (1987) *Democratizing Japan. The Allied Occupation*, Honolulu: University of Hawaii Press.

Watanuki Joji (1977) *Politics in Postwar Japanese Society*, Tokyo: University of Tokyo Press.

Woronoff, Jon (1985) *The Japan Syndrome*, Tokyo: Lotus.

—— (1986) *Asia's 'Miracle' Economies*, Tokyo: Lotus.

Yamamura Kozo (1967) *Economic Policy in Postwar Japan. Growth versus Economic Democracy*, Berkeley and Los Angeles: University of California Press.

Yasutomo, Dennis T. (1983) *Japan and the Asian Development Bank*, New York: Praeger.
—— (1986) *The Manner of Giving. Strategic Aid and Japanese Foreign Policy*, Massachusetts and Toronto: Lexington.
Yoshida Shigeru (1961) *The Yoshida Memoirs. The Story of Japan in Crisis*, Kingswood: Heinemann.
Yoshitsu, Michael M. (1983) *Japan and the San Francisco Peace Settlement*, New York: Columbia University Press.
Zahl, Karl F. (1973) *Die politische Elite Japans*, Wiesbaden: Harassowitz.

UNPUBLISHED MATERIAL

Interview with Kojima Kiyoshi, 21 September 1991, Musashikoganei.
Interview with Okita Saburo, 27 September 1991, Tokyo.
Letter from Kojima Kiyoshi, 18 April 1992.

Index

Note: All references are to Japan, unless otherwise indicated

Abe Masamichi 122–6, 128, 130
action, politics as 2–3
advanced countries *see* developed
Africa 89, 110, 136; African
    Common Market 115; and Asia as
    theme 70, 71; and growth 40, 41,
    42–3, 45
agriculture 157, 163–4; agricultural
    countries *see* developing
    countries; New Zealand
aid and investment 77, 82, 172; and
    international discussion 157, 158;
    by Japan to rest of Asia 27–8,
    77–8, 90, 124, 130, 158; lack of
    151
Akamatsu Kaname 6, 9, 34; and
    integration 97, 99–100, 101, 112,
    128; *see also* flying geese pattern
ALA (Asia and Latin America) 156
Allen, G.C. 28, 38, 40, 50
Amaterasu Omikami 47
Amaya Naohiro 14
APEC (Asia–Pacific Economic Co-
    operation) 179–80, 181
Appelbaum, Richard P. 63
Araki Tadao 122–6, 128, 130
Arisawa Hiromi 26, 27, 69
Aristotle 7
ASA (Association of Southeast
    Asia) 108, 115
Asanuma Inejiro 33
ASEAN (Association of Southeast
    Asian Nations) 19, 69, 147, 167,

174, 176; and APEC 179; and
    EAEC/EAEG 180; and Pacific
    Community 177–8; and PECC
    177–8
Ashiya Einosuke 157–8
Asia: Asian vs Pacific orientation
    113–28; as European
    geographical concept 68; and
    Japan as bridge 145–53; and Latin
    America (ALA) 156; relationship
    with *see* regional integration;
    theme 16, 63–71; *see also* China;
    Japan; NIEs; South Asia;
    Southeast Asia
Asia–Pacific Economic Co-
    operation 179–80, 181
Asian Development Bank 90, 178
Asian Development Fund
    proposed 88
Asian dynamism 128–33
Asian Economic Research Institute
    see Institute of Developing
    Economies
Asian Free Trade Area proposed
    122
Asian and Pacific Council 153–4
Asian Productivity Organization 90
ASPAC (Asian and Pacific Council)
    153–4
Association of Southeast Asia 108,
    115
Association of Southeast Asian
    Nations *see* ASEAN

Atlanticism/Atlantic Community proposals 119, 126, 136, 160, 172; *see also* NATO
Australia 167, 174; and Asia as theme 69–70, 71; and Asian vs Pacific orientation 116, 117, 120–1, 125; and growth 40, 41, 42–3; and international discussion 157–66 *passim* 153, 157, 160–2, 164–6; and Japan as bridge 147, 150–1, 152; and Kojima's concept of integration 98, 104, 110; and Pacific Community 175, 177; and re-entering world (by Japan) 74, 83; and regional co-operation 87; *see also* NAFTA; PAFTA
Austro-Hungary 20
Axelbank, Albert 13

Baerwald, Hans H. 22
balance of payments 47–9; *see also* trade
Balassa, Bela 144, 145
Bamba Nobuya 13
Bandung conference (1955) 5, 77, 88
Bangkok Resolution (1960) 88, 94
Bank of Japan 114
banks 90, 114, 178; *see also* World Bank
Belgium 46, 64, 74, 138
Benelux 138
Bey, Arifin 178
Bikini incident 33
Bodde, William, Jr 179
Boltho, Andrea 40
booms 47
Brazil 74
Bretton Woods 17, 81
bridge, Japan as 133–45, 173
Britain: and Asia as theme 67; and Asian vs Pacific orientation 115, 119, 120; colonialism 11, 64, 108; and development 56; and growth 44, 46, 49; and international discussion 154, 158, 160, 162, 165; and Japan as bridge 146; and Kojima's concept of integration 95, 100, 103, 106, 110; and PAFTA proposal 135, 136–7, 138, 142; and re-entering world (by Japan)

74, 78, 82–3, 85; and regional co-operation 87; and small country, Japan as 20, 25
Brunei 179
Burma 78, 107, 131

CACM (Central American Common Market) 72, 115
Calleo, David P. 85, 118, 119
Calvert, Peter 68
Cambodia 107
Canada 72, 167, 174, 180; and Asia as theme 69–70, 71; and Asian vs Pacific orientation 116, 119, 120, 125; and development 50, 53; and growth 40–3, 175; and international discussion 157–66 *passim*; and Japan as bridge 147, 150; and Kojima's concept of integration 98, 102, 104; and Pacific Community 175, 177; and PAFTA proposal 136–7; and re-entering world (by Japan) 74, 83; *see also* PAFTA
Castle, Leslie V. 162–4
Central America 136–7, 178, 180; Common Market 72, 115
Ceylon 107, 115, 131
cheap labour 92, 93, 132
Chile 178
China 24, 169, 175, 177, 178, 180; and APEC 179; and Asia as theme 16, 64–70, 71; and Asian dynamism 129–30, 131; and Asian vs Pacific orientation 114, 126; and development 52, 56, 60; and economism 32, 33; and international discussion 153, 160; and Japan as bridge 146–7; and regional co-operation 87; and small country, Japan as 19; Treaty of Peace and Friendship with Japan 174
Chinese Taipei *see* Taiwan
Chung Hoon-mok 143
Churchill, Winston 20
Cold War 87, 120; and Asia as theme 16, 64–5, 71, 168–9; and economism 32–3, 36–7; and re-entering world (by Japan) 77, 82;

and small country, Japan as 17, 22, 24–7
Colombo Plan 77–8
colonialism 11, 87, 170; *see also* decolonization
COMECON (Council for Mutual Economic Assistance) 1, 72, 115
Commonwealth, British 103, 137–8; and Asian vs Pacific orientation 115, 119, 120; *see also in particular* Australia; Canada; India; New Zealand
communism *see* socialist countries
comparative statistics on growth 38–49
Constitution, new (1946) 20, 22–3, 32
containment 153, 159–60
Cooper, Richard N. 159
co-operation *see* integration
Council for Mutual Economic Assistance 1, 72, 115
Crawford, Sir John 177
Cusumano, Michael A. 55

de Gaulle, Charles 136, 163
decolonization 64, 65, 67–9; and Kojima's concept of integration 99–100, 108; and regional co-operation 82, 92
deindustrialization 26
demilitarization 21, 22, 24, 26, 27, 30
Deng Xiaoping 174
depression *see* recession
Destler, I.M. 18
developed (advanced) countries: Japan as 114, 126–7, 171–2; *see also in particular* Australia; Europe; New Zealand; North America; OECD
developing countries and integration 98–100, 107–8, 110; and Asian vs Pacific orientation 114, 116, 117, 120; and international discussion 157–8; *see also* Africa; aid; Asia; Latin America
development 11, 15–16, 49–63, 165, 171–2; and Asian dynamism 129–32; and PAFTA proposal

143–4; quantitative *see* growth; and re-entering world (by Japan) 79–80, 83–4; and regional co-operation 92–3; stages and Asian dynamism 128–30
Drysdale, Peter 76, 165–6, 167
Dubro, Alec 13
dynamism, Asian 128–33

EAEC/EAEG (East Asia Economic Caucus and Group) proposed 180
East Asia 107, 108–9; *see also* Hong Kong; Japan; Philippines; South Korea; Taiwan
East Asia Economic Caucus and Group proposed 180
East–West problems 150–3
Eastern Europe 180
Ebihara Takekuni 110
EC/EEC (European Community/European Economic Community) 1, 12, 18, 72, 73, 89, 167, 168; and Asian vs Pacific orientation 115, 116, 119, 124; and growth 40, 42–4; and international discussion 155, 157, 159–60, 163; and Japan as bridge 146; and Kojima's concept of integration 96, 102–3, 104, 106, 107; and PAFTA proposal 134–8, 141, 155
ECAFE (Economic Commission for Asia and Far East *later* ESCAP) 24, 73, 75, 125, 167, 178; and PAFTA proposal 133; and regional co-operation 87–91, 94
Economic Counselling Board 75
Economic Planning Agency 34, 35, 75, 81, 114
Economic and Social Commission for Asia and Pacific (*formerly* ECAFE) 178
Economic Stabilization Board 75
economism 1–2, 4, 6, 10, 14–15, 28–37, 130, 131, 169–70; *see also* integration
Edström, Bert 14, 18, 28, 49
education 31, 41; re-education 21–9
EFTA (European Free Trade Association) 1, 40, 42–3, 72, 102,

103, 160, 180; and Asian vs Pacific
orientation 115, 119; and PAFTA
proposal 135, 136, 141
Eisenhower, Dwight D. 77, 82, 85,
118
Elsbree, Willard H. 20, 67
Eminent Persons Group 179
Emmerson, John K. 18, 49, 67
England *see* Britain
English, H. Edward 119, 136, 161–2
EPU (European Payments Union)
72, 75
equality of opportunity 97–8
Europe, Western 1, 167–8, 170, 174;
and Asia as theme 64, 65, 67,
70; and Asian dynamism 129; and
Asian vs Pacific orientation 115,
116–19, 121, 124; and
development 50, 53, 60; European
(Economic) Community *see* EC/
EEC; European Free Trade
Area *see* EFTA; and growth 40–3,
46–7; and international discussion
155, 157, 159–60, 163; and Japan
as bridge 146, 148, 152; and
Kojima's concept of integration
95–8, 100, 102–3, 105, 106, 110,
111–12; and PAFTA proposal
134–8, 140–2, 155; and re-
entering world (by Japan) 74, 75,
78, 82–3, 84–5; and regional co-
operation 89–90, 91
European Payments Union 72, 75
experts, group of 88–9
exports, Japanese 18; and Asia as
theme 66, 69–71; and
development 54, 55, 56; and
growth 46–8; and Kojima's
concept of integration 111; and
PAFTA proposal 139, 141; and
regional co-operation 91
eyewitness accounts 10

FAO (Food and Agriculture
Organization) 72
Far East concept 40, 41, 42–3, 68;
see also individual countries
Fiji 178
Finland 74, 100
First World War *see* World War I

flying geese pattern of development
15–16, 49–63, 171; and
integration 79, 92–3, 94, 98, 101,
109, 143
Food and Agriculture Organization
72
food imports *see* raw materials
under imports
foreign policies, types of 128
France: and integration 74, 87, 96,
106, 136, 138, 158; and themes
20, 47, 64, 67
Frank, Andre Gunder 62
Frazer, Malcolm 177
'free riders' 17; *see also* small
country
free trade *see* integration
Fujii Shigeru 74, 131–3
Fujino Shozaburo 148
future 148–50, 152–3, 170, 171

Galtung, Johan 11, 62, 63
GATT (General Agreement on
Trade and Tariffs) 17, 72, 73, 168,
180; and Asia as theme 70; and
Asian vs Pacific orientation
114–15, 119; and growth 15, 38,
45–9; and international
discussion 156, 160, 162; Kennedy
Round 5, 119, 144, 156, 159, 160,
167; and Kojima's concept of
integration 101, 104; and PAFTA
proposal 136, 142, 144, 145; and
re-entering world (by Japan) 74,
79; and regional co-operation
89, 94
GDP (gross domestic product)
40–3, 45
General Agreement on Trade and
Tariffs *see* GATT
geographical classification 9; Asia as
68; and Japan as bridge 145–53;
and small country, Japan as 19,
20–1
Germany (*mainly* Federal
Republic) 20, 46, 49, 50, 138, 158
Gilpin, Robert 16
global economic system *see* flying
geese
global integration 10–11; and Asian

vs Pacific orientation 114–15,
119; and Kojima's concept of
integration 94, 101–4, 107,
111–12
global organizations 72–3; *see also
in particular* GATT; IMF;
OECD; United Nations; World
Bank
GNP (gross national product): and
growth 38–9, 45–6; and
integration 137–8, 158, 172, 173
'Great Awakening' 99
Great Depression 38–9
Greater East Asian Co-prosperity
Sphere 20, 23, 88, 181
gross domestic product 40–3, 45
gross national product *see* GNP
growth, economic 15, 38–49, 62, 165,
169, 170; and economism 34–6;
and integration 102, 105, 114,
129–31; qualitative *see*
development; *see also* Income-
doubling
Guam doctrine 19

Haas, Ernst B. 94, 98
Halliday, Jon 11
Han Sung-joo 178
Haushofer, Karl 20
Hawaii Conference (1968) 166
He Xin 180–1
heavy industry: and development
55, 56, 61–2; and growth 39–40,
46, 48; and integration 92, 104,
111–12, 129, 131, 140–2
Hegel, G.W.F. 50, 59
hegemony 16–17; challenged *see*
Cold War; *see also* United States
Hemmi Kenzo 157
Henderson, Jeffrey 63
Hidaka Rokuro 13
Higgins, Benjamin 41, 51, 62
Hindmarsh, Albert E. 20, 55
Hiroshima 21
Hirschman, Albert O. 38, 62
homogeneity in integration 93
Hong Kong 177, 178; and APEC
179; and Asia as theme 66, 68,
69–71; and Asian dynamism
129–30, 131, 132; and

development 56, 105–6, 174; and
Kojima's concept of integration
107, 109; and PAFTA proposal
144, 173
horizontal integration 102
Howes, John F. 13
Hoyt, Edwin P. 67

IBRD *see* World Bank
Ienaga Saburo 20
Ikeda Hayato 6, 45, 175; and
economism 28–9, 34–6, 84; and
integration 80, 90, 91, 124, 126;
Plan *see* Income-doubling
IMF (International Monetary Fund)
17, 72, 82, 83, 101, 114
imperialism: structural 62–3; *see also*
colonialism
imperialism, economic 11
imports, Japanese: and Asia as
theme 66, 69–71; and Asian
dynamism 132; and Asian vs
Pacific orientation 120; of culture
60–1; and development 52, 54–5,
60–1; and growth 46–9; and
international discussion, exposure
to 158, 163; and Kojima's
concept of integration 105–6, 111;
of manufactured goods 52,
105–6, 132; and PAFTA proposal
139, 141; of raw materials and
food 29–30, 40, 47, 48, 54, 66,
69–71, 83, 106, 111, 120, 139, 163;
reduced 48; and re-entering world
(by Japan) 83; of technology and
capital 47, 48–9, 54–5, 71, 106,
111, 158
Income-doubling (Ikeda) Plan
(1960) 6, 34, 35–6, 45; and
integration 80–1, 84, 101, 149
independence: of colonies *see*
decolonization; of Japan *see* re-
entering world
India 24, 115, 144, 169, 174; and
Asian dynamism 129–30, 131;
and development 52, 56; and
Kojima's concept of integration
68, 107–8; and re-entering world
(by Japan) 74, 76, 77, 78, 82; and
regional co-operation 88, 105–6

Indonesia 78, 88, 107, 108, 173, 176, 177–8; and APEC 179; *see also* ASEAN
industry 16, 117; and Asian dynamism 129, 131–2; and international discussion, exposure to 163, 164, 165; and Kojima's concept of integration 97, 99, 104, 106, 107, 109, 111–12; and PAFTA proposal 140–2, 144; and regional co-operation 89, 92; and small country, Japan as 18, 19; *see also* development; growth; heavy industry; light industry; textiles
ingroups and outgroups 8–9
Inoguchi Takashi 17, 18
Institute of Developing Economies 5, 73, 91, 94, 110
integration 2, 7, 12, 72–166; Asian dynamism 128–33; Asian vs Pacific orientation 113–28; exposure to international discussions 153–66; and Japan as bridge 133–45, 175; Kojima's concept of *see under* Kojima; *see also* PAFTA; re-entering world; regional integration
international *see entries beginning* global
International Bank for Reconstruction and Development *see* World Bank
international discussions, exposure to 153–66
International Monetary Fund *see* IMF
internationalists *see* global integration
investment *see* aid and investment
Iriye Akira 20
Itagaki Yoichi 26
Italy 20, 46, 85, 138
Iwasaki Ikuo 5
Iwato boom 47
Izanagi 47
Izanami boom 47

JANFTA (Japanese–Australian–

New Zealand Free Trade Area) proposed 164–5
Japan *see* integration; themes
Japan Economic Investigating Committee 113–22
Japan Economic Research Center *see* JERC
Japan International Co-operation Agency 122
jargon 10
JERC (Japan Economic Research Center) 5, 131, 148, 154
JICA (Japan International Co-operation Agency) 122
Jimmu boom 47
Johnson, Chalmers 30, 34, 62, 81, 101
Johnson, Harry G. 159–60
Jones, F.C. 20

Kahn, Herman 19
Kajima Morinosuke 125–6
Kaplan, David E. 13
Karashima Kanesaburo 26, 66, 68
Kato Norihiro 27
Kennedy, John F. 85–6, 118–19; *see also* Kennedy Round *under* GATT
Kennedy, Paul 16
Keohane, Robert O. 16
Khamchoo, Chaiwat 64
Khrushchev, Nikita 82
Kierkegaard, Søren 4, 59
Kishi Nobusuke 33–4, 36, 88, 90, 101
Kjellén, Rudolf 20
Kobayashi Yoshimasa 24
Kojima Kiyoshi 2, 4, 5, 167, 175, 178; and development 50, 51, 58, 62; and economism 29, 34; and growth 50; and integration 73, 79–80, 87, 91–113, 132, 145, 155–6, 161; and small country, Japan as 19; *see also* PAFTA
Korea 24, 60, 66, 68; Korean War 25, 27, 32, 39, 44, 47; *see also* North Korea; South Korea
Korhonen, Pekka 4, 6, 50, 63, 130
Kosai Yutaka 39
Koyama Kenichi 148, 149
Krause, Lawrence B. 40

Kuno Osamu 25, 68
Kurimoto Hiroshi 133–44

labour, cheap 92, 93, 132
LAFTA (Latin American Free
   Trade Area) 72, 115
Lake, David A. 17
Lal, K.B. 88
Laos 107, 129, 153
Latin America 89, 110, 115, 177,
   178; and Asia as theme 70, 71;
   Free Trade Area 72, 115; and
   growth 40, 41, 42–3, 45; and
   international discussion 155, 156,
   158; and Japan as bridge 151; and
   PAFTA proposal 135, 136–7, 155;
   and re-entering world (by Japan)
   74, 83
leader and follower countries *see*
   flying geese pattern
Lebra, Joyce C. 20
Leviste, Jose P., Jr 178
Liberal-Democratic Party 36, 175
light industry 61; and integration 92,
   129, 131–2, 140–2, 144, 163; and
   Kojima's concept of integration
   106, 109, 111–12
Lincoln, Edward J. 18
Linder, Staffan Burenstam 178
living standards 41

Macao 68
McArthur, General 24
McCormack, Gavan 11
McDougall, Ian A. 163–5
Maddison, Angus 38
Maga, Timothy P. 118, 120
Malaya 107, 108, 115
Malaysia 88, 115, 131, 153, 176,
   177–8, 180; and APEC 179; *see
   also* ASEAN
Manchukuo 20, 65
manufacturing *see* industry
Marxism 50–1, 59
Masamura Kimihiro 21, 33
Masuda Ato 178
Matsumoto Kunio 149
Meiji period 23, 31, 38, 148–9
Mexico 178, 180
Middle East 48, 70–1, 115

Miki Takeo 2, 5, 12; and
   international discussion 74,
   153–5, 180; and Japan as bridge
   (Miki Plan) 145–53, 173
militarism: agreements 17, 18, 32,
   33–4, 126; arms industry 38–9;
   criticized 29; dislike for 6, 25, 172;
   lack of *see* peace; *see also*
   demilitarization; rearmament
Mills, C. Wright 10
Minami Ryoshin 58, 62
Ministries: of Finance 114, 175; of
   Foreign Affairs 30, 31, 114, 122,
   128, 175; of Forestry and Fisheries
   114; of Greater East Asia 29; of
   International Trade and Industry
   (MITI) 81, 114
Minobe Ryokichi 24
MITI (Ministry of International
   Trade and Industry) 81, 114
Mitrany, David 72, 94
Miyazawa Kiichi 145
Mommsen, Wolfgang J. 63
Momoi Makato 31
Momose Hiroshi 18
Mongolia 87
Monkasei 50
moral codes of international
   behaviour 157
Morgenthau, Hans 3
Murobuse Fumiro 148–9
Mutual Security Treaty *see under*
   United States
Myers, Ramon H. 20
Myrdal, Gunnar 9, 51, 62, 92, 94,
   97–102

NAFTA (Australia–New Zealand
   Free Trade Agreement) 120,
   163–4
NAFTA (North American Free
   Trade Agreement) 180
NAFTA (North Atlantic Free Trade
   Area) proposed 160
Nagano Shigeo 121
Nagasaki 21
Nagata Kiyoshi 26
Nakamura Takafusa 18, 19, 21, 65;
   and economism 31–2, 34, 36; and
   growth 39, 43, 47, 48–9, 141

Nakane Chie 9
Nakayama Ichiro 149
name of Japan changed 20
National Police Reserve 32
nationalism: economic 53, 63 (*see also* economism); enlightened 11; and integration 98, 101, 111; nationalists and internationalists, debate between *see* global integration; regional integration
NATO (North Atlantic Treaty Organization) 17, 119, 136
Netherlands 46, 60, 64, 67, 74, 87, 95
New Economic Program (US) 19
New Pacific Community proposed 119–20
New School of Internationalists *see* Myrdal
New Zealand 167, 174; and Asian vs Pacific orientation 116, 117, 120–1, 125; and growth 40, 41, 42–3; and integration 74, 87, 98; and international discussion 153, 157, 160, 161–4; and Japan as bridge 147, 150–1, 152; and Kojima's concept of integration 104; NAFTA (trade agreement with Australia) 120, 163–4; and Pacific Community 175, 177; *see also* PAFTA
Newby, Laura 67
newly independent countries *see* decolonization
NIEs (Newly-Industrialized Economies) 69; *see also* Hong Kong; Singapore; South Korea; Taiwan
Nish, Ian 28
Nixon, Richard 19
non-aligned countries 65
Nordquist, Gunilla 1
North America *see* Canada; United States
North American Free Trade Agreement 180
North Atlantic Free Trade Area proposed 160, 172
North Atlantic Treaty Organization *see* NATO
North Korea 20, 67, 87, 169

North Vietnam 87
North–South problems 150–1
NPR *see* National Police Reserve
Nurkse, Ragnar 62
Nye, Joseph S. 16, 144

OAEC *see* Organization for Asian Economic Co-operation
Occupation (1945–52) 14, 22–5, 28–33, 63–4, 168–9; *see also* 'reverse course'; small country
OECD (Organization for Economic Co-operation and Development): and Asian vs Pacific orientation 126–7; and growth 15, 38, 45; and integration 72, 91, 101, 126–7, 169, 178
OEEC *see* Organization for European Economic Co-operation
Ohira Masayoshi 126, 145, 175, 177, 180
Ohnishi Akira 158–9
oil 71; crisis (1973) 14, 19, 48, 174
Oki Hiroshi 68, 69, 78; and Asian dynamism 73–4, 128–30, 132
Okinawa 19, 21, 128
Okita Saburo 2, 5, 175, 177–9; and Asia as theme 66, 68–9; and Asian dynamism 131, 132; and Asian vs Pacific orientation 124, 126–8; and development 49, 61; and economism 28–9, 30, 34, 35, 36–7; and growth 45, 105; and international discussion 154, 158–9; and Japan as bridge 148–9; and re-entering world 73, 75–87; and regional co-operation 88–90, 104; and small country, Japan as 24, 26, 27, 28
Old School of Internationalists *see* Röpke
OPEC *see* Organization for Pacific Economic Co-operation
OPTAD (Organization for Pacific Aid and Development) proposed 157
Organization for Asian Economic Co-operation proposed 88–9, 90, 91

Organization for Economic Co-operation and Development *see* OECD
Organization for European Economic Co-operation 72, 75; *see also* OECD
Organization for Pacific Aid and Development proposed 157
Organization for Pacific Economic Co-operation proposed 116, 121, 122, 124–5, 128
Osaka 21
Osterhammel, Jurgen 63
Otake Hideo 30
Overseas Economic Co-operation Fund 90
Overseas Technical Co-operation Agency 90

Pacific Bank for Investment and Settlement proposed 157–8
Pacific Basin Economic Co-operation Committee 167, 174
Pacific Basin Economic Council 174, 177, 181
Pacific Common Market proposed 116, 121
Pacific Community proposed 175–7
Pacific Economic Co-operation Conference 50, 177–8, 181
Pacific Free Trade Area *see* PAFTA
Pacific rim concept 175
Pacific Trade and Development Conference (1968) 166
Pacific Trade Development Conferences 74, 167, 168, 173, 177, 178, 181
PAFTA (Pacific Free Trade Area) proposal 1–2, 5, 12, 74, 133–53, 172–3, 179, 181; and international discussion, exposure to 154–7, 160–1, 164, 165–6
PAFTAD *see* Pacific Trade Development Conferences
Pakistan 78, 88, 107, 115, 129, 131
Palonen, Kari 3, 4, 8, 11
Papinot, E. 47
Papua New Guinea 165, 178
Patrick, Hugh 39

PBEC *see* Pacific Basin Economic Council
peace 169–70; and Japan as bridge 149–51; 'overall' and 'one-sided' 33; Peace and Friendship Treaty (China and Japan) 174; Peace Treaty *see under* United States; peaceful foreign policy 128; -researching economists *see* Myrdal; Röpke
Peattie, Mark R. 20
PECC *see* Pacific Economic Co-operation Conference
Penrose, E.F. 50
Perelman, Chaim 7, 8, 9
Peru 178
Philippines 24, 78, 88, 115, 153; and APEC 179; and integration 176, 177–8; and Kojima's concept of integration 107, 108, 109; and PAFTA proposal 173; *see also* ASEAN
Plan for Doubling National Income *see* Income-doubling
Plan for Reconstructing the Post-war Japanese Economy (1946) 6
politics 1–4; and economism 31–7; and integration 82, 88; and international discussion 153, 154, 155–6, 159–60; political foreign policy 128; and small country, Japan as 25–6
population 18, 19, 30, 39–40, 82, 103, 137–8
Portugal 60
poverty 21
presence 9
prestige 9–10, 171
protectionism 53, 156, 163–5
psychological factors 6, 169, 170; and small country, Japan as 18, 25–6, 27
public opinion poll 24–5

Ranis, Gustav 159
Rapp, William V. 50, 58
raw materials *see under* imports
rearmament 23, 32–3
recession and economic depression 38–9; *see also* oil crisis

re-education and reform of Japan 21–9
re-entering world 74–87, 168–9
reform *see* re-education
regional integration and co-operation 87–94, 167, 168–81; and Asian dynamism 131; and Asian vs Pacific orientation 115–28; and Kojima's concept of integration 94, 100, 103–11, 113–14; *see also in particular* EC/EEC; PAFTA
Reischauer, Edwin O. 22, 31
reparations, war 78–9, 90, 130
'reverse course' in Occupation 22, 23, 24, 32
rhetoric 7–8
Ricardo, David 56
Röpke, Wilhelm 9, 55, 62; and Kojima 94–7, 98, 101, 102, 106
Rosovsky, Henry 39
Rostow, W.W. 62
Rowland, Robert C. 7
Royama Masamichi 25–6
Russia *see* Soviet Union/Russia
Ryu Shintaro 26

Sabah 115
Sakamoto Jiro 149–50
Sakamoto Yoshikazu 11, 13, 22, 23, 64
San Francisco Peace Treaty *see* Peace *under* United States
Sarawak 115
Sasaki Ryuji 67
Sato Eisaku 45
SEATO (Southeast Asia Treaty Organization) 17
Second World War *see* World War II
sectoral understanding of politics 2–3
security concept 76; Security Treaty *see under* United States; *see also* militarism
Seki Hiroharu 178
Sekiguchi Keitaro 25
Sekiguchi Sueo 40
Self-Defence Force 32
self-reliance concept 63
Senghaas, Dieter 63

Seow, Greg 177
Serita Hitoshi 25
Sethaphanichakan, Luang Thavil 88
Shibusawa Masahide: and integration 124, 130, 153; and themes 18, 19, 28, 36
Shimizu Ikutaro 24–5
Shimla Conference (1955) 77, 88
Shinohara Miyohei 62, 148
Shiraishi Takashi 73, 74, 79, 85, 87
Singapore: and APEC 179; and Asia as theme 69–71; and integration 107, 115, 130, 144, 170, 176, 177–8; *see also* ASEAN
Singh, Lalita Prasad 76, 77–8, 88–9, 90–1
small country, Japan as 3–4, 14, 16–28, 168
socialist countries 33, 65, 71; combating 119–20, 153 (*see also* Cold War); COMECON 1, 72, 115; excluded 125, 170; *see also* China; Soviet Union
Socialist Party, Japan 33
South Africa 40, 41, 42–3
South America *see* Latin America
South Asia *see* Burma; Ceylon; India; Pakistan
South Korea 88, 126, 151, 153, 169, 177, 178; and APEC 179; and Asia as theme 67, 69–71; and Asian dynamism 129–30, 131; and growth 174; and Kojima's concept of integration 107; and PAFTA proposal 173
South Vietnam 78, 107, 153
Southeast Asia 41, 63, 153, 167, 169, 176; ASEAN 19, 69; and Asia as theme 64, 68–70; and Asian dynamism 129, 131; and Asian vs Pacific orientation 114, 115, 117, 121, 123, 126; and growth 170, 174; and Kojima's concept of integration 107–8, 110; and PAFTA proposal 139–40, 173; and re-entering world (by Japan) 78, 83; and regional co-operation 88, 89, 91–3; Treaty Organization 17
Soviet Union/Russia 87, 96, 106,

177, 178; and Asia as theme 66, 70, and Asian vs Pacific orientation 114, 115; and development 50; and economism 32, 33, 37; and growth 170; and Japan as bridge 146, 147; and PAFTA proposal 173; and re-entering world (by Japan) 82; Russo-Japanese war 38, 79; and small country, Japan as 17, 20–1, 25; collapse 180
Sri Lanka *see* Ceylon
stability 35, 165
Stalin, Josef 20
standards of living 123, 127
Steven, Rob 11
Storry, Richard 31, 33–4
Sugi Takashi 25, 69
Summa, Hilkka 7
sunrise and sunset industries 61–2, 112
supporter countries 17, 18; *see also* small country
Sweden 74, 95, 100
Switzerland 74, 95
'synthetic dialectics' 56–7

Taipei *see* Taiwan
Taira Teizo 30
Taiwan 88, 151, 153, 169, 177, 178; and APEC 179; and Asia as theme 66–7, 68, 69–71; and Asian dynamism 129–30, 131, 132; and growth 174; and Kojima's concept of integration 107; and PAFTA proposal 144, 173
'take-off' of growth 62
tariffs *see* GATT; protectionism
technology, new 61, 92, 117; *see also under* imports
textiles: and integration 104, 109; and themes 18, 38, 48, 52, 54–6, 61
Thailand 5, 70–1, 74, 88, 107, 108, 153, 176, 177–8; and APEC 179; and Asian dynamism 129, 131; and Asian vs Pacific orientation 115, 123; *see also* ASEAN
Thayer, Nathaniel B. 30
themes 8, 13–71, 168–70; Asia 16,

63–71; *see also* development; economism; growth; small country
threats to development 59–60
time: and Japan as bridge 147–50, 152–3; -lag in development pattern 56, 171
Tinbergen, Jan 62
Tokyo 21; Conferences 120, 121; future 149
Tonga 178
Toulmin, Stephen 8
trade 18; and re-entering world (by Japan) 74–87; *see also* exports; imports; integration
Trade and Development Board of UNCTAD 127
Trade Expansion Act (US) 119
transport, ocean 117–18
Truman, Harry 20
Tsuchiya Kiyoshi 26
Tsukamoto Masao 122–6, 128, 130
Tsuneishi, Warren M. 30
Turkey 24
Turner, Barry 1

Uchida Kenzo 30
UNCTAD *see* Conference *under* United Nations
unemployment 93
UNESCO 72
United Kingdom *see* Britain
United Nations: and Asian vs Pacific orientation 115, 127, 131; Conference on Trade and Development (UNCTAD) 127, 131, 137, 151, 171–2; and development 44, 51, 168, 169; Development Decade (1960s) 44, 51, 169; Economic and Social Commission for Asia and Pacific (*formerly* ECAFE) 178; Educational, Scientific and Cultural Organization (UNESCO) 72; and growth 15, 38, 40–5; and integration 72, 73, 82, 128; and Japan as bridge 151; and PAFTA proposal 137, 151; and regional co-operation 87; and

small country, Japan as 24, 25, 27;
see also ECAFE
United States 2, 3, 5, 72, 167, 170,
171, 172, 174, 180, 181; and Asia
as theme 65–7, 69–71; and Asian
dynamism 129, 132; and Asian vs
Pacific orientation 114–20, 124,
125; and development 50, 53; and
economism 32–4, 37; and growth
39, 40–4, 47, 49; and international
discussion 156, 158–60, 162, 163,
164, 165, 166; and Japan as bridge
146–8, 150–2; and Kojima's
concept of integration 96, 98,
101–6, 110; Mutual Security
Treaty with Japan 18, 32, 33–4,
126; and Pacific Community 175,
177; Peace Treaty with Japan 32,
33; and re-entering world (by
Japan) 74, 77, 78, 82, 84, 85–6;
and regional co-operation 87, 88,
89–90, 91; and small country,
Japan as 14, 16–27; *see also*
Occupation
USSR *see* Soviet Union/Russia

Väyrynen, Raimo 18
Vernon, Raymond 62
Vietnam 78, 87, 151, 153; War 146,
174, 175

Ward, Robert E. 22
wars: Russo-Japanese 38, 79;
Vietnam 146; world *see* World
War; *see also* reparations *and
under* Korea

Watanuki Joji 30
welfare state approach *see* Myrdal
West *see* developed countries
West Asia 40, 42–4
Western Europe *see* Europe
White Papers 35
Whitlam, E. Gough 178
WHO (World Health
Organization) 72
Wilkinson, Bruce 161, 166
'Wise Mens' Commission 88–9
Wolff, Lester L. 176
world *see entries beginning* global
World Bank 72, 82, 83
World Health Organization 72
World War I: and integration 82, 85,
95, 147; and themes 20, 30, 39,
61, 63, 70
World War II: and integration 83,
95, 147; and themes 3, 20–1, 24,
29, 33, 168; *see also* Occupation
World War III, fear of 25; *see also*
Cold War
Woronoff, Jon 62

Yamaguchi Shogo 26
Yamamura Kozo 22
Yasutomo, Dennis T. Y. 18, 88, 90
Yen Block 65
Yokota Kisaburo 25
Yoshida Shigeru 24, 31, 32–3, 67
Yoshitsu, Michael M. 22, 32–3, 67
Youth Volunteer Corps 90
Yugoslavia 74

Zahl, Karl F. 29, 30